LINES OF DEVELOPMENT

ANALYSIS, GEOMETRY,
ARCHITECTURE

CAMERON WU

ACTAR PUBLISHERS
BARCELONA, SPAIN
NEW YORK, NY

LINES OF DEVELOPMENT
ANALYSIS, GEOMETRY, ARCHITECTURE

Published by
Actar Publishers
New York, Barcelona
www.actar.com

Author
Cameron Wu

Graphic Design
Olga Pipnik

Copy editing and proofreading
Lee Onbargi

Printing and binding
Arlequin & Pierrot

This publication is made possible in part by the Barr Ferree Foundation Fund for Publications, Department of Art and Archaeology, Princeton University.

Distribution
Actar D, Inc. New York, Barcelona

New York
440 Park Avenue South, 17th Floor
New York, NY 10016, USA
T+1 2129 662 207
salesnewyork@actar-d.com

Barcelona
Roca i Batlle 2-4
08023 Barcelona, Spain
T +34 933 282 183
eurosales@actar-d.com

Indexing
ISBN: 978-1-63840-041-7
Library of Congress Control Number: 2022942867

Printed in Europe

Publication date: January 2024

Cover image: "Geodesic Leveling 03"
© 2015 Cameron Wu & Iman Fayyad

for Imogen
and Lucy

CONTENTS

LINES OF DEVELOPMENT

Mathematicians and architects have traditionally used two distinct methods for the authoring and study of geometric form. Analytic geometry, also known as coordinate geometry, describes and modulates form through algebraic equations. Descriptive geometry, related to the subject known since antiquity as *solid geometry*, operates via more direct graphic means—constructing projective representations with the drawing tools of straightedge and compass. Although analytic geometry gave rise to the invention of other mathematical spaces of operation such as *elliptical* and *hyperbolic* geometries, architects have little practical use for these non-Euclidean spaces.[1] Terms used in this book such as "two-dimensional drawing plane" and "three-dimensional space" shall henceforth refer exclusively to those of Euclidean, or *parabolic*, geometry. The writing and manipulation of analytic geometry primarily occurs in algebraic notation, but the visualization of its function curves and surfaces through drawing and modeling has always been a fundamental part of the discipline. Equations can be graphically represented by points, curves, and surfaces. Conversely, related sets of geometric points, curves, and surfaces can generally be defined efficiently via parametric or implicit equations. The analytic geometer maintains command of the algebraic expressions of description in addition to the geometric forms to which these expressions refer—understanding both models of mathematical and spatial articulation as equivalent and reciprocally interchangeable. Enabled by relatively recent and powerful digital methods, contemporary architects can operate in either analytical or descriptive modes, though most still default to the latter. Due to specific geometric attributes, *ruled surfaces* have endured as significant protagonists in the history and progression of both disciplines.[2] This is particularly true of cones and cylinders as related to architectural design, representation, and construction. The presence of straight ruling lines on these surfaces imbues them with a mathematical and material intelligence that predicates the geometric techniques and architectural proposals in this book.

Certain types of historical and contemporary graphic representation superimpose linguistic code on top of associated geometric forms. Eighteenth-century Baroque dance notation describes the spatial displacement of dancers in orthographic plan (**01**) or perspective (**02**) while simultaneously indexing coded information for the placement and timing of local individual moves—spins, pauses, leg sweeps, etc. Unlike algebraic curves and surfaces, the geometric lineaments of the displacement paths are not equivalent and interchangeable with the overlaid linguistic code, but rather the two representational modes are complementary, operating at both macro and micro scales. In architectural and urban design, a similar superimposition occurs in geographic information systems (GIS)

1 Bernard Cache, "A Plea for Euclid" *ANY: Architecture New York*, No. 24, Design After Mies: BOXING THE LONG SHADOW AT IIT (1999), pp. 54-59. An exception to this statement is *spherical geometry*, a non-Euclidean two-dimensional space that can be represented in Euclidean three-dimensional space.

2 Ruled surfaces contain straight ruling lines at least one direction of their *UV curve field*. In contemporary terms, geometric surfaces are subdivided with a grid of perpendicular lines, whose opposing orientations are referred to as *U* and *V*.

01

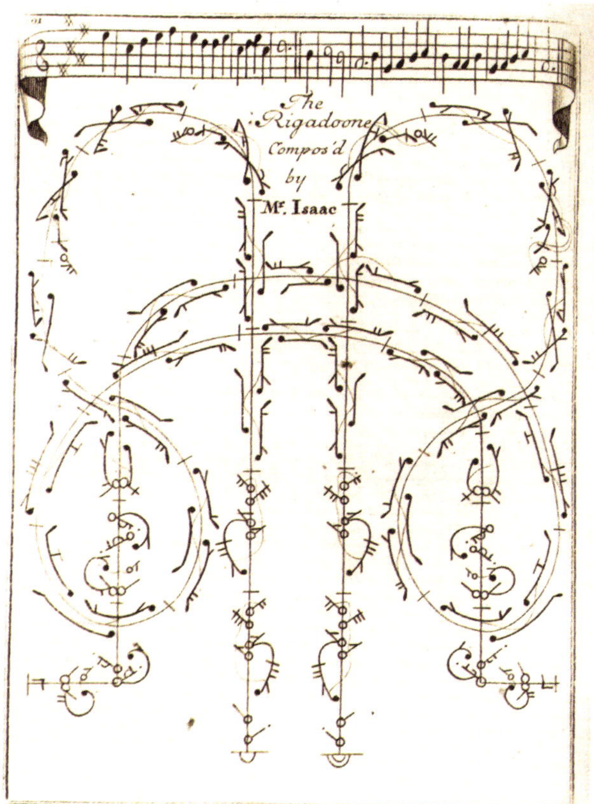

02

Raoul Auger Feuillet (1660-1710). Dance notation for a rigadoon by Isaac from *Chorégraphie*, 1700 Source: John Weaver, Orchesography: *An Exact and Just Translation from the French of Monsieur Feuillet*, 1721.

Kellom Tomlinson (1693-1753), George Bickham (1684-1758) engraver. Illustration for *passacaille* from *The art of dancing explained by readings and figures*, 1735. Source: Typ 705.35.842, Houghton Library, Harvard University.

03

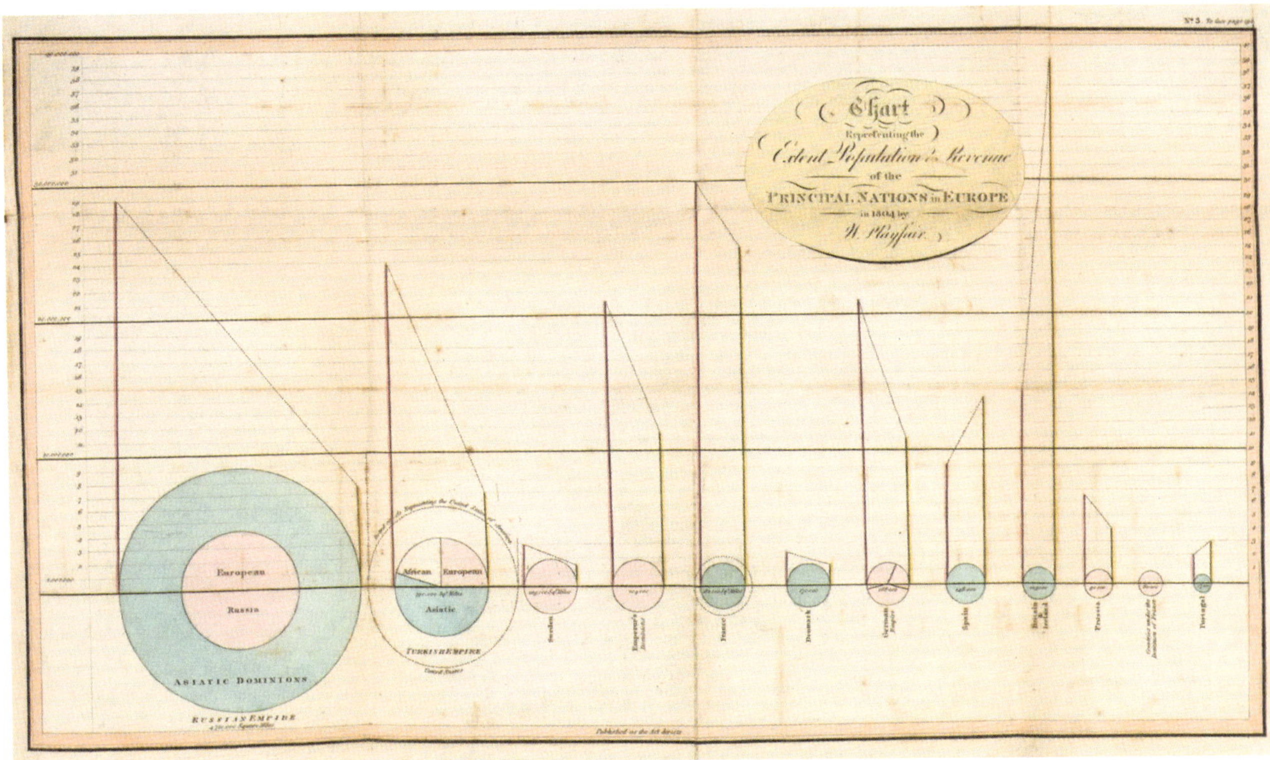

Extent, Population, and Revenue of the Principal Nations of Europe in the order of their Magnitude, 1804.
Source: William Playfair (1759-1823), *Inquiry Into the Permanent Causes of the Decline and Fall of Powerful and Wealthy Nations: Designed to Shew[!] How the Prosperity of the British Empire May Be Prolonged.*
2nd ed. London: Printed for Greenland and Norris, 1807.

mapping. Quantitative data related to specific locales may be represented numerically, by color, or by other coded means and visually integrated into cartographic representations of the physical environment. This overlay of multiple sets of coded data onto geographic space enables the perception of natural, economic, social, and demographic patterns subject to further analysis. With the publication of *The Visual Display of Quantitative Information* (1983) and *Envisioning Information* (1990), statistician Edward Tufte (b. 1942) demonstrated how representations of quantitative data can be effectively dissociated from any physical or geographic forms to which the data might refer. These visual data-spaces are flexible and reconfigurable, allowing design imperatives to vary depending on the thesis and intention of the author. The geometric shape, magnitude, and color of the graphics may not represent physical attributes of spaces or objects, but rather convey quantities and classifications of various non-visual information (**03**). Of course, many examples cited by Tufte also show notations and data projected onto actual spaces, objects, or geographies—similar to the aforementioned Baroque dance notation and GIS mapping. Although multiple layers of information may be mapped onto specific forms, this data may not directly describe the originating or spatial characteristics of the latter and are often incidental to the processes of formation. Euclidean two-dimensional and three-dimensional space thus remains the de facto milieu of spatial description and perception, with additional coded information simply hitching a ride.

René Descartes (1596-1650) is generally credited with the invention of analytic geometry. His concise mathematical text *La Géométrie,* published in 1637, provided methods to fuse algebra and geometry through the crucial idea of a coordinate system, enabling the graphing of polynomial expressions in two and three dimensions.[3] To reiterate, algebraic expressions of analytic geometry and the curves and surfaces they describe are interchangeable representations of equivalent entities, bound together inextricably by the axiomatic language of mathematics. Although Descartes's unparalleled contributions occurred in the 17th century, the origins of analytic geometry date back to ancient Greece. Of three problems of classical Greek geometry, perhaps the most relevant here is that of *cube duplication*, otherwise known as the Delian problem.[4] The story goes that the people of Athens, in efforts to counteract an ensuing plague, were asked by the oracle of Apollo at Delos to double the volume of the cubical altar in his temple. Determining this scale factor simply amounts to solving the modest algebraic equation $x^3 = 2$, with the solution of the cube root of 2—an irrational number (~1.259921....). Having disallowed notions of variability and arithmetic continuity (the use of non-whole or irrational numbers) the Greeks

3 Descartes was known as a philosopher as much as mathematician. *La Géométrie,* one of the most important mathematical texts of all time, was published as an appendix to *Discours de la Méthode* (*Discourse on Method*).

4 The three classical Greek problems: 1. squaring the circle (construction of circle and square of equal area) 2. angle tri-section 3. Delian problem, or cube duplication.

never developed an algebra appropriate for the methods of coordinate geometry.[5] Using only techniques of solid geometry, Menaechmus (380-320 BC), a tutor of Alexander the Great, devised an elegant solution involving the construction and intersection of two curves, a parabola and a hyperbola—both conic sections. Although he did not know it, Menaechmus had solved for the unique solution of the simple algebraic curves $y= x^2$ (a parabola) and $x*y=2$ (a hyperbola)[6], yet he had come to this solution via solid geometry construction, or via *descriptive* means.

The Greeks continued for centuries to study conic sections entirely with the methods of solid geometry without referencing algebraic considerations (**04**). It turned out that conics were critical to the development of analytic geometry, related to a wide range of engineering and computational problems. The equations defining conic sections are second order polynomial expressions whose solution spaces model significant behaviors of Newtonian mechanics. From celestial orbits (elliptical), to gravitational acceleration, projectiles, optics, and acoustics (parabolic), to GPS tracking and sundials (hyperbolic), the breadth of their usefulness cannot be overstated. Cones are *geometric embodiments of quantitative relationships* governed by algebraic expressions, with instantiations of variables dictating specific planes that slice them, and whose solutions are determined by intersection points of the resulting conic sections. For the analytic geometer, this is self-evident. From the contemporary architect's point of view of parametric versioning and computational variability, this is a provocative notion. The cone is a geometric solution space of computational relationships distilled into a simple and discernable form. Yet as many contemporary architects seek to devise intelligent algorithms to translate quantitative data into performance-oriented design proposals, it is important to note that often the visually compelling surfaces of analytic solution spaces are formally *unrelated* to viable architectural schemes. Consider again the Delian problem and the elegant descriptive solution of conic sections constructed by Menaechmus, yet the comparatively basic design solution was to simply increase the cubic altar dimensions by ~26%.

While the techniques of analytic geometry alternate between algebraic notation and visual representation, the methods of descriptive geometry are firmly ensconced in the latter. Not surprisingly, architects have historically gravitated toward descriptive methods due to the direct graphic definition and manipulation of form through projective drawing. With the publication of *Géométrie Descriptive* in 1799, Gaspard Monge (1746-1818) codified pragmatic techniques to represent objects in three-dimensional Euclidean space. These elegant and economical

5 Carl Boyer, *History of Analytic Geometry*, Yeshiva University Press (New York, NY) 1956, p.16.
6 Eliminating the y variable from the two equations, parabola $y= x^2$ and hyperbola $x*y=2$, we are left with $x*x^2 = x^3 = 2$ (algebraic definition of the Delian problem) whose solution is the x coordinate of the intersection point of the two curves.

04

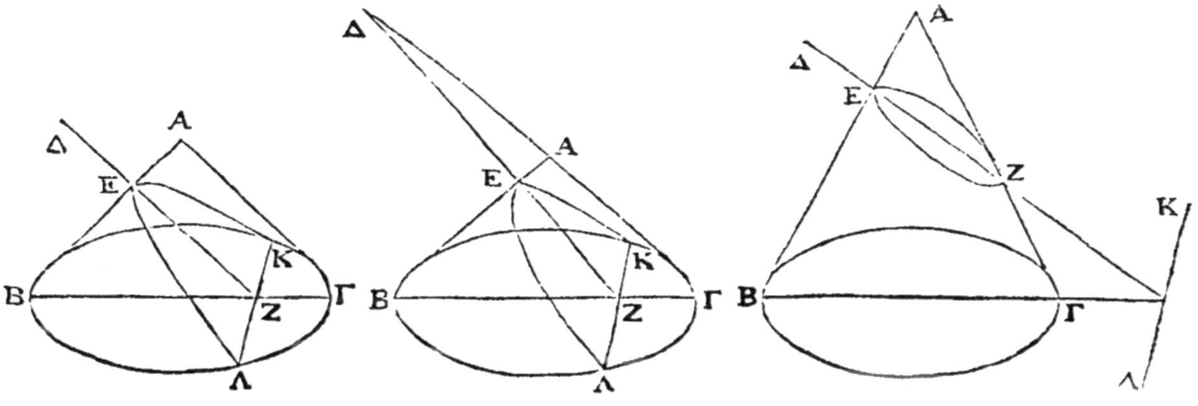

Three different conic sections from Edmund Halley's reconstruction of the original *Conics* text by Apollonius of Perga (c. 240-190 BC). The Greek mathematician Apollonius showed that by varying the angle of the cutting plane, a single right or oblique cone can yield all three types of curves. He gave the names ellipse, parabola, and hyperbola, meaning "less than", "the same as", and "more than", respectively, yielding the etymology of ellipsis, parable, and hyperbole. Source: Edmund Halley (1656-1742), *Apollonii Pergaei Conicorum (Conics of Apollonius)*, 1710.

05

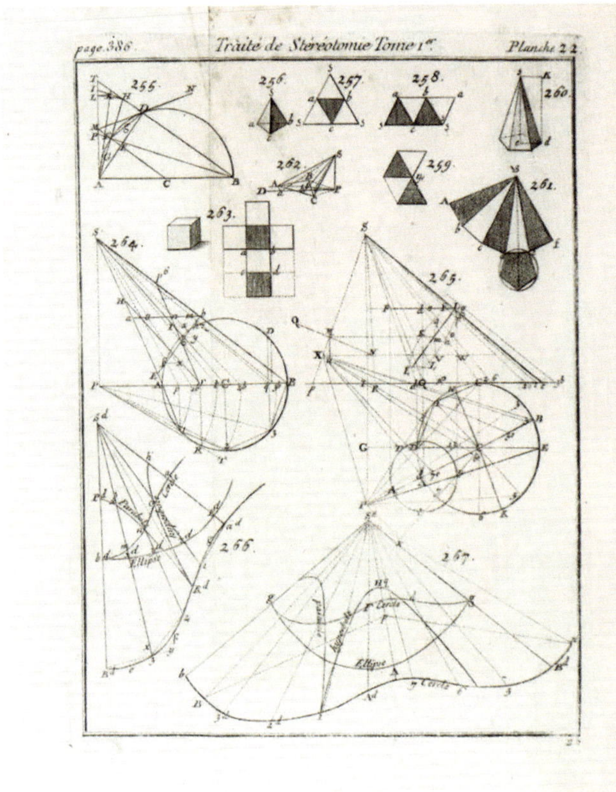

Projection and development of various geometric solids: regular tetrahedron, faceted pentagonal cone, cube, oblique circular cone with developed conic sections. Source: Amédée-François Frézier (1682-1773), *La Théorie et la Pratique de la Coupe des Pierres*, 1738, Tome I, plate 22. © Bibliothèque nationale de France.

06

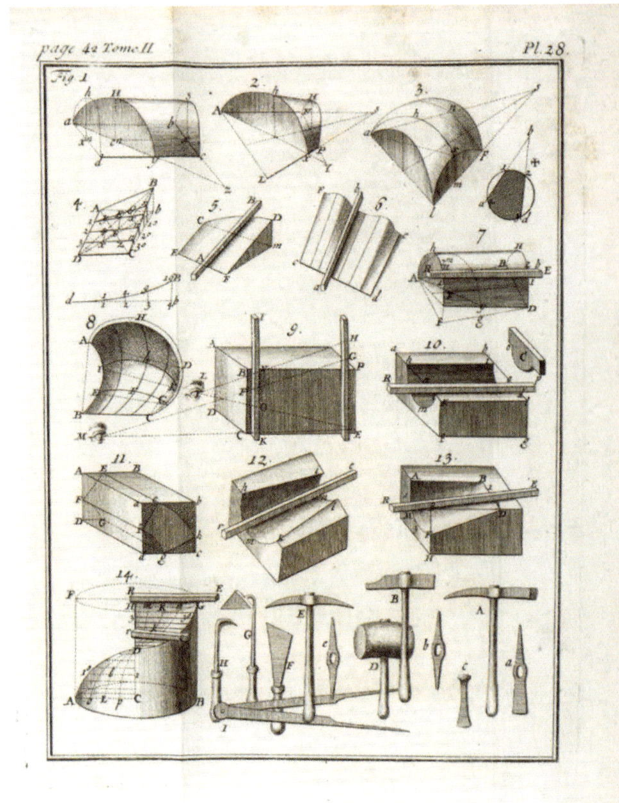

Generalized notation for stereotomic solids: domical and conical vaults, including ruling line extensions, voussoir bounding box, and straightedge verification. Source: Amédée-François Frézier (1682-1773), *La Théorie et la Pratique de la Coupe des Pierres* 1738, Tome II, plate 28. © Bibliothèque nationale de France.

drawing methods allowed the architect and engineer to parse projective information onto two perpendicular planes of projection, which divided three-dimensional space into four quadrants. These planes, carrying metric information from horizontal and vertical projections, could conceptually rotate about their intersection axis and flatten onto the single plane of the drawing surface. This enabled facile representation and manipulation of non-planar entities and objects not aligned with the planes of projection. Monge famously used his descriptive methods for the defiladement of military fortresses with oblique stone walls, designing voussoir geometries that had been previously determined algebraically. As a radical restatement of solid geometry[7], descriptive geometry allowed the architect to move adeptly between perpendicular projections while maintaining a dexterous command of all three dimensions of Euclidean space. Architects and engineers were empowered to explore an expanded range of challenging architectural forms and geometric ideas. Descriptive geometry became the preferred method of design inquiry for the architect, while also serving to further the estrangement between architecture and mathematics after the 18th-century rise of differential calculus.[8]

Vaulted forms have been present in architectural construction since antiquity, and it is not surprising that ruled surfaces such as cones and cylinders were surface types of great interest to the descriptive geometer, especially given the increased repertoire and dexterity provided by Monge. In fact, projective studies of ruled surfaces similar to those found in Monge's text—cones, cylinders, conoids, helicoids—appeared in many architectural treatises over 100 years before *Géométrie Descriptive* (**05**). As singly ruled surfaces, cones and cylinders bend in only one axis, with only one curve field composed of straight lines. For the analytic geometer, these surfaces manifest relationships between linear (straight) and exponential (curved) algebraic terms. For the descriptive geometer, these surfaces can directly transition between doubly curved spherical domes and planar walls. The presence of straight lines on cones and cylinders allowed easier representation and study of curved, non-planar surfaces. Simply put, straight lines are efficient geometric vehicles to keep track of an infinite number of points in three-dimensional space. Only two projections of two discrete points define the location of any (oblique) line with Monge's methods. The geometric properties of ruled surfaces that enabled expedient projection were also indispensable for stereotomic construction, which became more precise and structurally daring with the augmentation of descriptive techniques. Exposed outer surfaces of stone voussoirs are often singly ruled, in contrast to their interior contiguous and planar faces. The singly ruled nature of these exposed surfaces allowed masons to precisely cut and dimensionally

7 Robin Evans, "Forms Lost and Found Again", *The Projective Cast: Architecture and Its Three Geometries*, The MIT press (Cambridge, MA) 1995, p.324.

8 Antoine Picon, "Architecture and Mathematics: Between Hubris and Restraint", *AD Architectural Design, No. 212, July/August 2011, Mathematics of Space*, p.31.

07

Conical trompe. Maison des Anges. Saumur, France, 17thc. Source: Structurae International Database and Gallery of Structures. © Jacques Mossot.

verify the fidelity of the surface with linear construction tools (**06**). The equally pragmatic necessities of stereotomic construction thus reinforced the tendencies of descriptive drawing techniques to promote the interest and use of ruled surfaces.

Even though Monge is best known in architectural discourse for the codification and publication of descriptive geometry, he was additionally renowned for his contributions to analytic geometry.[9] The 19th century witnessed a rapid expansion of definition and visualization of analytic surfaces, not only in the primary milieus of parametric and implicit equations, but also in the realm of physical modeling. Théodore Olivier (1793-1853), a pupil of Monge, produced exquisitely crafted string models to visualize various classes of analytic surfaces (**08**). These analog models of mechanical ingenuity were often transformable—allowing modulation of the mathematical surfaces through a range of input variations. Arrays of colored and weighted tensile strings physically manifested curve fields of ruling lines. Variations included not only singly ruled cylinders and cones, but also doubly ruled hyperbolic paraboloids (hypars) and hyperboloids of revolution.[10] With a pragmatic resonance similar to the expedient projection of linear points or the precision of a stonemason's straightedge, two discrete points tensioning any given string of these models induced an analog material bias, predisposing them to exclusively represent ruled surface classes.

Ruled surfaces were only a subset of the rapidly expanding and diverse catalog of 19th-century mathematical geometries. The broader range explored by analytic geometers included those exhibiting complex double curvature, with curve fields bending in both orientations. The visualization and modeling of this larger mathematical repertoire demanded copious effort and attention, leading to physical representations fabricated via cast plaster and carved wood. Unlike Olivier's string models, the opaque and volumetric nature of these material solutions meant that only one side of the mathematical surface was perceptible. Straight lines occurring on these complex surfaces numbered far fewer, and often indicated the periodic degenerate, or "zero" conditions (**09**). Alexander Brill (1842-1935), a German mathematician who had also studied architecture and descriptive geometry in the 1860s, owned a business producing mathematical models for researchers and universities. Among his most successful sellers were his series of "carton" models—notched assemblies of perpendicular sets of uniformly offset planes (**10**). Similar to wood and plaster models, the resulting volumetric expression

9 Carl Boyer, "The Invention of Analytic Geometry", *Scientific American, vol. 180, issue 1, January 1949,* p.45. Like Descartes, Monge was a polymath of many talents, in addition to his contributions to analytic geometry, he was an experimental chemist, and shares the credit for discovering the chemical composition of water.

10 Doubly ruled surfaces have straight ruling lines on *both* curve field directions, and include the hyperbolic paraboloid (hypar), the hyperboloid of revolution, and the plane.

08

Théodore Olivier (1793-1853). Ruled surface string model: hyperboloid and hypar. Source: Cornell University Collection of Olivier String Models for Descriptive Geometry; Model CUCE04; 1884.

necessarily biased the presentation of a single side. The mathematical surface was not explicitly rendered, but effectively implied by multiple silhouettes of intersecting planar sections using the carton method. The production of these various types of models continued until the 20th century, documenting the progressive advancement and representation of mathematical form. The expertise of mathematicians operating within axiomatic systems of authorship and visualization lead to prolific invention and discovery during this period. The generative methods of analytical geometry were potent, as even modest modulations of equations could produce profound variations of form.

Without comparable form generators such as algebraic modulation within Descartes's coordinate system, design and formal innovation advanced at an arguably slower pace with the descriptive methods of the architect. During this same period of rapid knowledge expansion in analytic geometry, the essential structural and typological dispositions of architecture remained relatively stable, cycling through various styles up until the industrial revolution. In the decades before and after Mies van der Rohe's 20th-century project of a distilled hegemonic classicism painted the discipline into a linguistic and tectonic corner, however, other architects had been searching for new modes of architectural form making. With the increased publication and availability of mathematical model catalogs, visual engineering manuals, biological compilations in the 19th and early 20th century, artists and architects had access to abundant ready-made source books from which they could liberally draw endless architectural inspiration.[11] With such an expansive range of scientific and mathematical material to choose from, it is both remarkable and obvious that architects gravitated toward ruled surface the geometries. As previously noted, many of these geometric surfaces had already been subjects of investigation in architectural treatises for centuries. Given new methods of construction in concrete and steel, issues of constructability weighed heavily in favor of ruled surfaces, and renewed interest in these forms would take them to new levels of sophistication and expression.

Antoni Gaudí (1852-1926) departed from pre-modern vernacular with more free-form surfaces in the Casa Milà (1906). The undulating periodic roof of the Sagrada Familia School (1909, reconstructed 2002) exhibited a more disciplined singly ruled conoidal surface, enabling successive linear rafters at variable slopes to support the vaulted roof (**11**). Gaudi ultimately became obsessed with the doubly ruled surfaces of the hyperboloid of revolution and hyperbolic paraboloid (hypar) as evidenced in the basilica of Sagrada Familia (begun 1915). In *Vers Une Architecture*

11 Andrew Witt, *Formulations, Ch. 3: Theorems Made Flesh: the Architectonics of the Mathematical Model*, MIT Press (Cambridge, MA) 2021, pp. 61-99.

10

Carton models of second order (quadric) surfaces, authored by Alexander Brill (1842-1935), 1877. Each plane of the models represents one of the variables *x*, *y*, or *z* set to equally spaced constant values for parallel or intersecting section cuts. Source: Mathematical model collection, Phillips University of Marburg, Germany. Photo: Ramona Trusheim.

09

Plaster model of Clebsch diagonal cubic surface, c.1884. Source: Collections de l'Institut Henri Poincaré, © Institut Henri Poincaré.

(1923), Le Corbusier wrote, "A volume is enveloped by a surface, a surface divided by the directrices and generatices of the volume, and this gives the volume individuality."[12] While not surprising that an architect might use technical language to describe general conditions, this statement shows that Le Corbusier understood architecture's potential for geometric abstraction and he was predisposed to adopt new forms in languages he already understood. Works such as the hyperboloid at Chandigarh (1954) were simple and rigorously defined. More architectural considerations such as light, program, and structure motivated the inflections of geometry in later works, including the Philips Pavilion (1959), the Firminy Chapel (begun 1963), and the conoid roof at Notre-Dame du Haut Ronchamp (1955), which had ruling lines which were manageable in projection, yet produced a voluptuous form in three-dimensional space.[13]

Numerous 20th-century architect/engineers including Eduardo Torroja (1899-1961), Pier Luigi Nervi (1891-1979), Felix Candela (1910-1997) also tested the structural limits of ruled surface design and construction. Their training as structural engineers enabled these designers to engage the analytic space of structural performance of their spatial forms more than most architects. Felix Candela, the great Mexican engineer, architect, and structural artist, focused almost exclusively on the hyperbolic paraboloid, or hypar. Candela wrote in 1958 that the hypar "is the *only* warped surface whose equation is simple enough to permit stress calculation by elementary mathematics."[14] The ruling lines of the surface were not only useful for their descriptive and fabrication attributes—expedient visual projection and manageable formwork construction—but were also instrumental to specific mathematical attributes which enabled Candela to perform accurate pre-digital structural analysis.[15] With specific loading and support conditions, the form of the hypar is geometrically similar to the analytic surface describing its membrane surface stresses. In other words, an architectural proposition and the shape of its analytical performance model *can* be geometrically comparable, bound together through form as well as numeric magnitudes. The formal correlation between these two models depends on how the hypar surfaces are permuted, loaded, and supported. As Candela's schemes became more complex with less symmetrical hypars, the correspondence decreases. The most explicitly typological work of his career was the Church of Our Lady of the Miraculous Medal (1953-55). In order to produce the architectural and spatial hierarchies demanded by the cathedral type, the contiguous hypars comprising the nave and aisles became more asymmetrical and eccentric, inducing some of the highest stresses in any of his works and distancing the architectural form from its

12 Le Corbusier, *Towards a New Architecture,* Dover Publications Inc. (New York, NY) 1986, p. 24.

13 Robin Evans, "Comic Lines", *The Projective Cast: Architecture and Its Three Geometries*, The MIT press (Cambridge, MA) 1995, p.308.

14 From Felix Candela's unpublished autobiography, Maillart Archives, Department of Civil & Environmental Engineering, Princeton University (Princeton, NJ)

15 Felix Candela, "General Formulations for Membrane Stresses in Hyperbolic Paraboloid Shells", *Journal of the American Concrete Institute, vol. 57, issue 10,* (October 1960), pp.353-372.

structural solution space. There are other architectural idioms directly mimetic of the analytic spaces which describe them. The most didactic of these manifestations typically relate to structural performance. The Magazzini Warehouse in Chiasso, Switzerland (1925) by the Swiss engineer and bridge-builder Robert Maillart (1872-1940), exhibits a roof truss section nearly identical to its bending moment stress diagram, with a simple bisection and sloping of each half to form a gable **(14)**. Because its structural depth is correspondent with the stresses at every span location, the truss is able to negotiate the distance with evenly distributed stress and material economy. Frei Otto (1925-2015) used soap bubble experiments to empirically study minimal surface forms of tensile membrane structures, most notably for the 1972 Munich Olympic Stadium. Minimal surfaces were a subject of great interest for 19th-century analytic geometers, including Heinrich Scherk (1798-1885) and Hermann Schwarz (1843-1921). These surfaces are so named because they define the minimum surface area that can span between any given closed-loop boundaries **(15)**. As architectural form, they equalize and distribute structural forces evenly across the tensile surface, covering the greatest area with the least embodied stresses. Additionally, they maintain minimum surface area to volume ratios, which have direct implications for energy conservation and thermodynamics. Unlike Candela's simple hypars or Maillart's warehouse trusses, these tensile membrane forms are not geometrically comparable to the mathematical solution spaces of their structural or energy performance, yet they do represent quantitatively optimized versions.

Digital computation and visualization methods have afforded contemporary mathematicians the ability to produce analytic forms with unprecedented quickness and precision. Not surprisingly, a significant resurgence of interest by the architectural discipline has followed, enabled by the availability of three-dimensional modeling and computational software beginning in the 1990s. Unlike the co-option of mathematical geometries that occurred during the 20th century, the ease and availability of digital methods has enabled the architect to directly author mathematical forms expediently and iteratively, using non-descriptive means. Most often these techniques are deployed without an understanding of the underlying processes of formation, especially regarding the mathematics of spline curves and surfaces. While practitioners may translate generative algorithms directly into architectural proposals in order to bolster rhetoric of performance, architects are primarily drawn to these analytic surfaces for their aesthetic value and capacity for spatial invention. Toward the end of the 20th century, digital design mediums enabled the architect to

11

12

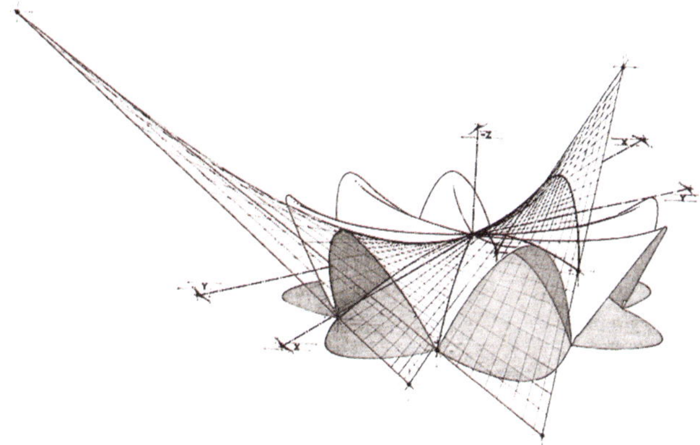

Antoni Gaudí (1852-1926). Sagrada Familia School, 1909, rebuilt 2002. Linear rafters support the undulating singly ruled conoidal ceiling.Source: Photo courtesy the author.

Drawing by Felix Candela (1910-1997) for Los Manantiales restaurant in Xochimilco, Mexico, 1958. Hyperbolic paraboloid (hypar) geometries permute radially with ruling line extensions for two bays that share a single hypar. Source: Felix Candela, *Casabella* 306, 1966, p. 28.

13

Robert Maillart (1872-1940). Warehouse Magazzini generali. Chiasso, Switzerland, 1924-25. Source: ETH-Bibliothek Zürich, Bildarchiv, Hs_1085-1924-25-1-1-1

14

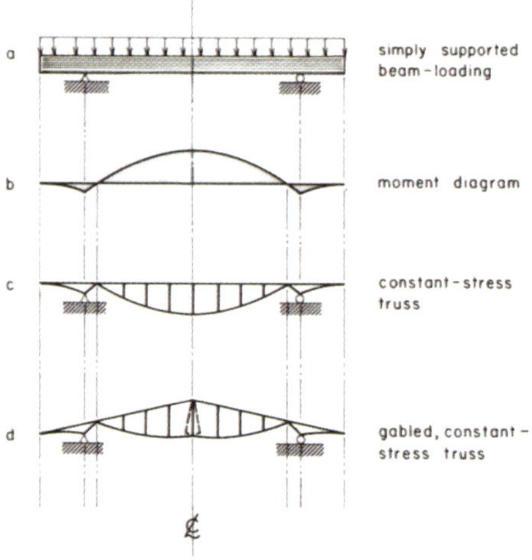

Warehouse Magazzini structural diagrams showing: b) bending moment for beam with cantilevered ends, c) constant force truss, d) gabled constant force truss. Source: Billington, David (1928-2018). *Robert Maillart's Bridges: The Art of Engineering*. Princeton University Press, 1979, 67.

15

Frei Otto (1925-2015). Minimal surface soap film experiments. 1962. Source: Institute for Lightweight Structures (ILEK). Stuttgart, Germany.

16

J. Mayer H. Architects. Metropole Parasol. Seville, Spain, 2011. Many early architectural manifestations of digital forms did not construct the complex curvature of the surface, but effectively implied it with planar assemblies similar to 19th century mathematical carton models. Source: Photo courtesy the author.

author complex forms, perhaps finally eradicating the cumbersome constraints of Mongean projection and stereotomic construction, which conspired to insist that we draw and build with at least *some* straight ruling lines. Architects are now liberated to draw or model nearly anything, but left with diminished means for previous disciplinary expertise to remain relevant. Early experiments in the construction of digitally designed non-planar forms relied on techniques visually and tectonically akin to Alexander Brill's 19th century carton models. The inability of this technique to explicitly construct the curving surface it implies became more conspicuous as the scale of these experimental projects increased along with the need for a weather barrier. The Brill mathematical models generally exhibited sets of planes parallel to the *xy*, *yz*, and *xz* origin planes, with section cuts defined by implicit equations aligned with the Cartesian axes of the original surface equation. The parallel and perpendicular sets of cutting planes in works like Jürgen Mayer's Metropole Parasol (2011) have less to do with the mathematical definition of the NURBS surface it implies (**16**). The cutting planes' orientations and spacing are instead calibrated in response to architectural, urban, or environmental issues.

New constrained and reciprocal relationships have emerged between design geometry and material construction with curving architectural forms, especially given the requirement to construct environmental envelopes and the building industry's longer-term transition toward fabrication methods based on sheet materials. Unless there is material deformation, the accurate construction of curved surfaces depends largely on the geometric properties of isometric developability.[16] Much attention has been paid to developable surfaces in building technology recently, especially in the area of digital geometric consultancy. The architectural practice largely credited for significantly advancing digital processes for the construction of complex surfaces is also known for embracing design methods that are decidedly analog. There exists a mythology surrounding Gehry Partners using paper study models for concept and schematic design phases, and subsequently digitizing them for further refinement and detailing during construction document delivery. Even though the specific contingencies of these signature configurations may be challenging to describe mathematically, embedded in the models is the material property of developability, making them predisposed to amenably accept methods of contemporary surface construction. Put more directly, because the scale models are made of sheet material, it is easier to construct the 1:1 building in an industry based on sheet material construction. All developable surfaces are

16 A *developable* surface is one that can be unrolled flat to a plane without distortion. All such surfaces are singly ruled (with ruling lines in only one curve field orientation) and include cones, cylinders, and tangent developables.

singly ruled, meaning there are numerous straight ruling lines traversing Gehry's calligraphic forms, though it may not be immediately apparent from panel orientations and seam design. Once again, the descriptive and material virtues of ruled surfaces become useful and relevant, albeit dispersed and camouflaged in these cases.

Perhaps more than other developable and ruled surfaces, cones have maintained relevance for both analytical and descriptive geometry. In analytic terms, they still operate as basic solution spaces for classical and current computational problems. In descriptive terms, they have remained persistent design forms familiar and useful to the architect. Originally, this may have been due to geometric qualities enabling facile drawing and projection. However, it is the fabrication advantages that have kept singly ruled developable surfaces critically relevant in the digital age—enduring despite the shift from volumetric stereotomy to sheet-based construction. The advent of complex forms in contemporary architecture has necessitated the use of developable surfaces to post-rationalize geometries of double curvature for economy and constructability. They have become the unavoidable corrective means to rectify geometrically undisciplined architectural form. The research and geometric techniques in this book aim to produce new combinatory techniques and architectural idioms, using developable and doubly ruled surfaces to serve as the *a priori* vocabulary of a spatial and tectonic language.

The sequence begins with a collection of short case studies examining various types of singly and doubly ruled surfaces found in historical and contemporary architectural precedents. These observations are not exhaustive analyses, but concise visual and written synopses exhibiting previous and effective deployment of these geometries. Following is a geometric primer that samples combinatory techniques authored and refined to produce new formal idioms using these surfaces. These geometric design techniques mainly focus on piecewise continuous and smooth aggregations of ruled surfaces, typically joined along native ruling lines. Most of these aggregate figures, except those composed of doubly ruled surfaces, are then subject to *geodesic planking*—a subdivision method to subdivide the overall host surface into developable strips for fabrication and construction (17). Finally, a series of architectural design projects explores the range of these geometric techniques, from domestic figural compositions of tangent continuity to larger scale aggregations and periodic fields. Unlikely to be combined in arbitrary ways using these techniques, ruled surface geometries require specific knowledge of their curvature and isometry for successful deployment. They offer productive resistance in terms of how they combine, leading to motivated geometric grammars and legible syntaxes—attributes necessary to bring their virtues into a discursive frame.

17

Geodesic plank of right circular cone with Frenet frames.

RULED SURFACE CASE STUDIES

The following investigations consider historical and contemporary architectural precedents that employ ruled surfaces in their designs. Variations of scale, surface class, materiality, and tectonics exhibit the applicable range of (singly ruled) developable and doubly ruled surfaces. While not exhaustive, the brief analyses posit observations that reveal how these forms negotiate between architectural, material, and geometric requirements.

Sickergill Bridge

Renwick, United Kingdom (1898)

01

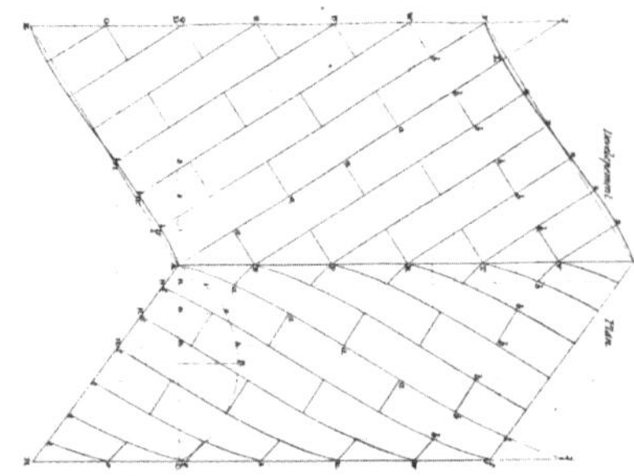

03 Plan projection of a helicoidal skew arch vault (below) and its flat development (above) from Peter Nicholson's *Treatise On the Oblique Arch with Spiral Joints* (3rd ed. 1847)

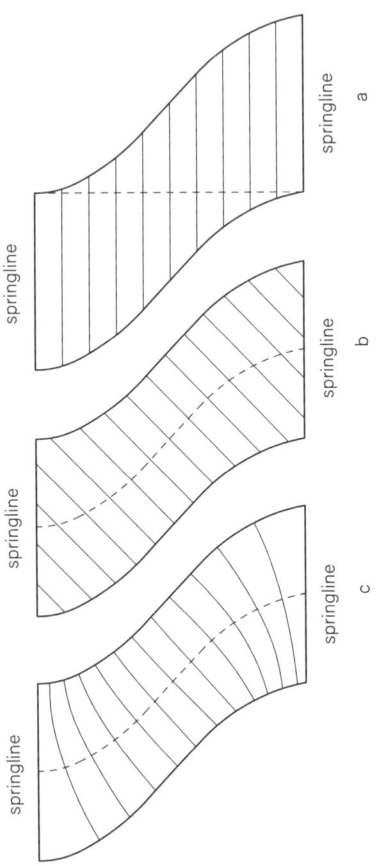

02 Development of three types of skew arch construction: a) false skew, b) helicoidal, and c) logarithmic

Completed in 1898, the Sickergill Bridge demonstrates the helicoidal method for constructing a skew arch bridge. Skew arch bridges negotiate the overpass between two paths (typically road and stream) which are *not* perpendicular in plan. Large angular deviations present difficulties in structure, geometric resolution, and methods of construction for the intrados of the masonry arch.

Peter Nicholson (1765-1844) published his helicoidal method in *Popular and Practical Treatise on Masonry and Stone-cutting* (1828), which described how standardized stones could be cut off-site and placed in a dynamic arrangement during construction. Other notable options for constructing skew arches include the structurally optimized logarithmic method, invented by Edward Sang (1805-1890), and the"false skew" method, which results in the most uniform and conventional stone pattern by arranging straight courses parallel to the springline. The logarithmic method requires every voussoir to be cut to a unique stereotomic shape, whereas the conventional coursing of the false skew method results in structural weakness, especially as the spanning angle increases.[1] The helicoidal method is an intermediate solution between bespoke structural optimization and ease of repeatable construction. The mid-surface stones can all be cut from the same eccentric pattern, resulting in helical coursing lines.

The ability for the stone coursing grain to rotate to different orientations over the fixed geometry of the host cylinder is an important concept for the architectural design work in this book. The helical edges of the stone are geometrically comparable to the edges of geodesic surface planks, used in most of the designs. In both cases, the orientation of the tectonic construction grain need not align with the host geometry's major axes and ruling lines, and can be designed to address other architectural and aesthetic issues.

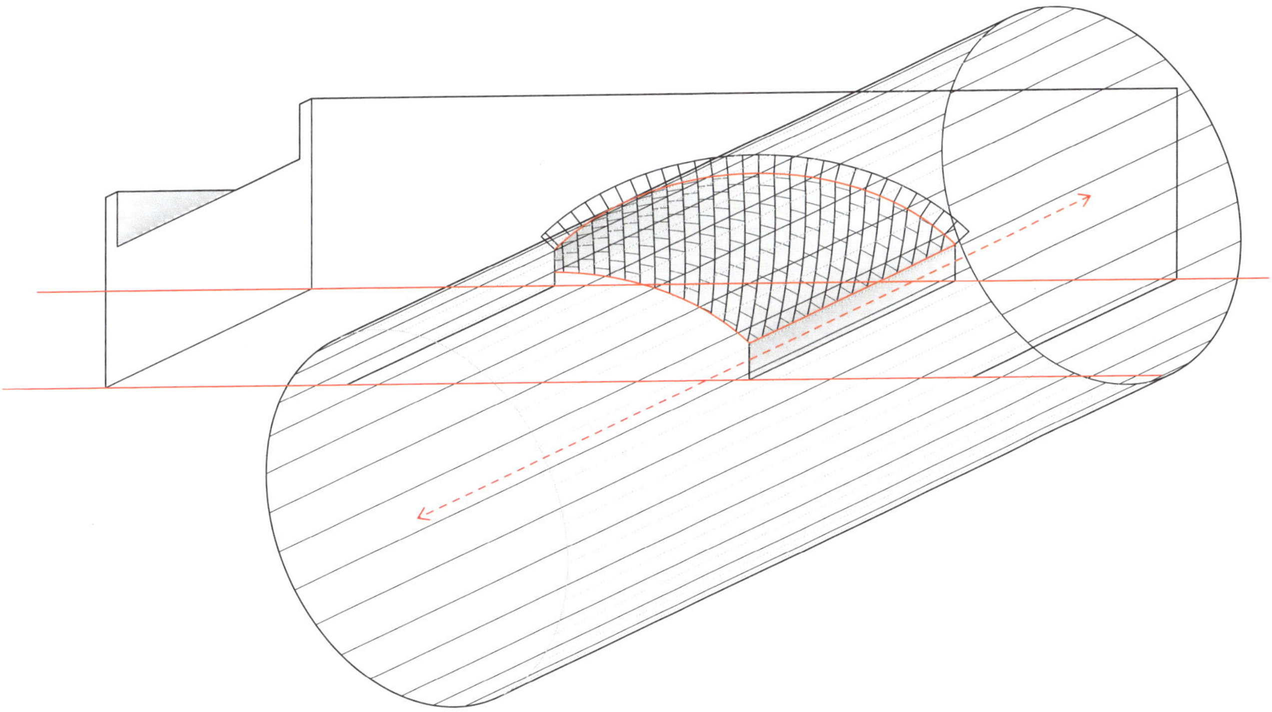

04 Cylindrical vault surface subdivided into helicoidal coursing independent of ruling lines

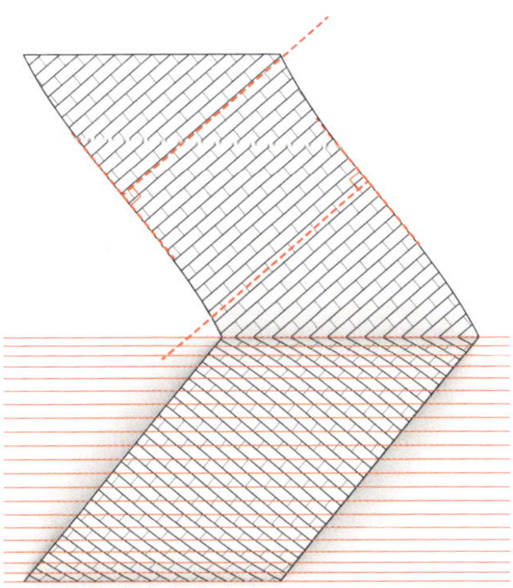

05 Sickergill Bridge vault plan (below) and helicoidal development (above)

06 Stone orientation is independent from the ruling line formwork

HELICAL COURSING

The construction formwork for the barrell arch manifests the straight ruling lines of the cylinder. The angle at which the stones are laid is dependent on the degree of skew angle, radius and length of arch, and the resulting surface development. The rotated helicoidal arrangement demonstrates that the coursing of tectonic units can deviate from the primary orientation of the host geometry.

1 Peter Nicholson, "Treatise On the Oblique Arch with Spiral Joints" from *The Guide to Railway Masonry*, 3rd ed. Groombridge & Sons (London, 1847), p. XIXXX.

01

Trompe At Abbaye Toussaint d'Angers

Angers, France (orig 13c. restored 1980)

Trompes and squinches are early architectural examples that demonstrate the utility of developable surfaces when addressing problems of structure and plan. Their reduced formal expression often contrasts with decorative and stylistic elements of traditional vernaculars, highlighting the interplay between geometry and architecture.

The trompe at Abbaye Toussaint d'Angers is one of the simplest examples of a conical trompe. The longitudinal edges of its voussoirs that mark the ruling line generators converge at the cone apex located on the vertical intersection line of the two side walls (**01**). The conical surface is tangent to the walls along two of these ruling line generators. While fabrication of cone apexes can be problematic due to inadequate minimum bending radii of sheet materials, the plastic nature of stereotomic construction is well suited to express these small and precise geometries. The local area proximate to the apex becomes a stucco surface, yet it is rendered with great precision. Often the numerous ruling lines of stone will terminate into a single idiosyncratic voussoir that serves as the structural and geometric springing point of the trompe, as in the Hôtel d'Angoulême Lamoignon (**03**).

Better known examples such as Hôtel de Bullioud by Philibert de l'Orme (**04**) have molding or other architectural elements which obscure the lines of tangency between the trompe and the supporting walls. The Toussaint Abbey trompe is unadorned, allowing an uninterrupted transition from the stereotomic voussoirs of the conical surface to the planar stucco wall. The non-planar space curve intersection between the cylindrical turret above and the conical trompe produces a crisp edge which hangs precisely in space. Coupled with the refined contiguous stonework and tangent transition to the stucco wall, the trompe achieves the qualitative effects of a delicate architectural drawing which is counterintuitively made of heavy stone.

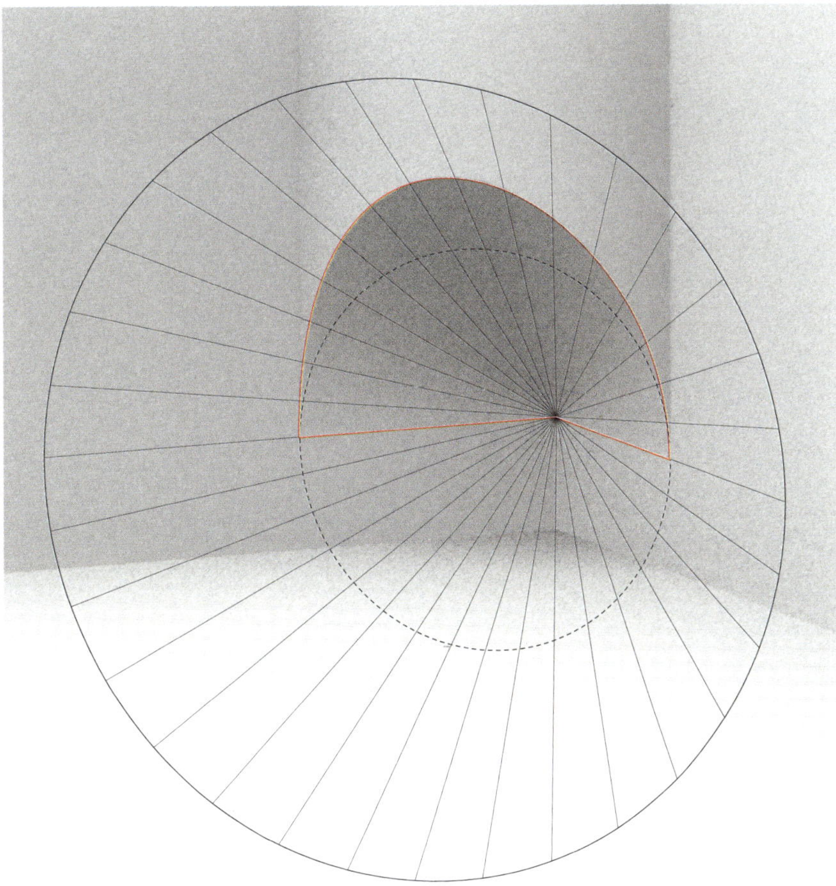

THIN AND THICK

The refined stereotomic edge of the trompe and its tangent transition from conical stone voussoirs to the planar stucco wall conveys the precision of an infinitesimally thin surface. It is simultaneously reminiscent of a delicately projected architectural drawing while also maintaining a strong volumetric expression.

02 Conical trompe surface is tangent to vertical walls along two ruling line generators

03 Hôtel d'Angoulême Lamoignon, Baptiste Androuet du Cerceau Paris France (1589)

04 Hôtel de Bullioud Philibert de l'Orme Lyons France (1536)

01

Église Saint-Pierre

Le Corbusier & José Oubrerie
Firminy, France (1973-2006)

Completed in 2006, forty-one years after Le Corbusier's death, the Saint-Pierre church in Firminy, France is the last major work of the architect. The large silhouette appears as a monolithic frustum with tapering filleted edges. Closer inspection of concrete seams reveals the discrete geometric elements which comprise the piecewise continuous compound surface of the exterior figure. The design and occurrence of massive and truly solid poché has diminished in recent centuries of architectural construction. Deep volumetric expression is now necessarily more concept than reality, and must be achieved through the composition and manipulation of surfaces via continuity, tangency, convexity, and concavity.

The main volume of Saint-Pierre is composed of four cones and four trapezoidal planar figures, arranged tangently to form the continuous exterior surface. The four cones serve as variable radius fillets between the four leaning planes and converge to crisp apex corners of the horizontal base. The frustum mass is counterintuitively set upon a more porous plinth comprised of planes and voids, making the former appear to levitate above grade. More delicate additive elements including a parabolic rain hood, linear wrap-around gutters, and the geometric primitives of the skylight embrasures may challenge the initial reading of a singular solid. However, the relative thinness and scale of these additional masses and lineaments remain secondary to the monolith to which they are attached. Similar juxtapositions of volume, surface, and line play out on the interior, albeit inverted. Apertures punctured through the envelope allow access to light from the side and high above, as if embedded in a deep subterranean grotto. The extruded embrasures protrude proud of the interior surface, revealing the dimension of their wall thickness without betraying the volumetric reading of smaller solids lodged in the poché.

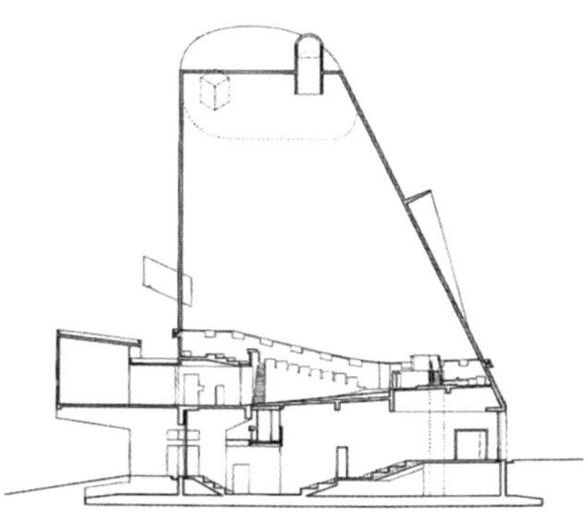

02 The robust volumetric presence of the exterior belies the delicate nature of the section

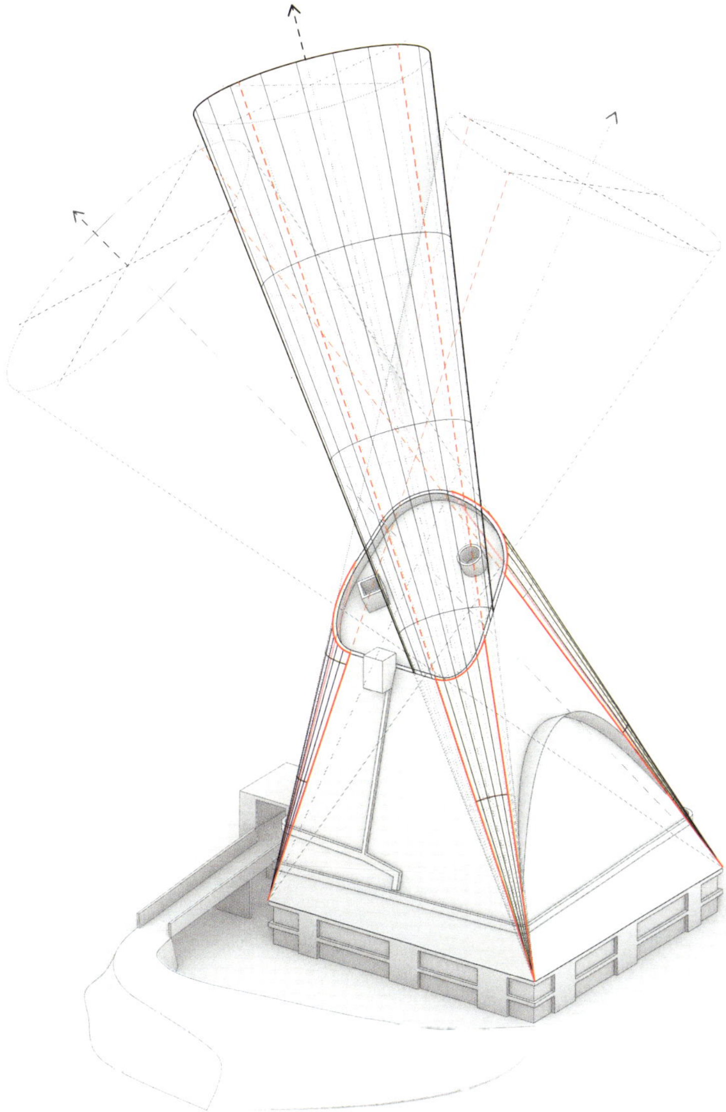

03

04

SOLID AND VOID

The piecewise continuous surface conveys two opposing readings–the solid monolith of the exterior and the subtractive void of the interior. As truly solid poché has become less prevalent in contemporary design and construction, deep volumetric expression of either type must be achieved through the composition of continuous surfaces.

IKMZ Brandenburg University of Technology

Herzog & de Meuron
Cottbus, Germany (2004)

01

The Cottbus Library by Herzog & de Meuron is an example of piecewise continuous circular cylinders trimmed and joined tangently along ruling line generators to produce a single undulating form. Each of the four exterior convex portions of the vertical façade convey the presence of a discrete centrifugal cylinder inside, pulling away from the centroid. Conversely, the four intermediate concave portions read as tensile membrane, inflecting inward from the negative pressure of a continuous shrink-wrapped skin.

The plan diagram (**04**) is reminiscent of a well-known comparison made by Greg Lynn between the composite curvature of several piecewise continuous, tangent arcs (often used in Baroque architecture) and a more contemporary inflected spline curve with weighted control vertices (**02**). Both manifest a formal dialectic between the continuous and discrete, and this comparison showcases the variable resolution of curvature methodology in mathematical geometry and architectural representation.

Though Lynn would disagree that the (lower resolution) of Baroque piecewise assembly is the antecedant of contemporary (higher resolution) calculus-based spline forms[1], both examples represent quantitative variations of the same geometric method. In terms of differential calculus, the former exhibits discrete and tangent non-zero subdivisions of constant curvature (G1 continuity) while the latter spline curve represents infinitesimal subdivision (limit approaching zero) of constantly changing curvature (G2 continuity).

Though not as finely differentiated as a weighted spline curve, the constant curvatures of the piecewise method make the discrete primitives and local centers of the Cottbus massing clear and legible. Most of the architectural design in this book uses comparable piecewise techniques when assembling developable surfaces for geodesic planking subdivision, as more uniform curvatures offer key advantages for material bending and tectonic construction.

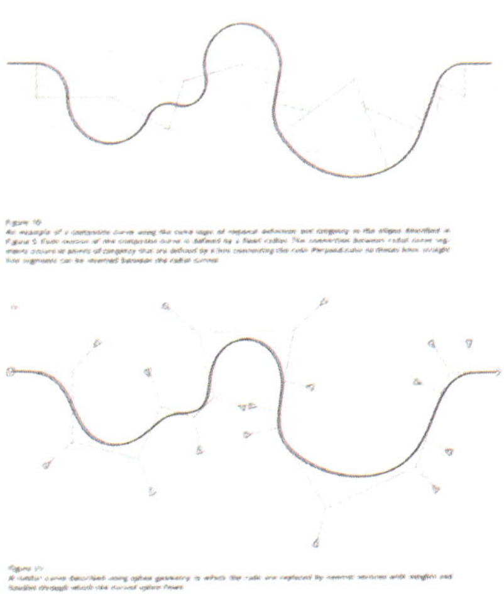

02 Comparison of piecewise continuous arcs and NURBS curve from Greg Lynn's *Animate Form* (1999)

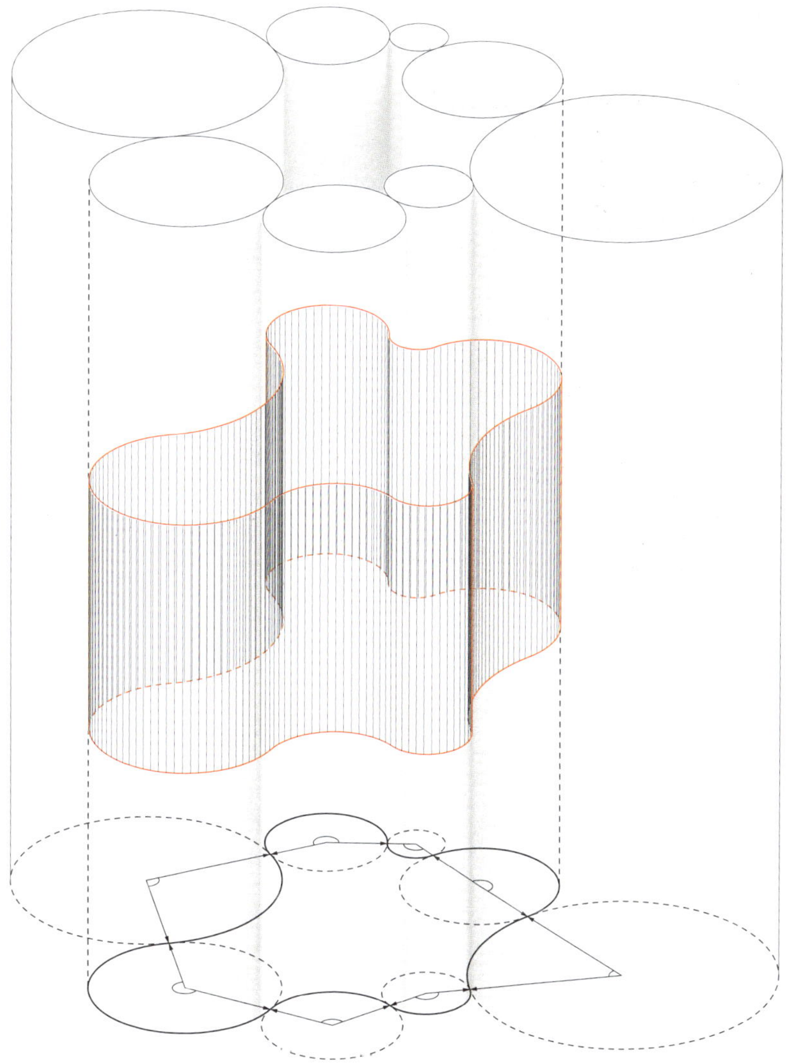

03

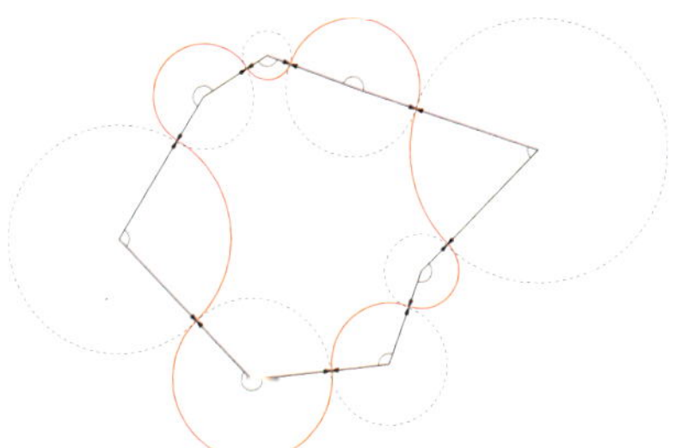

04 Plan diagram

05 Interior continuity

PART AND WHOLE

Cottbus Library is an exemplar of piecewise continuity–both in the two dimensional lineaments of the plan and the volumetric reading of the continuous extruded façade. Discrete geometric primitives and their centers are locally legible and simultaneously integral to the larger whole.

1 Greg Lynn, *Animate Form*, Princeton Architectural Press (New York NY, 1999) p.20.

01

Aula Medica

Wingårdh Arkitektkontor
Solna, Sweden (2013)

The façade the Aula Medica, designed by Wingårdh Arkitektkontor, is a piecewise continuous assembly of geometric surfaces, most of which are developable. Two vertical cylinders, two plumb planes, and a slender oblique cone comprise the majority of the façade with one hyperbolic paraboloid (hypar) completing the circuit. The hypar surface spans between the large vertical cylinder and the smaller leaning cone. If the hypar has a plumb ruling line edge conicident with a vertical generator of the large cylinder (**03**), the surfaces would be contiguous, but not tangent (G0 continuity). All of the surface normals along the cylinder generator lie in a single plane (a requirement for developability) whereas the normals along the hypar edge do not–evidence of the non-smooth transition. If the upper and lower ruling lines of the hypar are designed to be tangent to the horizontal circular/elliptical cuts of the cylinder and cone (i.e. the surfaces are not stitched along ruling lines), minor discrepancies between the idealized surfaces become apparent (**02**).

The primary subdivision of the façade reinforces the native UV curve field for each geometric element while also binding the totality with a continuous grid. Horizontal subdivisions are straight for the planes and hypar, and circular/elliptical for the cylinder/cone, respectively. Verticals are straight for all geometries. Further division of each quadrilateral into a triangular tesselation has considerable benefits. Not only can the triangulated façade accomodate the double-curvature of the mid-surface hypar, its faceting allows a discrete and incremental transition of surface normals between the hypar and the flanking cylinder and cone, producing the perception of smoothness.

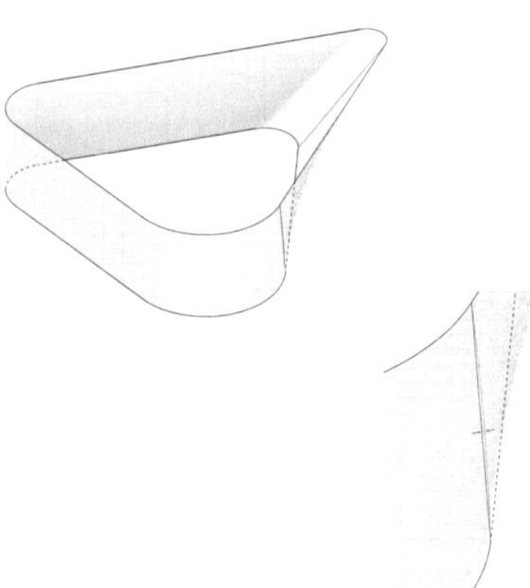

02 Surfaces exhibit discrepancies when not joined along ruling lines.

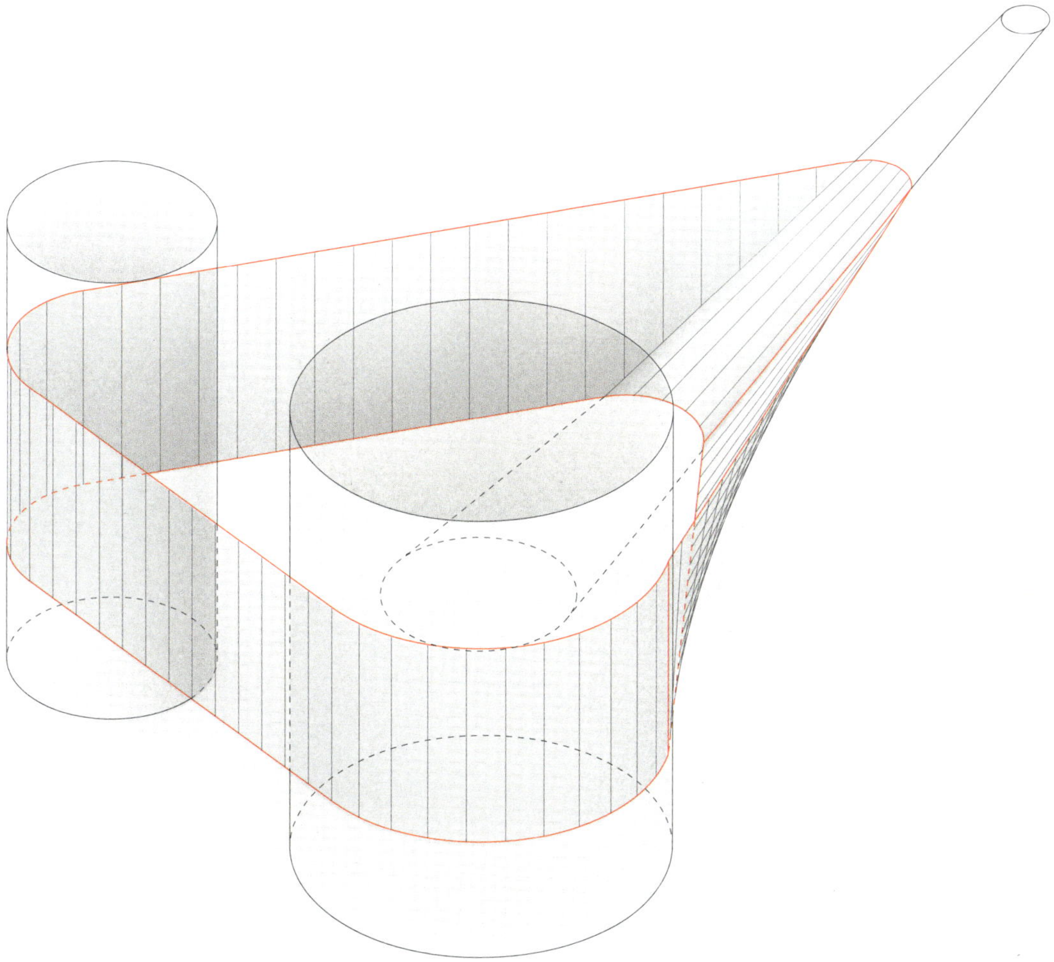

03 Hypar with G0 continuity along ruling line generators of cylinder and cone.

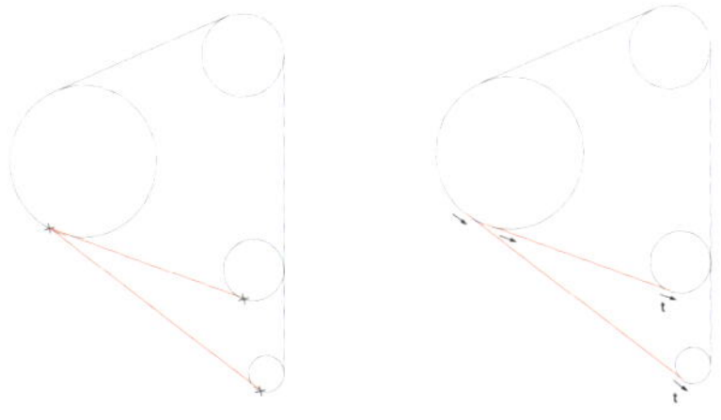

04 Plan diagrams: minor variation of connection and tangency points.

05

TECTONIC MOSAIC

The subdivision the UV curve field into faceted triangles allows the façade to abosorb the double curvature of the hyperbolic paraboloid, while also rectifying geometric discrepanices of the idealized surfaces.

01

Saint-Andrew the Apostle Parish Church

Leandro Locsin
Makati, Philippines (1967)

02 Interior structural ribs

Any open or closed linear shape can serve as a profile for tapered extrusion to produce a generalized cone–a developable surface with one curve field of ruling lines that converge to a point. Saint-Andrew the Apostle Parish Church by Leandro Locsin deploys generalized cones trimmed and joined tangently along ruling line generators to produce several compound forms at many scales. The reflected ceiling plan of the church (**05**) shows the range of curvature of the discrete perimeter segments which collectively comprise the bilaterally symmetrical butterfly shape. The two long edges of the plan (left and right) are nearly straight, with large radii of curvature, dictating that the tapering surfaces extruded above these edges are nearly planar. Conversely, areas with tighter radii of curvature produce cones more visually conventional in their curved appearance (**03**). Though the discrete arcs of the church plan may be nearly circular/elliptical, the half-butterfly profiles can be understood as specific, yet arbitrary, non-circular shapes which extrude and taper to produce the two generalized cones of the roof.

As singly ruled surfaces, developables are curved in one direction and straight in the other, providing structural rigidity in the curved axis and relative weakness in the flat linear axis. The advantages of developable surface fabrication are somewhat offset by structural liabilities. Beam-like ribs of the interior are oriented along the ruling lines of the cone to compensate (**02**), spanning from the perimeter arches and support portals to the roof apex, transferring the load to the massive cruciform bracing of the exterior (**03**). The uneven transition of varying density of these structural ribs belies the abrupt change of curvature in the plan. Converging ruling lines also draw visual attention to the single occulus above the altar, reading as a node of light that pulls the roof surface upward, as if gathering tensile fabric.

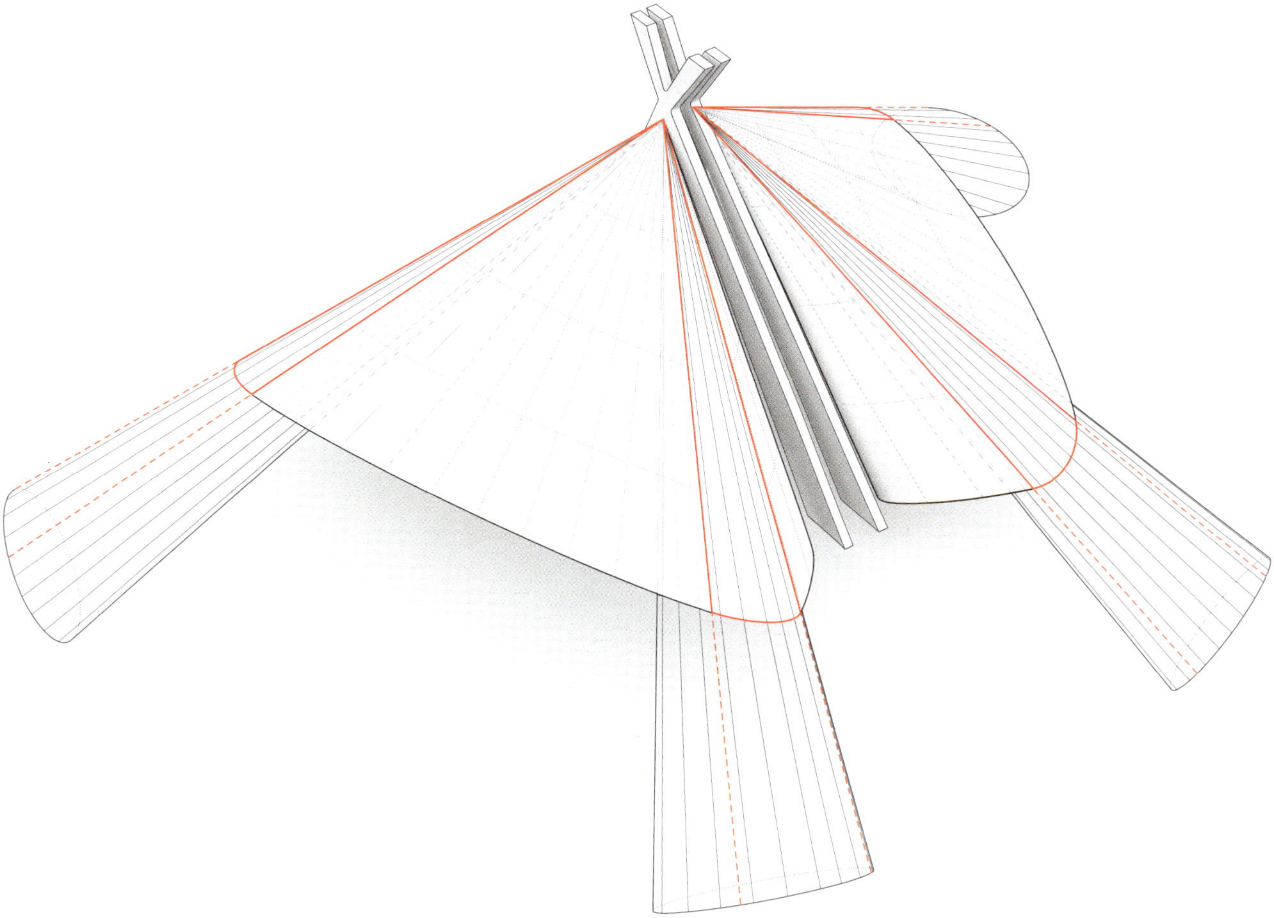

03

04 Entry detail

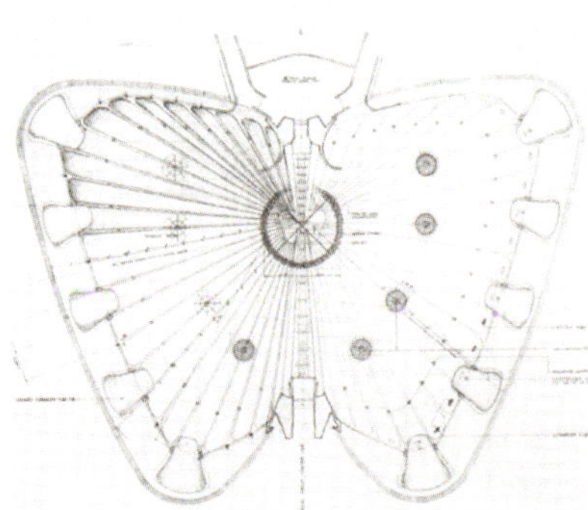

05 Reflected ceiling plan

ECCENTRIC SURFACE CLIPPING

Piecewise continous concrete surfaces of varying radii (conic and cylindrical) form numerous entry portals in addition to the main roof of the church. Eccentric clipping of these compound forms (independent of axes/orientations) obfuscates their piecewise nature while visually augmenting the curvature of some surfaces which are relatively flat.

01

Springtecture B

Shuhei Endo
Shiga-Ken, Japan (2002)

Springtecture B produces multiple interior and exterior spaces by modulating a single continuous geodesic planking surface. Though the geodesic ribbon is actually composed of multiple pieces of joined corrugated steel, it behaves as a single geometric entity, winding through space to define the parti. Planar areas of the ribbon are either horizontal or vertical. The smooth and continuous transitions between level and plumb planes are negotiated by several quarter-turn geodesic helices. The location and radii of these helical fillets are defined by a set of horizontal cylinders.

Because right circular cylinders have constant curvature in the lateral axis, geodesic lines on their surface are always helices (except for two special cases of the circle and line) whose angular relationship with the central axis remains constant. This dictates that the angle of incidence in plan for incoming horizontal planks (tangent to the cylinder) is exactly the same as the elevational angle of vertical planks which diverge from the cylinder. This would not be the case if the strip was bending around a tapering cone or other developable surface. Nor would it be the case if the planar portions of the roofs and walls were sloped or canted, which would produce a variety of different plan and elevational rotations.

Though the angle is consistent in Springtecture B, the modulation of the single geodesic strip produces a variety of spaces that deftly manage privacy, views, and light. Paradoxically, the continuous geodesic ribbon connects spaces that are largely discrete and discontinuous in terms of architectural circulation. These spaces are bounded primarily by planes, and the understated filleting of their dihedral corners is not only local stylization, but integral to a strategy of geometric continuity. Axiomatic material and geometric behavior is required for this continuity to govern the overall volumetric distribution. It imbricates the plan and section together, and enables the rhythmic and constrained plays of solid/void, surface/volume, interior/exterior, and convex/concave.

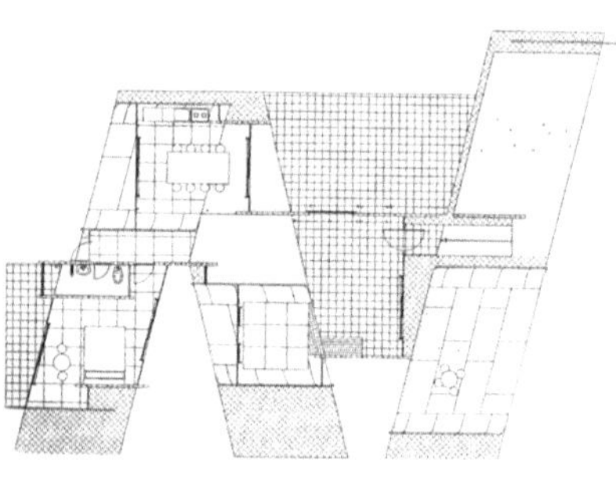

02 Plan

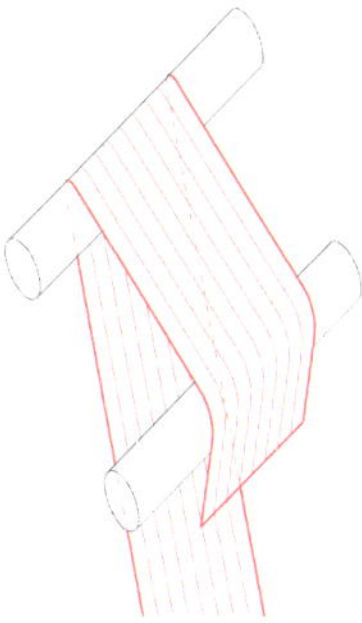

03 Geodesic plank sequence

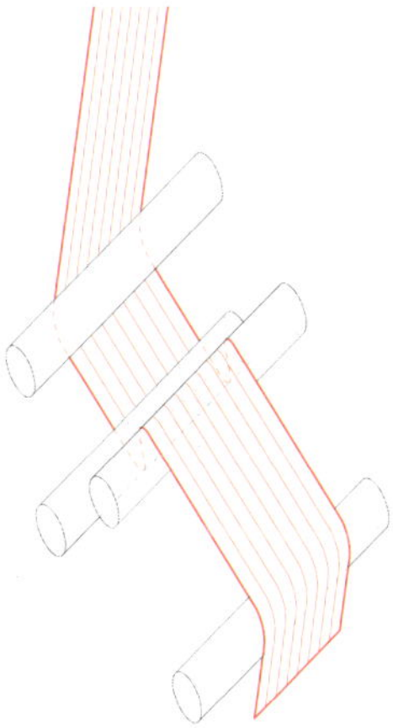

04

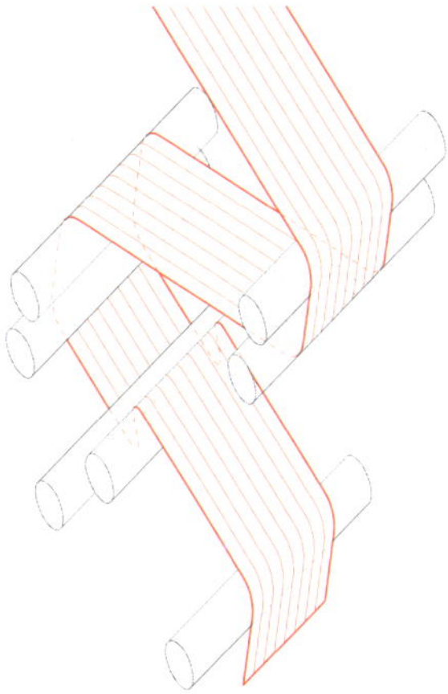

05

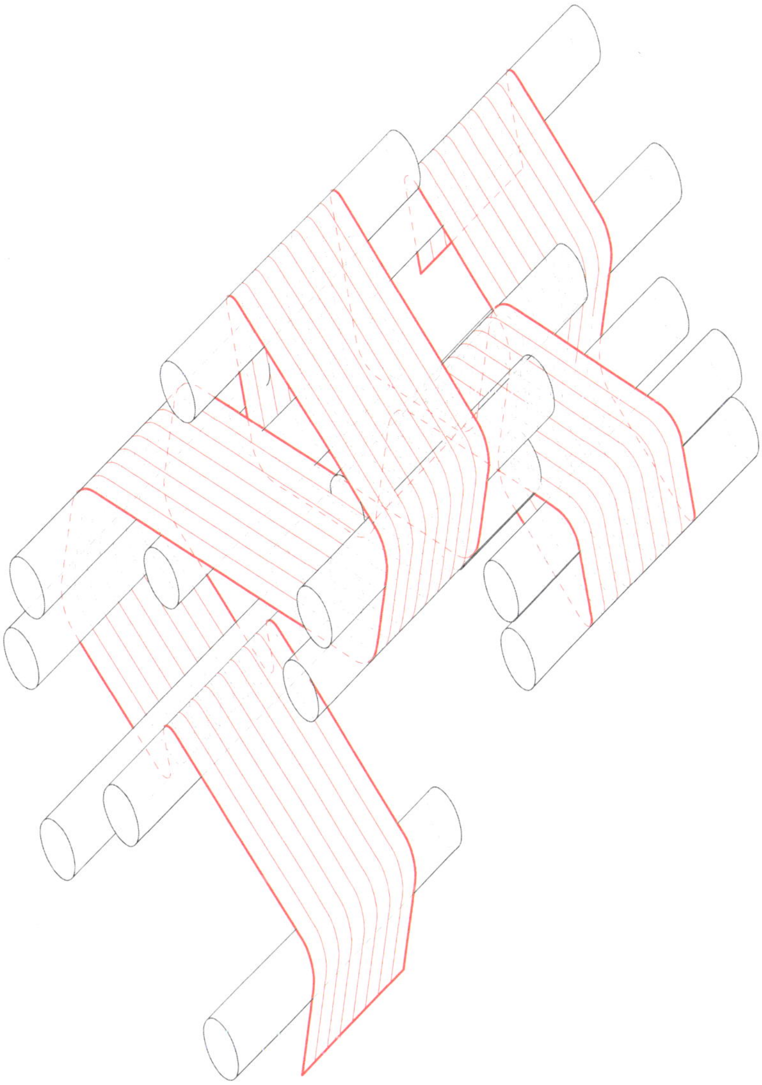

06 Geodesic plank sequence (final)

PLAN/SECTION RECIPROCITY

The constant curvature of the helical fillets behaves axiomatically and predictably, yet produces an unexpected variety of indoor and outdoor spaces.

07 Elevational view

01 Southeast view

520 West 28th Street

Zaha Hadid Architects
New York, New York (2016)

The façade of 520 West 28th Street exhibits treatments of geometry, congruence, and repetition that declare the autonomy of each floor as part of an aggregate massing. The semicircular moldings that laterally terminate the expanses of floor-to-ceiling glass express the containment of each discrete level (**01**). On the south and north façades, however, the glazed floors shift in section by a half-level, disrupting the regularity of the serial stacks.

A compound stitching surface provides façade continuity to ameliorate this sectional displacement. It appears as a type of geometric sinew akin to a spanning minimal surface under tension. This tensile webbing, apparently subject to plastic distortion, is actually a combinatory assembly of trimmed conic surfaces. A stack of elongated cones alternates the orientation of its apexes, allowing the axes to remain horizontal while the trimmed surfaces are nested efficiently and contiguously. Each cone intersects with its neighbor above and below along straight ruling line generators. Nested profiles of hyperbolas, a type of conic section, are evident in the bas-relief depth of the façade webbing. One set of hyperbolas defines the edge shape of the curtain wall glass. The other set defines the boundary of material transition between the lighter surface of the webbing and the darker volumetric edges, which are fused with the spandrel moldings separating each floor (**06**).

Contemporary architecture often uses developable surface patches to post-rationalize forms of double curvature for economy and constructability. The serial conic forms here serve as a primary formal and tectonic language, leveraging geometric expertise to address formal and typological issues.

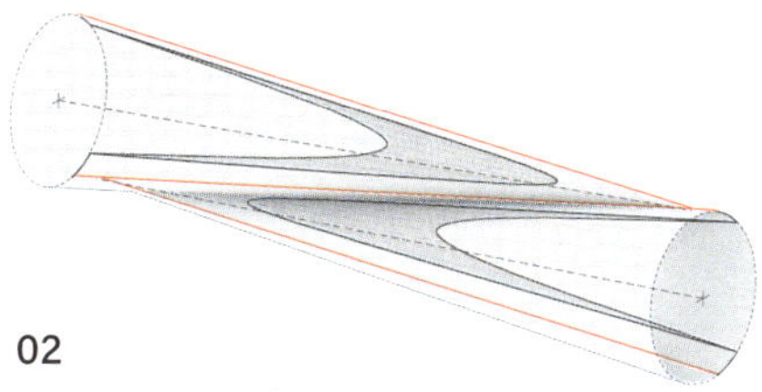

02

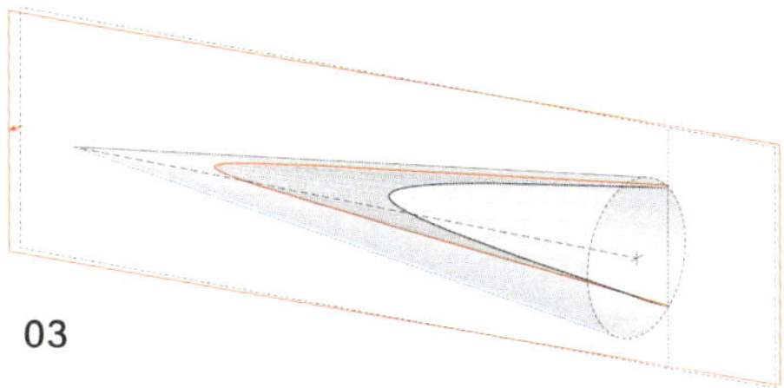

03

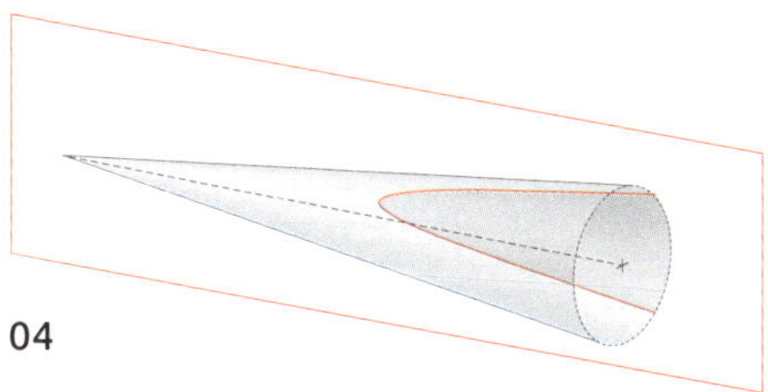

04

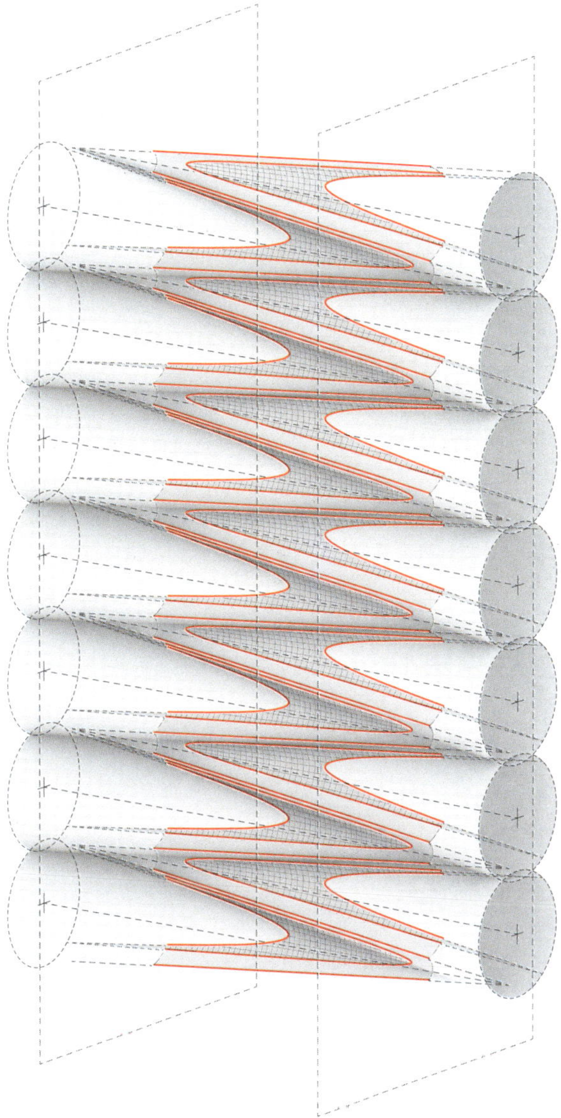

05

06

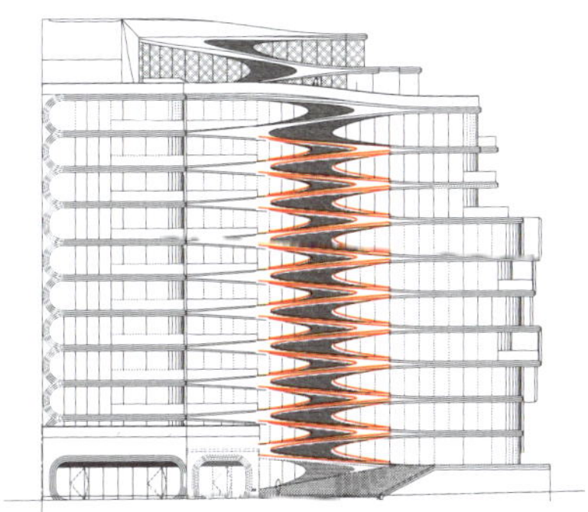

07 Elevation

PLANAR AND VOLUMETRIC

The conic surfaces provide the elevational graphic of the hyperbola edges of the curtain wall, while also producing the volumetric language and aesthetic of the plastic façade.

Precious Blood Parish Church

Étienne Gaboury
Winnepeg, MB, Canada (1968)

01

The main roof of the Precious Blood Parish Church by Étienne Gaboury (1930-2022) is a physical approximation of a more precise geometric idea. The form resembles a helical developable–a type of surface visually and geometrically similar to a cone, except that the gathering linear generators never converge at a single apex. Instead, the curve field ruling lines are perpetually distributed with serial tangency to a helical "edge of regression" (**03**). This swept surface is capable of nesting with itself multiple times according to the periodicity of the helix, yet the roof framing of the Precious Blood Church manifests slightly less than one full rotation, resulting in an overall form that appears more singular than periodic.

The exterior is predominantly covered with wood shakes, which convey less geometric infomation about the surface than directional cladding would. However, the interior chamber exhibits robust framing rafters that mark the major ruling lines of the surface. Proximate to the tapered waist, these rafters converge into a dense arrangement, jostling for proper geometric positioning with the imaginary helix that organizes them in space. The substantial timber dimension precludes that each and/or all rafter axes can be exactly tangent to the single edge of regression. Unable to occupy the same three-dimensional space, the "thick lines" of the rafters displace each other and rest contiguously in a pinwheel organization–a close approximation of a helical developable. While material thickness precipitates a negotiation between the ideal geometry and the building's structure and tectonics, the dynamic spatial qualities are successfully conveyed.

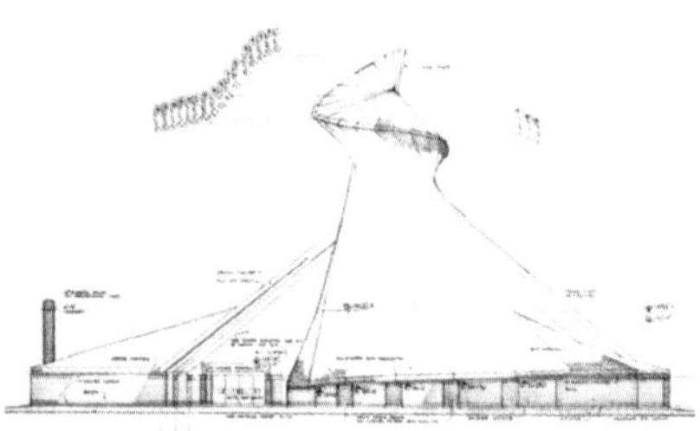

02 Elevation

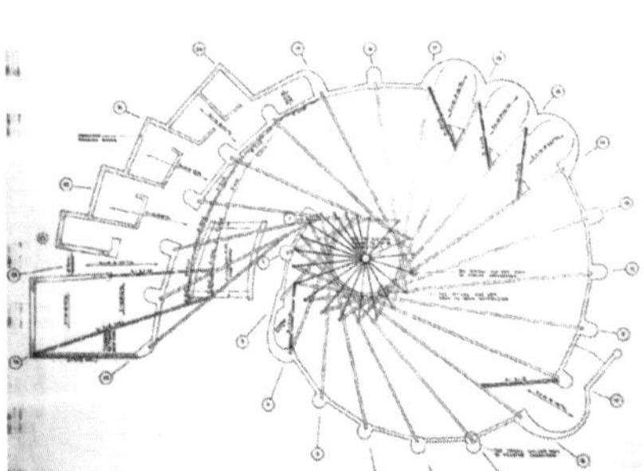

03 Base wall and rafter plan

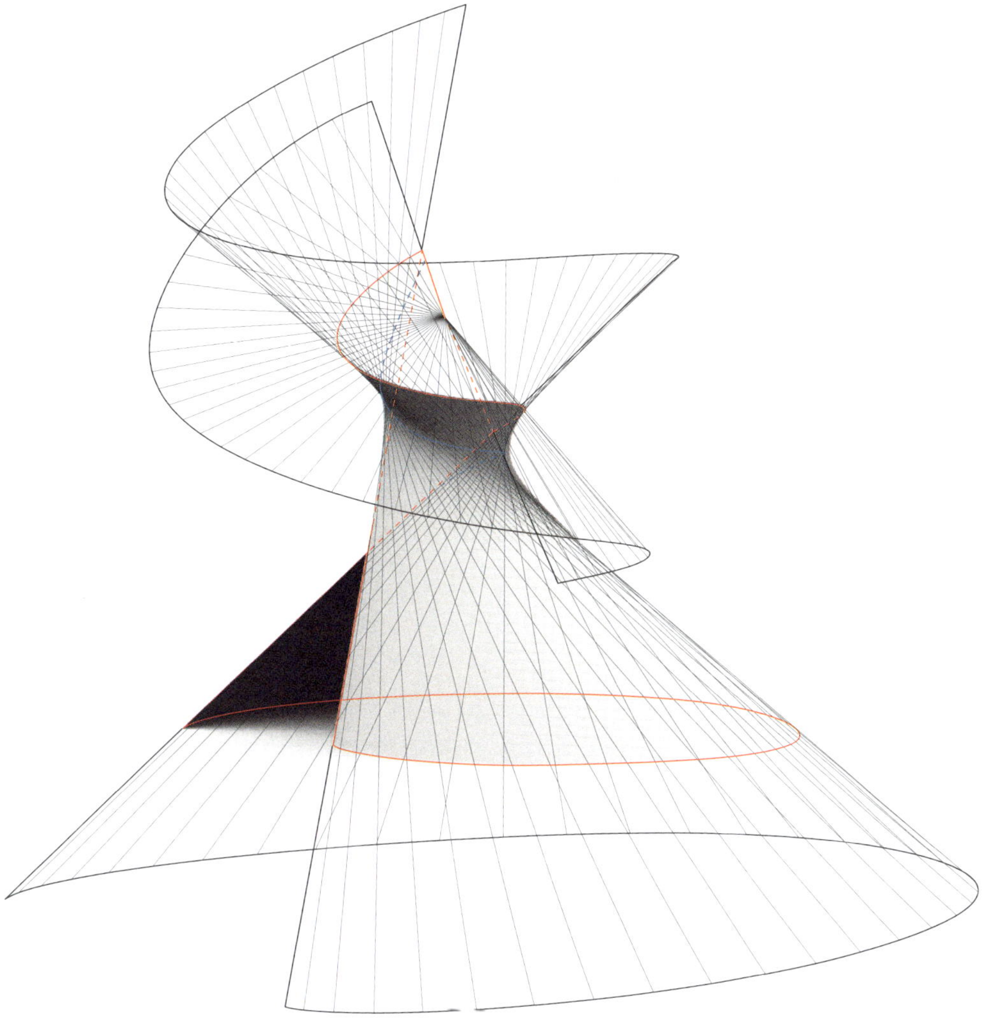

04

05 Rafters during construction

06 Interior timber framing

MATERIAL APPROXIMATION

The non-zero dimension of the structural rafters does not allow for the multiple axial tangencies required for the helical developable, but the close approximation conveys its spatial and geometric qualities.

Catalano House

Eduardo Catalano
Raleigh, North Carolina (1954)

01

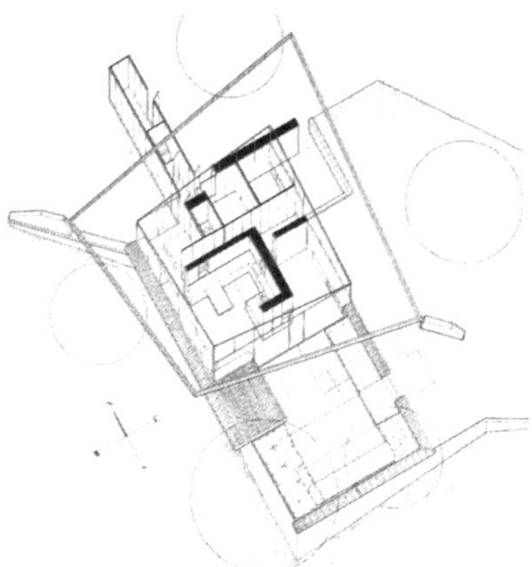

02 Axonometric

03 Interior

The signature roof of the Eduardo Catalano House (1954) is a hyperbolic paraboloid (hypar), a doubly ruled surface with a UV curve field of straight ruling lines in both directions. The hypar defines the projective orientation of the roof edges and orthogonal interior geometry. The plan is a square, with two lower corners anchoring the hypar to concrete butresses on the ground and two elevated corners cantilevering to form deep eaves (**01**). The roof is self-supporting, floating aloft and touched by a minimum of interior partitions only for structural stabilization (**02**).

The structural roof framing utilizes the ruling lines in both directions of the UV curve field (**05**). However, the normal vectors (perpendicular to the surface) along any given ruling line of a hypar do not lie in a single plane–a geometric requirement for all developable surfaces. Doubly ruled hypars are thus *not* developable, even with straight lines in both directions. Cladding planks oriented parallel to ruling lines would necessarily twist about their longitudinal axis in order to form the hypar surface. As an alternative, the orientation of the roof, subroof, and ceiling cladding are rotated 45° (in plan) from the ruling line grid. This rotated grain highlights the gentle curvature of the surface (**01, 06**). Due to the symmetry and mild eccentricity of the hypar, the shiplap boards can mantain contiguous edges with minimal deflection about their long axis. The gently curving boards render a continuous surface which is structurally rigid due to double-curvature shell action, while also containing implicit and ubiquitous straight lines. The ceiling grain appears at odds with the interior plan elements defined by the ruling line grid. However, at locales where the lower geometries make contact with the ceiling, the presence of straight lines on the curved surface becomes explicit. This is especially true at the perimeter, where the rotated grain of the ceiling amenably receives the inclined top edge of the trapezoidal glazing (**03**).

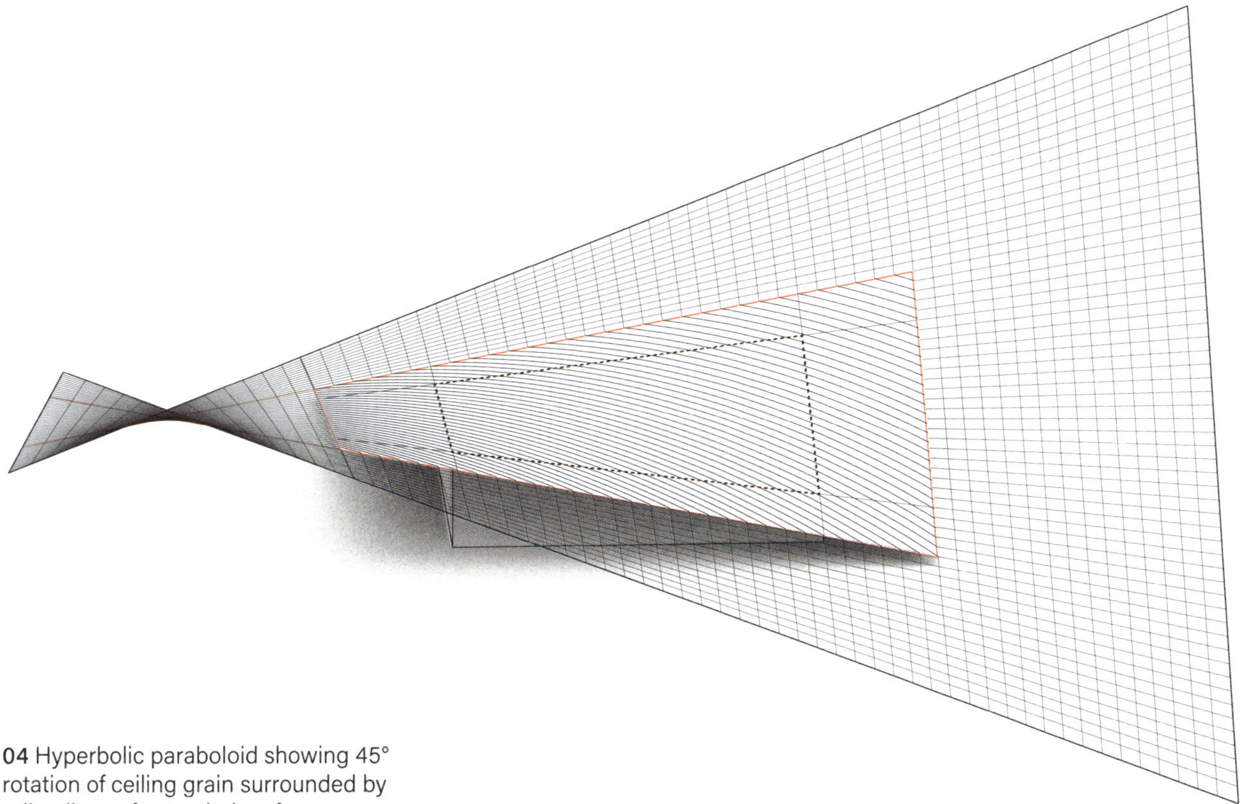

04 Hyperbolic paraboloid showing 45° rotation of ceiling grain surrounded by ruling lines of extended surface

05 Roof framing along ruling lines

06 Subroof planks rotated 45°

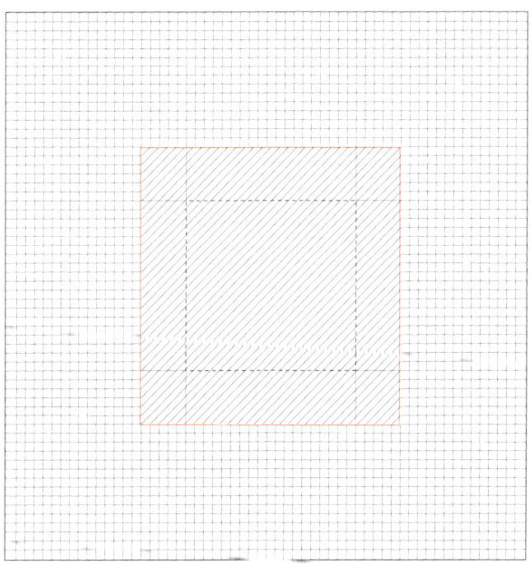

07 Plan diagram

DUAL ORIENTATION

Four perimeter edges and structural rafters of the roof align with the native ruling line subdivisions of the hypar geometry. The roof, subroof, and ceiling cladding are rotated 45° to address material bending and tectonic concerns. Both grains manifest different readings of the surface while negotiating between architectural and geometric requirements.

Luce Memorial Chapel

I.M. Pei & Chi-kwan Chen
Taichung, Taiwan (1963)

01

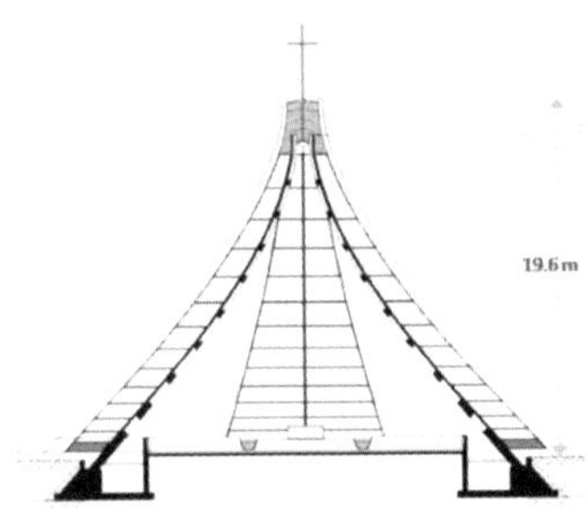

02 Section

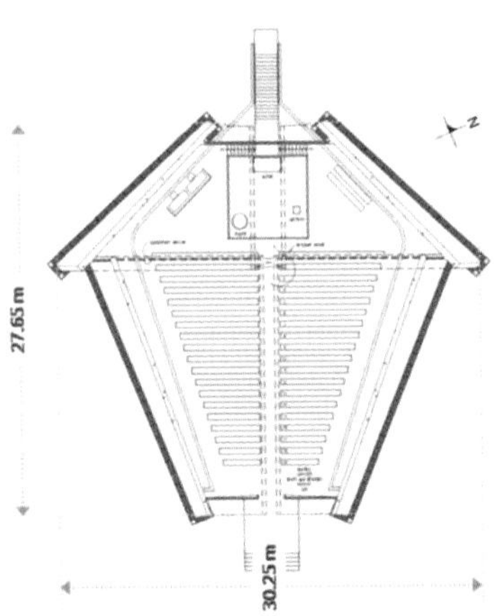

03 Plan

The Luce Memorial Chapel designed by I.M. Pei (1917-2019) and Chi-kuan Chen (1921-2007) is composed of four hyperbolic paraboloids (hypars) placed in symmetrical pairs, producing an enclosure with curved and glazed gaps that allow light to enter the sanctuary. The linear concrete ridge beams and straight walls of the plan cut and footprint disclose the presence of horizontal ruling lines. Its design and construction was contemporaneous with many other examples of hypar architecture during the mid 20th century, including buildings by Marcel Breuer, Felix Candela, and Miguel Fisac. While these works typically expressed straight ruling lines or parabolas as the architectural subdivisions and limits of the hypar surfaces, the curved vertical profile edges of Luce Chapel walls are hyperbolas.

Planar section cuts of hypar surfaces can produce parabolas, hyperbolas, and straight lines–all possible conic sections except for circles and ellipses. Cutting planes parallel to the saddle normal will only intersect the hypar once, with two specific orientations intersecting along the UV ruling lines (**06**), and others producing open parabolas (**07**). Nearly all other cutting planes (not parallel to the saddle normal) will intersect the hypar twice to yield symmetrical hyperbolas (**04**).

The limited samplings of the hyperbola curves of the Luce Chapel wall edges do not allow us to perceive the overall symmetry and coherence of the conic sections, but rather convey a softer calligraphic composition. Material and tectonic decisions also belie the mathematical characteristics of the forms, such as the interior diamond coffering which obfuscates the implicit ruling lines of the hypars (**05**). The Luce Chapel demonstrates how architecture can leverage the well-known construction advantages of ruled surface geometries, while also remaining formally and aesthetically distinct by deploying specific tectonic methods and uncommon surface trimming.

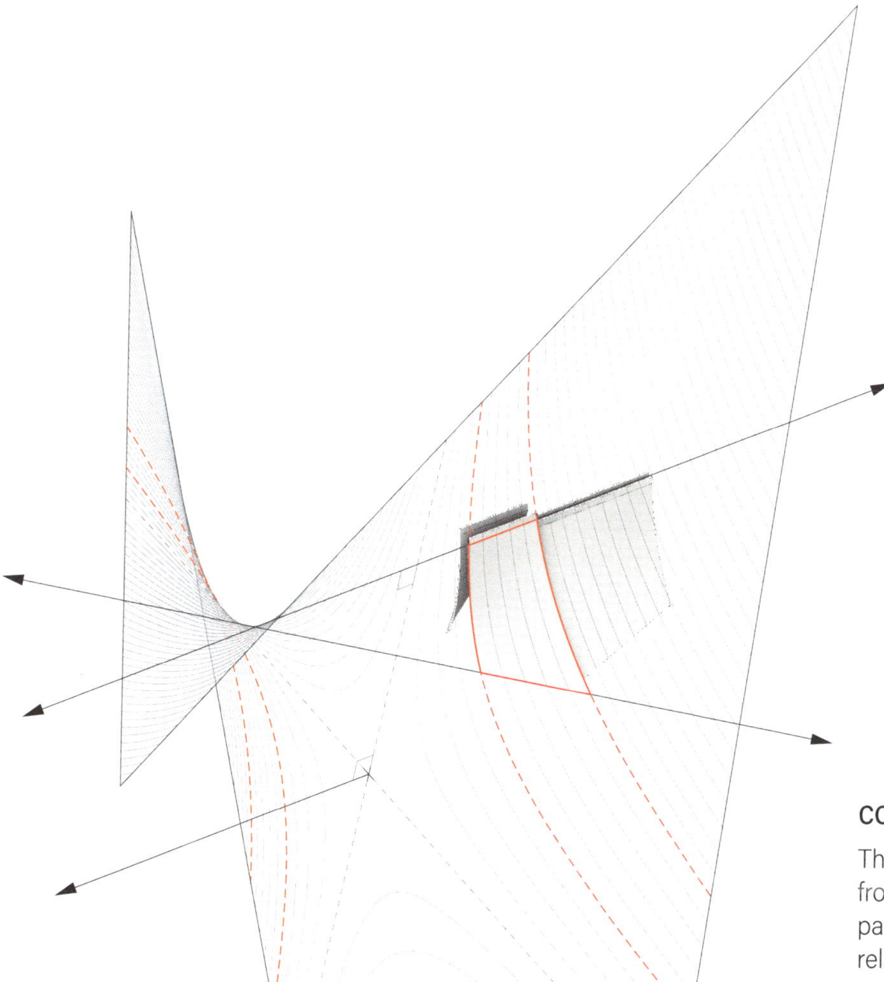

04 Hyperbola subdivision

CONIC RELATIONSHIPS

Though formally and visually distinct from cones and cylinders, hyperbolic paraboloids are mathematically related to developable surfaces and are able to produce conic sections.

05 Interior concrete coffering

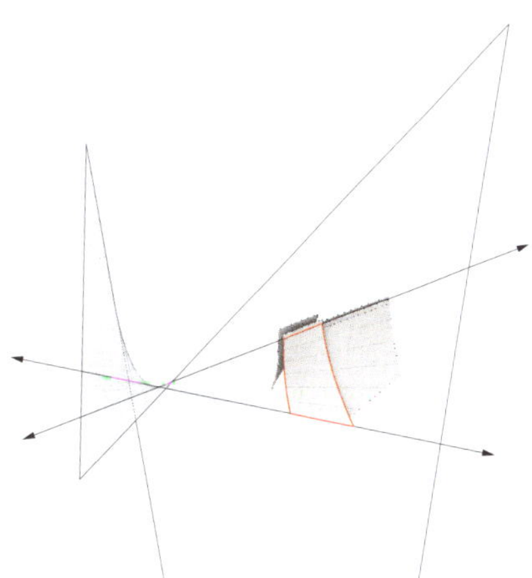

06 Ruling line subdivision

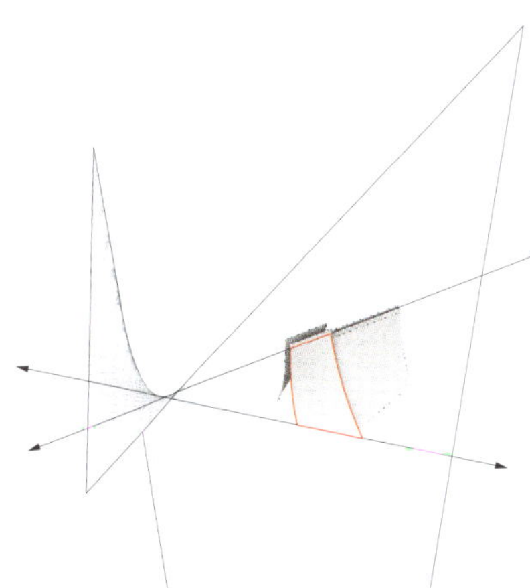

07 Parabola subdivision

01 View from southwest

VIA 57 West

Bjarke Ingels Group
New York, New York (2016)

The most straightforward U and V curve field subdivision for a hyperbolic paraboloid (hypar) uses its two sets of straight ruling lines. The four perimeter edges of VIA 57's roof are comprised of low horizontals on the south and west sides and steep inclined edges of the east and north sides that meet at the apex of the northeast corner. The uppermost four edges of the central courtyard are also linear, unambiguously comfirming that the roof/façade is a doubly-ruled hypar.

Subject to different subdivision logics, the interior seams do not adhere to these native ruling lines. The most noticeable departure occurs as one entire curve field U is replaced by intersection curves of the hypar surface with a series of horizontal planes (**03**).

The resulting topographic lines are hyperbolas, emerging as the upshot of architecture's intractable demand for flat floors–a criterion extrinsic to geometry. A complimentary curve field V would typically be (near) perpendicular to U, thus avoiding acute/obtuse intersection angles for panel shapes easier to fabricate and install. The two seams that divide the three easternmost bays of the roof/façade are parallel to the adjacent edges of the building and courtyard. These two lines are the only interior subdivisions that are ruled and straight (**04**).

The remainder of the curve field V rotates away from the ruling line orientation, with seams generally oriented along the fall line, and nearly perpendicular to the horizontal hyperbolas. The resulting pattern of the southwest corner is decidedly radial, with seams rotating progressively westward toward the river. Departing from the ruling line subdivision thus has architectural benefits: flat floors, well-behaved panel shapes, and better views.

The hypar surface conflates conventional notions of projective orientation, requiring architecture and geometry to negotiate in a play of surface seams–each jockeying for primacy of function and expression on a single three-dimensional edifice.

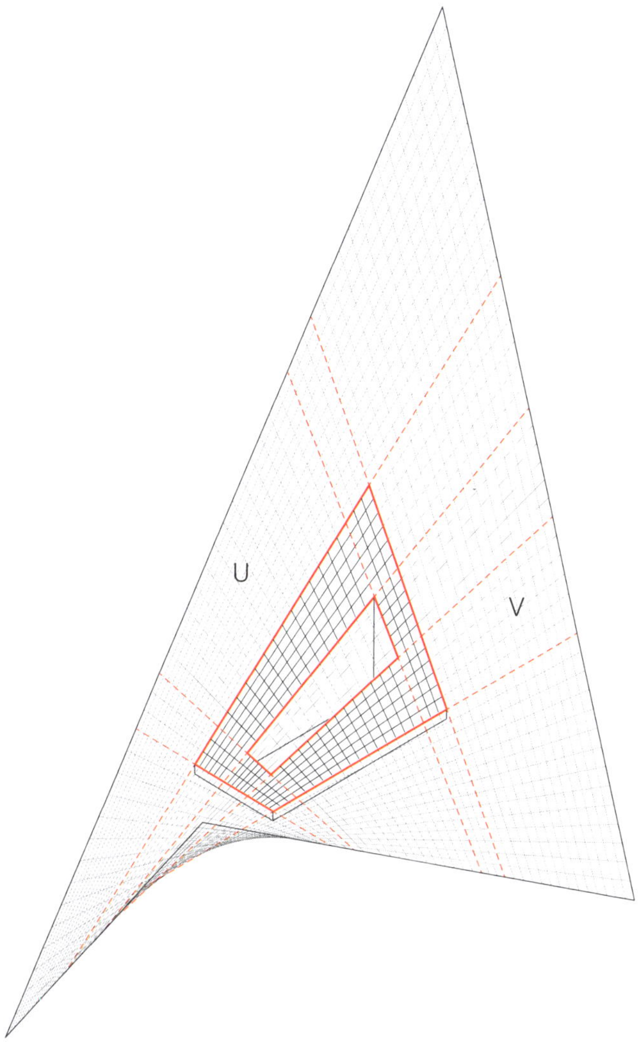

02 Extended hyperbolic paraboloid

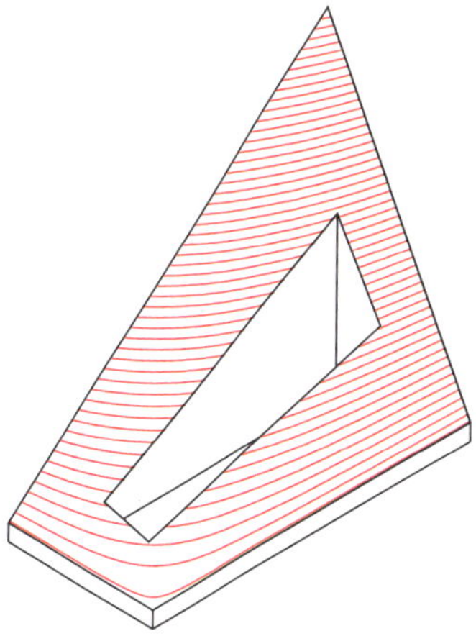

03 Horizontal hyperbola cuts

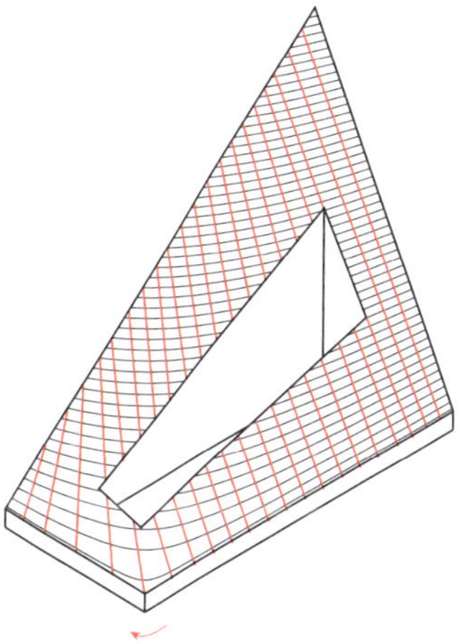

04 Transition from ruling lines to fall lines

05 Aerial view

ARCHITECTURE VS. GEOMETRY

VIA 57 West does not produce differentiated space through aggregation of a geometric unit but through subdivision of the figural whole. The seams of the hyperbolic paraboloid subdivision explicitly convey the coincidence and/or friction between the competing imperatives of architecture and geometry.

GEOMETRY PRIMER: RULED SURFACE IDIOMS AND COMBINATORY TECHNIQUES

COMBINATORY TECHNIQUES FOR DEVELOPABLE (SINGLY RULED) AND DOUBLY RULED SURFACES

In differential geometry, developable surfaces are defined as those with zero Gaussian curvature which can be unrolled, or "developed", to a plane without distortion. These surfaces are singly ruled (they have straight ruling lines in one direction of the UV curve field) and commonly include cones, cylinders, and tangent developables. The advent of complex curvilinear forms in architecture has necessitated the use of developable surfaces to post-rationalize designs of double curvature for economy and constructability, using them as the unavoidable means to rectify geometrically undisciplined form.

In lieu of such measures, these studies speculate on techniques to produce new architectural idioms of developable and doubly ruled (non-developable) surfaces to serve as the a priori building blocks of a formal and tectonic language. Capable of combinatorial variation within geometric constraints, these forms require specific knowledge of their curvature and isometry for successful deployment.

Although these surface classes only comprise a small subset of all Euclidean geometries, they are capable of producing an infinite variety of figural compositions or aggregated periodic fields. Their capacity to produce calligraphic lines and space is complimented by geometric properties amenable for fabrication and construction. They unroll without distortion, which is advantageous because the vast majority of construction is made from flat sheet materials.

For any three-dimensional surface, a "geodesic line" is the shortest distance between any two points on that surface. For developables, geodesics unroll to a plane as straight lines. It follows that sets of similar geodesics on a developable surface can unroll as parallel lines, thus defining a series of two-dimensional strips that serve as a flat map of the three-dimensional surface. This method of subdivision is known as "geodesic planking". The following pages show several combinatory techniques of geodesic planking which serve as the geometric bases for many of the architectural projects to follow. Additional techniques are also shown for doubly ruled geometries (hyperbolic paraboloids and hyperboloids).

GEODESIC LEVELING (56-61)

The technique of "geodesic leveling" allows smooth and continuous transitions of geodesic subdivisions from horizontal, to sloped/inclined, and back to horizontal again. A piecewise continuous "host" surface is defined using cones, cylinders, and/or planes. The curved developable surfaces are trimmed along ruling line generators and arranged tangently to plane figures or other developables. Horizontal geodesic lines typically occur on planar surfaces, transitioning to curved and sloping geodesics on the developables, and returning to horizontal on another planar surface. The orientation and slope of the curving geodesic lines (or planks) is a function of the radius, slant angle, orientation, and angular sweep of the developable surface on which it is drawn. The calibration of these variable slopes can correspond to the incline of stairs, ramps, or other architectural spaces of the interior—tracing the trajectory of circulatory movement within.

DIHEDRAL CONE INSCRIPTION (62-65)

An infinite number of (right circular) cones can be inscribed inside any dihedral angle between two intersecting planes. Surface normals along any ruling generatrix of the cone are co-planar—a geometric property of singly ruled developable surfaces. This allows the cone to achieve tangency to both intersecting planes along two separate ruling lines, producing a variable radius fillet around the dihedral corner.

HYPAR HYPERBOLOID STITCHING (68-73)

A surface is doubly ruled if it contains straight ruling lines in two directions—i.e. through any given point there are two distinct lines that lie on the surface. There are only three types of these surfaces: the hyperbolic paraboloid (hypar), the hyperboloid of one sheet, and the plane. Although both directions of the UV curve field are comprised of straight lines, the hypar and the hyperboloid are not developable. The variations shown here exhibit smooth and piecewise continuous assemblies of hyperbolic paraboloids (hypars) and hyperboloids of revolution.

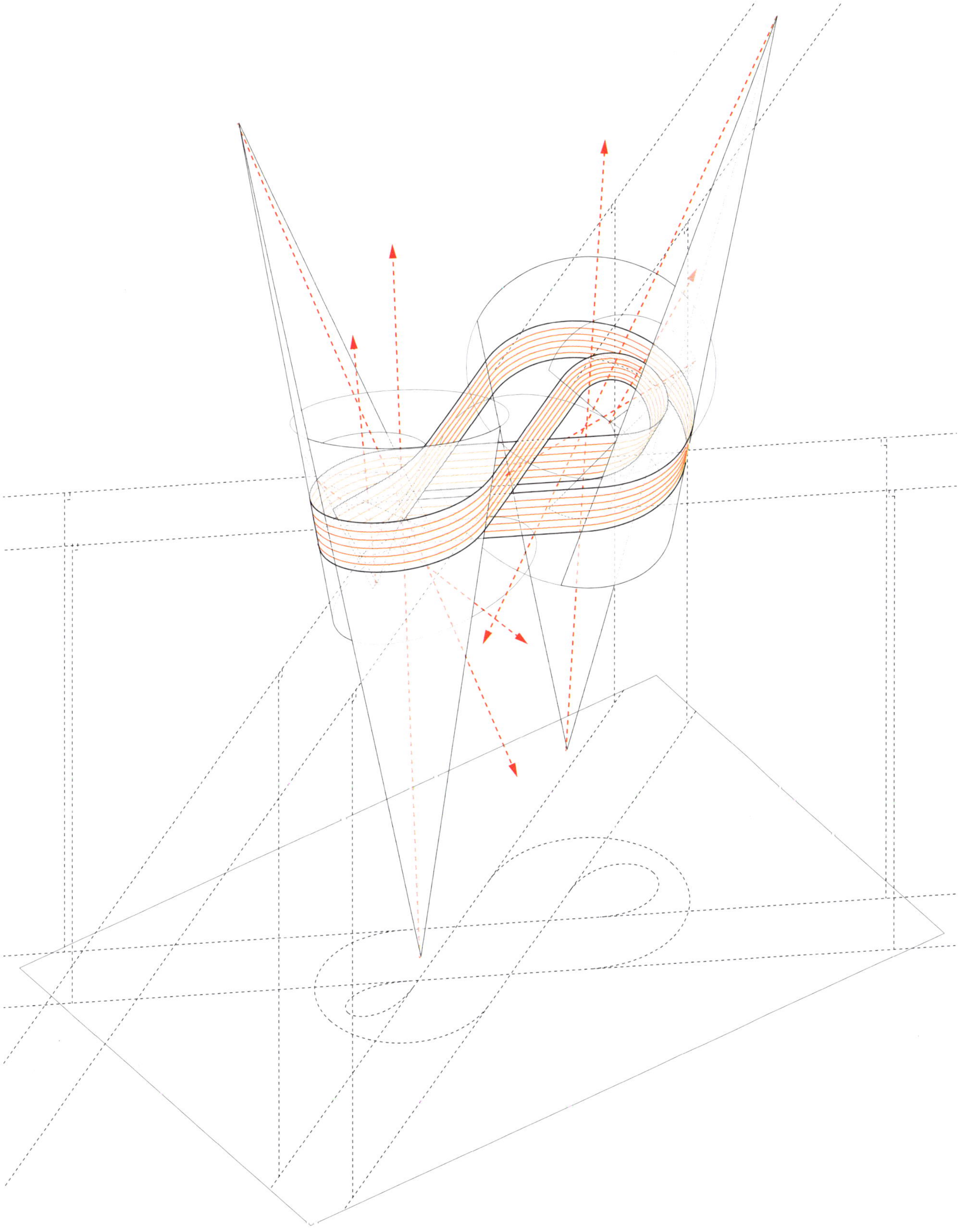

GEODESIC LEVELING 01
INVERTED CONES

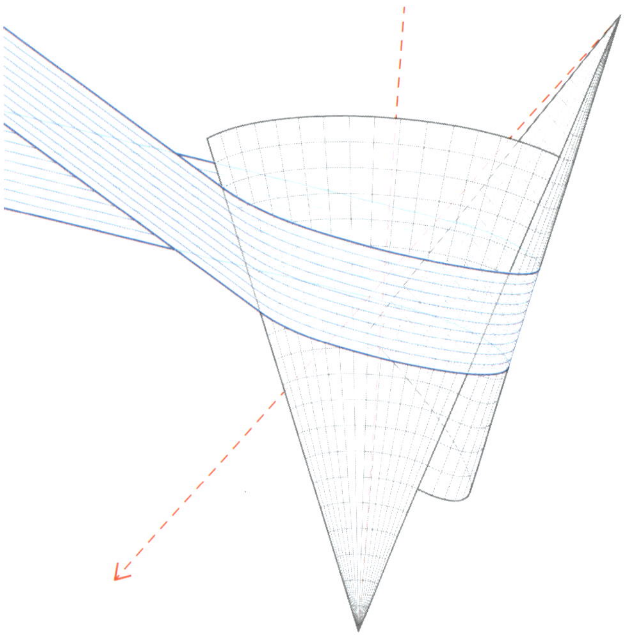

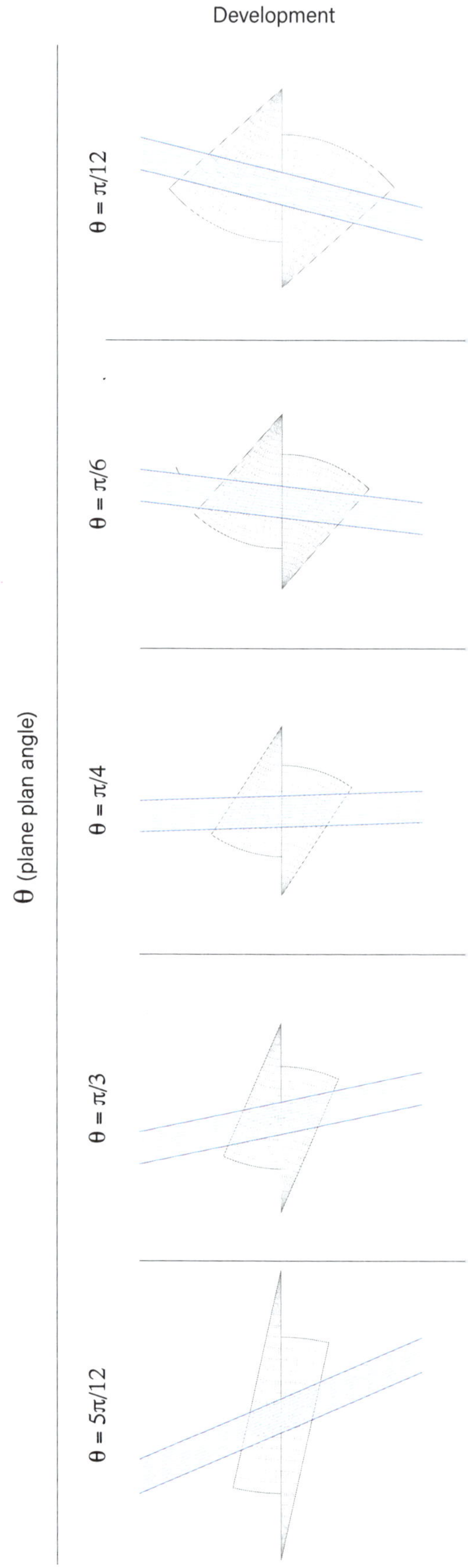

In cases shown here, the piecewise continuous host surface is comprised of two partial cones trimmed along their ruling line generators arranged tangent to two plumb planes. The horizontal geodesic lines occur on one planar surface, transition to curved and sloping geodesics on the cones, and return to horizontal on the other tangent plane. These examples show variations of the angle (θ) between the plan projections of the plumb planes. Compositions deploy two congruent cones with apexes in opposing orientations. This arrangement allows one conic surface to induce the slope of the curved geodesic lines, while the other conic surface subsequently conteracts this action in an equal and opposite manner, leveling the slope back to horizontal before connecting to the opposite planar surface.

Elevation 01 | Elevation 02 | Plan | Oblique

GEODESIC LEVELING 02
SINGLE CYLINDER (270° PLAN)

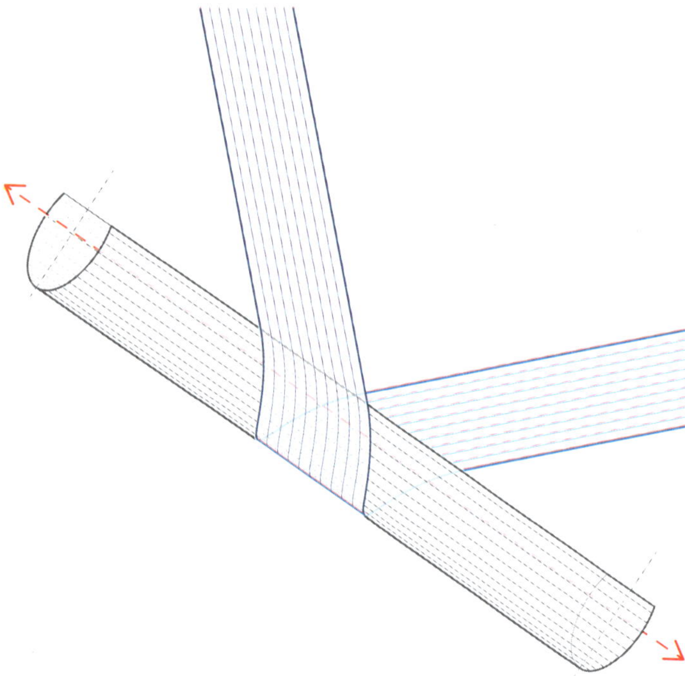

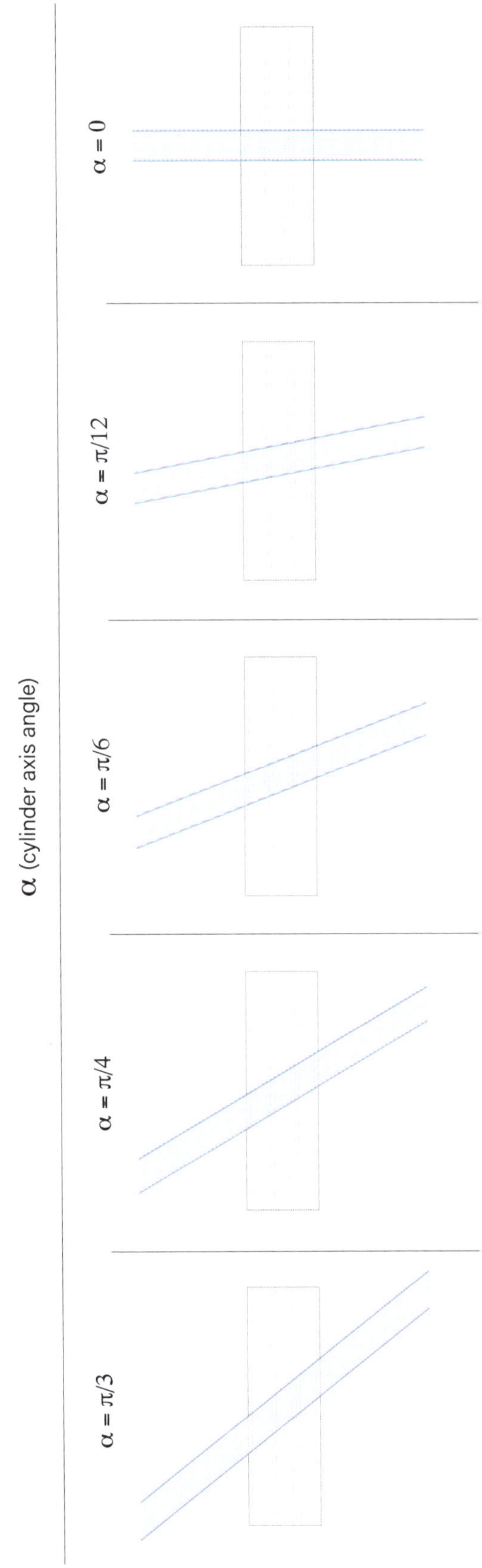

In cases shown here, the piecewise continuous host surface is comprised of a single cylinder trimmed along its ruling line generators (parallel to its axis) arranged tangent to two non-plumb planes. The horizontal geodesic lines occur on one planar surface, and transition to curved and sloping geodesics on the cylinder, and return to horizontal on the other tangent plane. The orientation and slope of the curving geodesic lines (or planks) is a function of the radius, tilt angle, and angular sweep of the cylindrical surface. These examples show variations in the tilt angle (α) of the cylinder while the angle between the plan projections of the planes is held fixed at 270° (or -90°), making these combinations amenable in orthogonal architectural plans. Although the single cylinder can both induce the slope of the geodesic curves and return them to horizontal, the planar surfaces in these geometric arrangements cannot be plumb.

Elevation 01
Elevation 02
Plan
Oblique

GEODESIC LEVELING 03
SINGLE CYLINDER (360° PLAN)

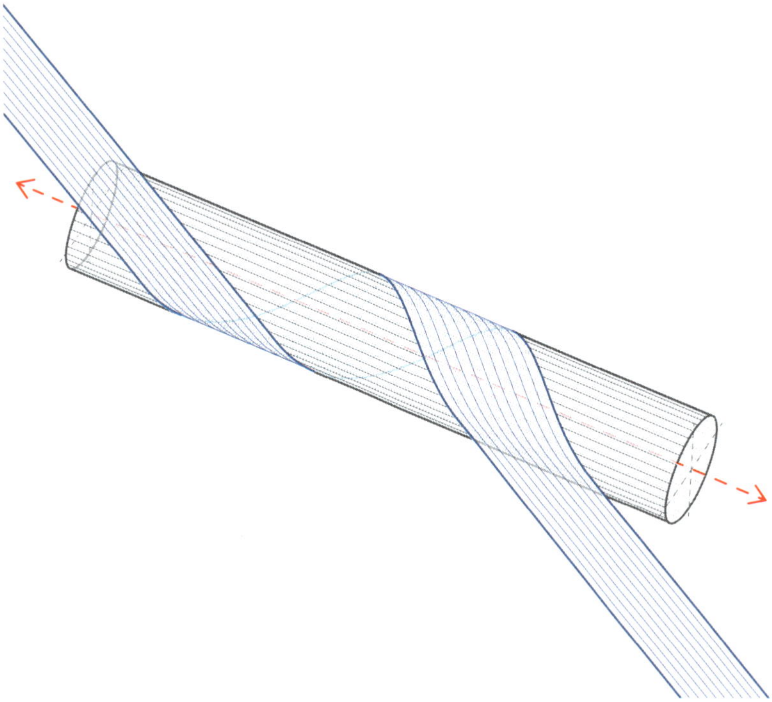

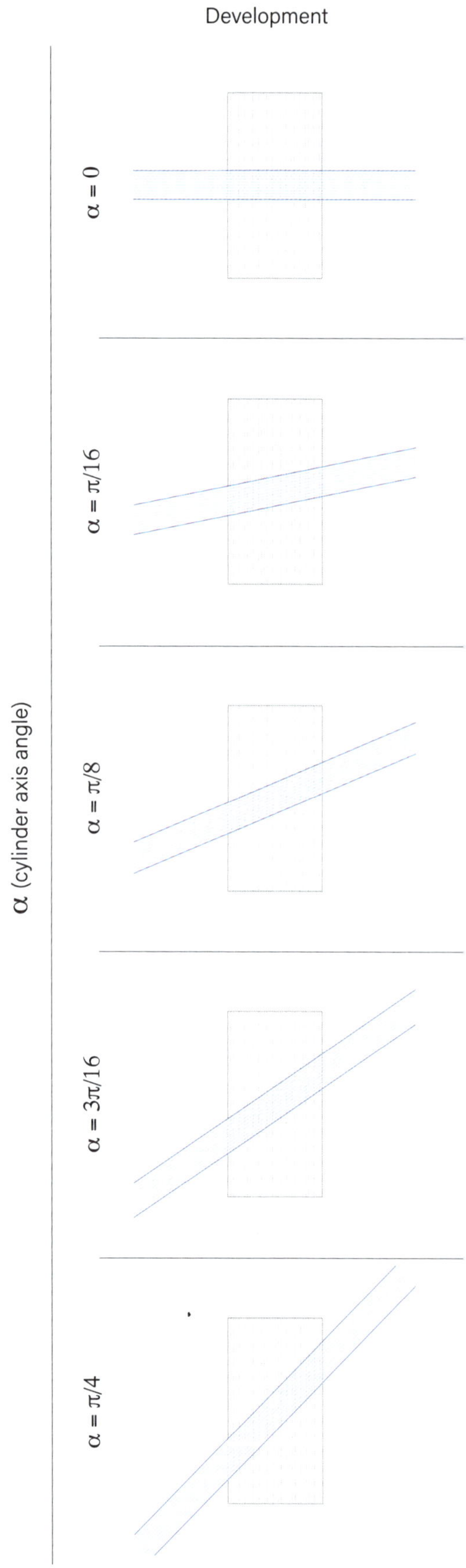

In cases shown here, the piecewise continuous host surface is comprised of a single cylinder arranged tangently to a single plumb plane along a ruling line. The horizontal geodesic lines occur on the planar surface, and transition to curved and sloping geodesics on the cylinder for a full helical rotation, and return to horizontal on the same tangent plane (in a different location). These examples show variations in the tilt angle (α) of the cylinder with a full 360° helical sweep, dictating that the level geodesics lie in the same plane. This is the only arrangement of geodesic leveling using a single cylinder in which the host plane of the horizontal lines can be plumb.

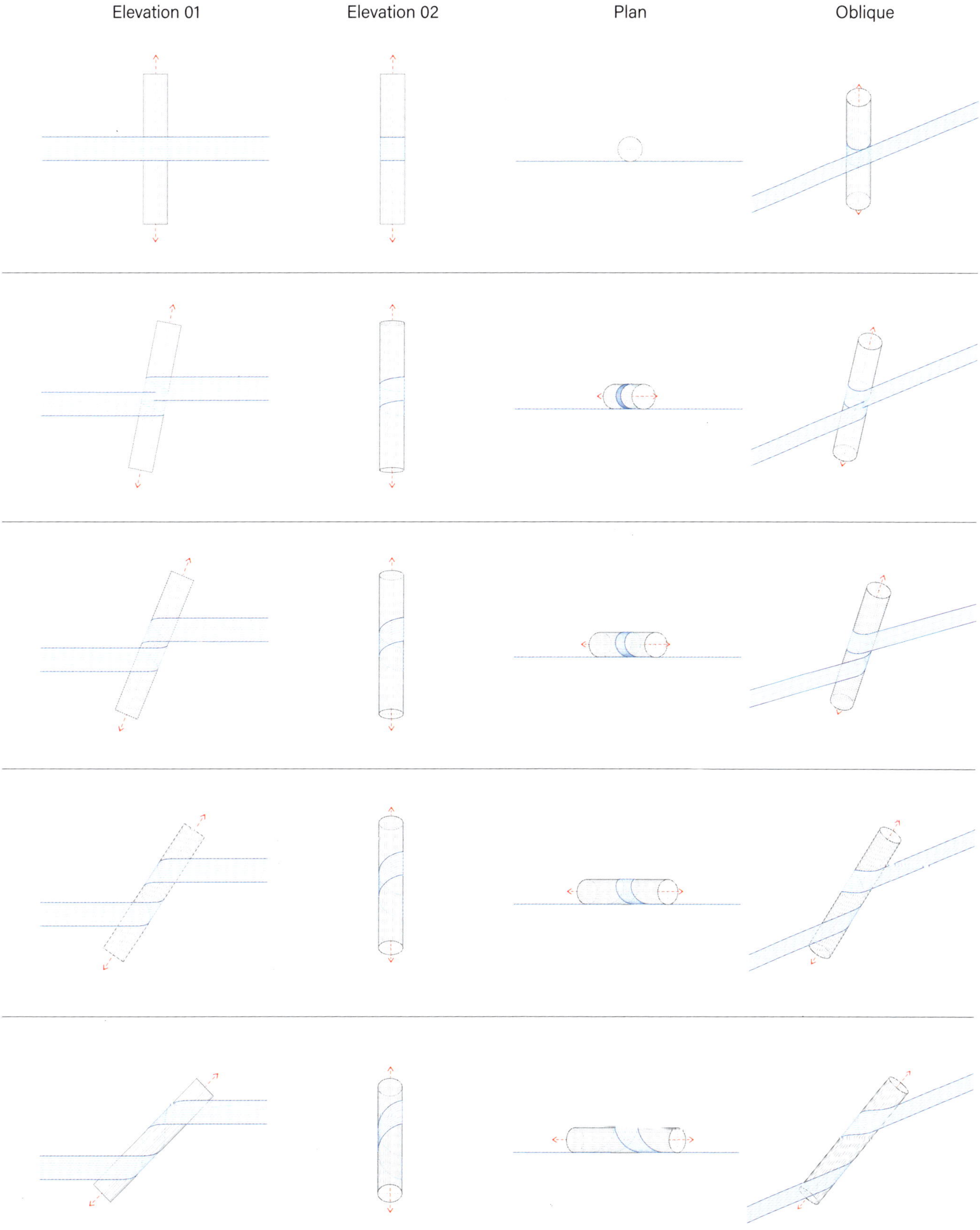
Elevation 01
Elevation 02
Plan
Oblique

DIHEDRAL CONE INSCRIPTION 01
CONSTANT GEODESIC SLOPE / VARIABLE CONE ANGLE

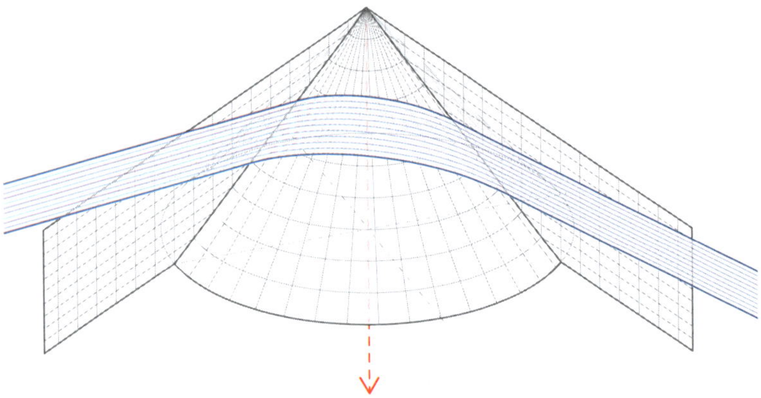

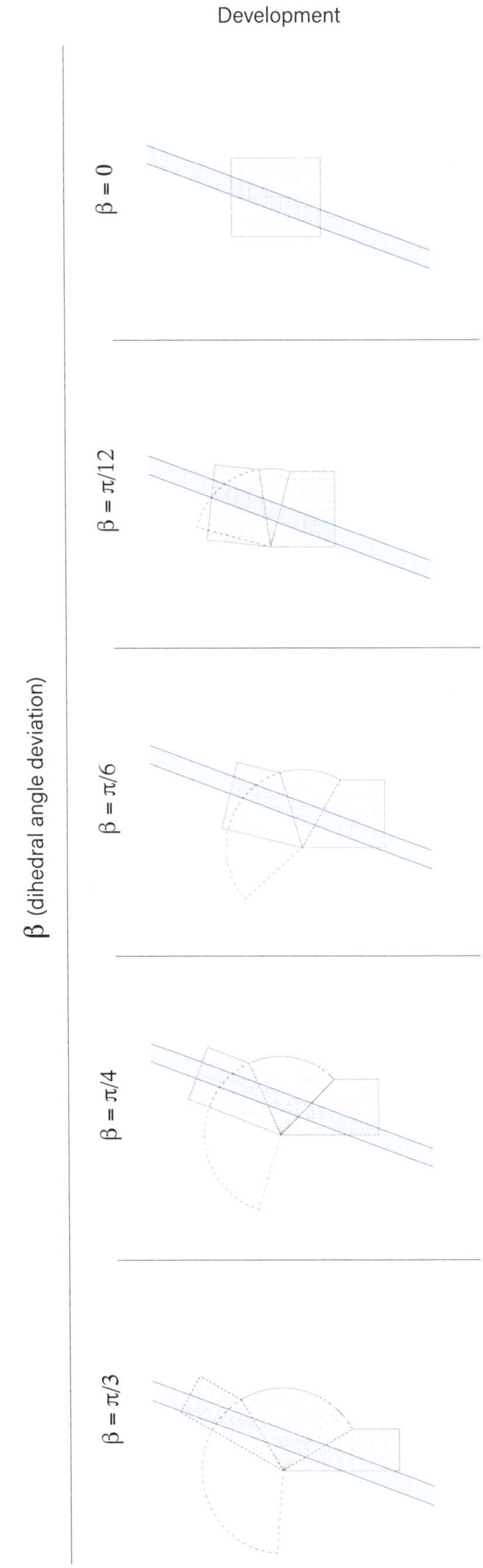

In cases where the developed (unrolled) state of the conical surface is less than ϖ radians (180°), continuous geodesic lines can migrate around the smoothed dihedral corner. The change of orientation and slope of the geodesics is a function of the profile angle, tilt, and angular sweep of the conic surface. The examples shown here use a constant inclination for the geodesic lines entering the corner, while the resultant deviations of slope vary when traced across the different conic inscriptions.

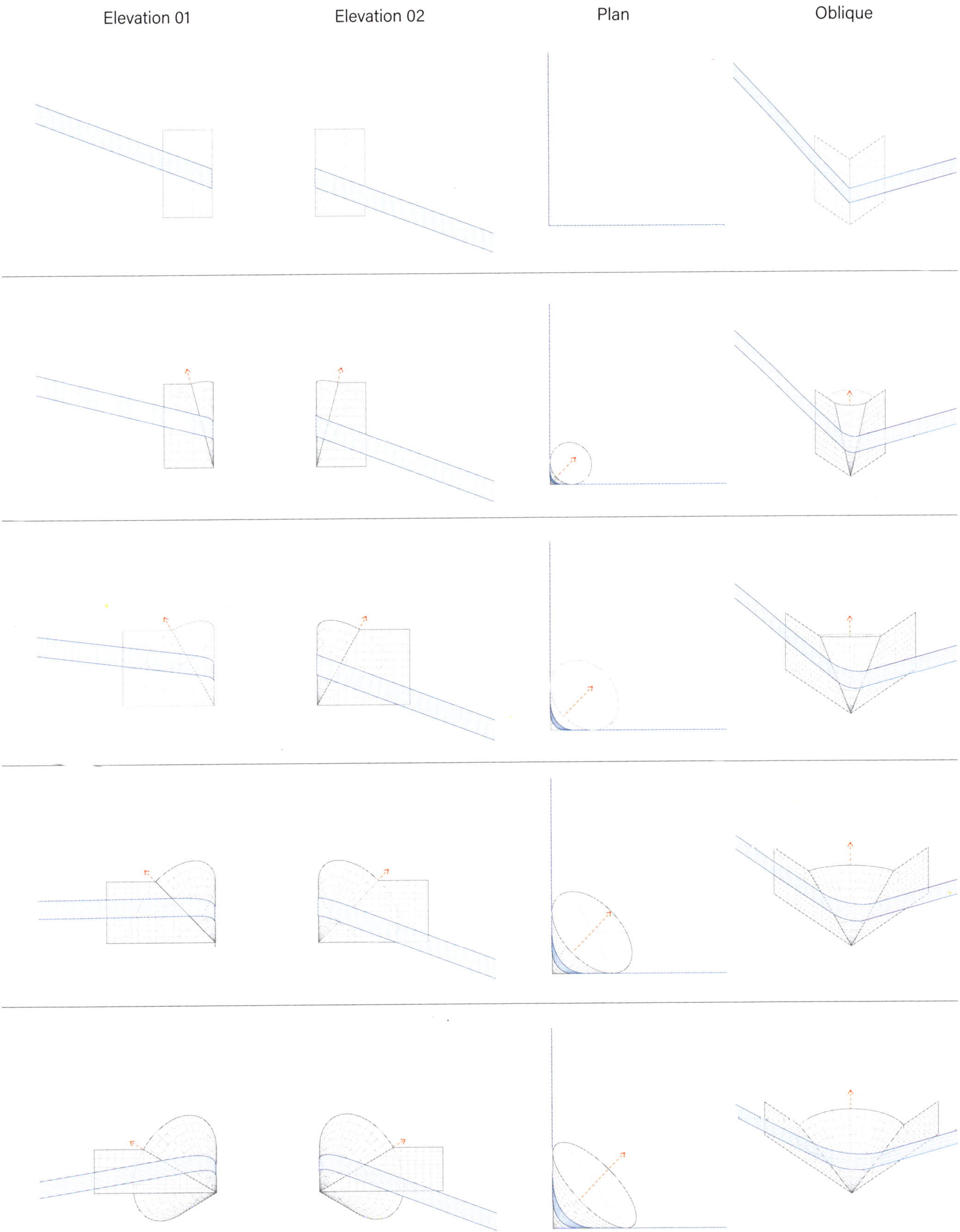
Elevation 01
Elevation 02
Plan
Oblique

DIHEDRAL CONE INSCRIPTION 02
VARIABLE GEODESIC SLOPE / CONSTANT CONE ANGLE

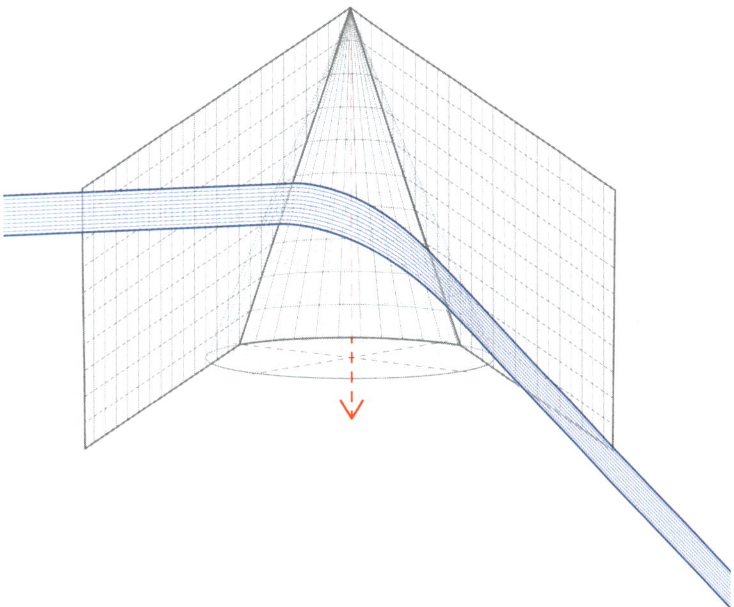

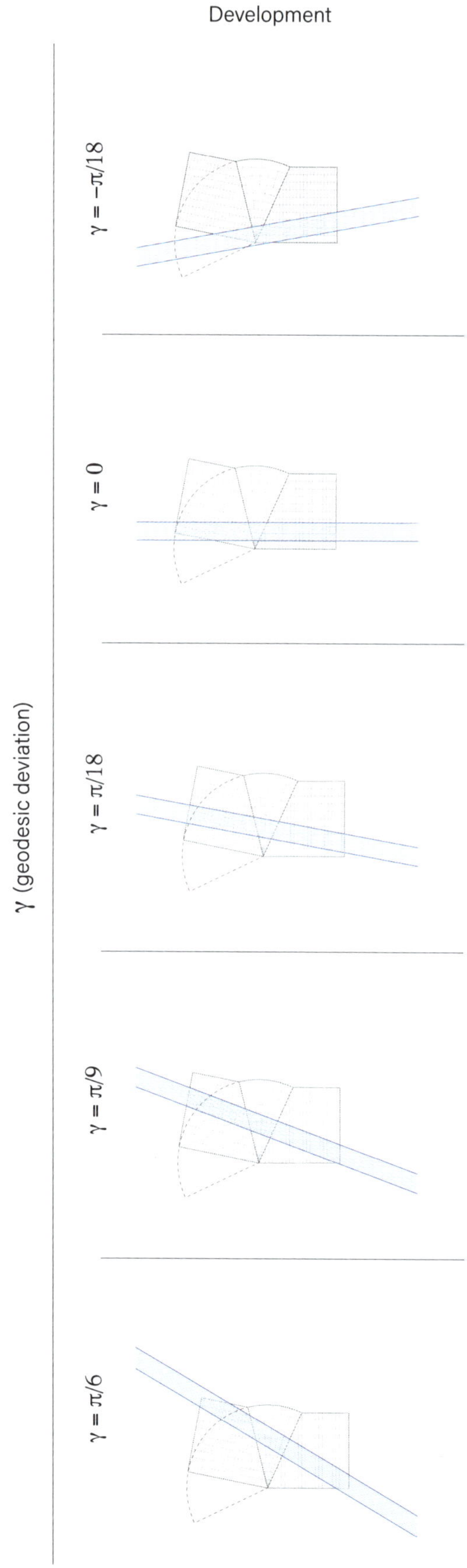

In cases where the developed (unrolled) state of the conical surface is less than ϖ radians (180°), continuous geodesic lines can migrate around the smoothed dihedral corner. The change of orientation and slope of the geodesics is a function of the profile angle, tilt, and angular sweep of the conic surface. The examples here show variations of input angles and resultant deviations of geodesic line slopes when traced across identical conic inscriptions.

Elevation 01	Elevation 02	Plan	Oblique

GEODESIC LOOPING 01
CYLINDER-TETRAHEDRON

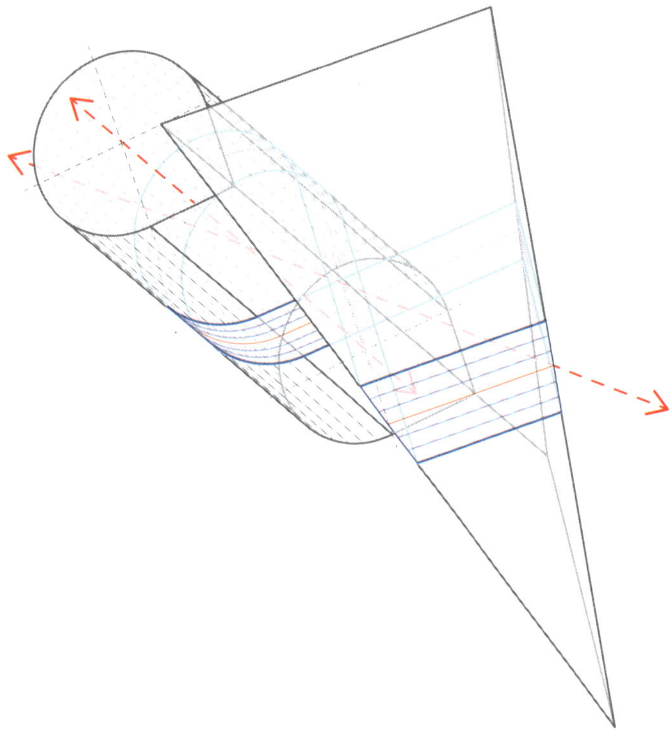

The technique of "geodesic looping" uses continuous transitions of geodesic subdivisions of a piecewise continuous host surface to produce a closed figural loop or a periodically repetitive array. In cases shown here, the host surface is comprised of a cylinder, a tetrahedron, and two auxiliary planar figures. The cylinder is trimmed by two ruling line generators, along which the tangent stitching planes are attached. These planes are coplanar with two sides of the tetrahedron, thus making all seams smooth and continuous.
The geodesic planks migrate across one volume before transitioning to the other and then back again in an endless cycle. The non-zero curvature of the cylinder is constant, causing different geodesic lines to bend into helices of varying eccentricity. For the tetrahedron, the zero curvature of each plane dictates that the only change in direction of the geodesic lines occurs at the three dihedral folds. Despite their geometric differences, the cylinder and the tetrahedron are calibrated to "turn" the ribbon in space in equal and opposite directions. These examples show variations in the tilt angle (α) of the cylinder, which produce different eccentricities of the 270° helical sweeps. The tetrahedron must necessarily transform its proportions and orientation to facilitate the closed loop.

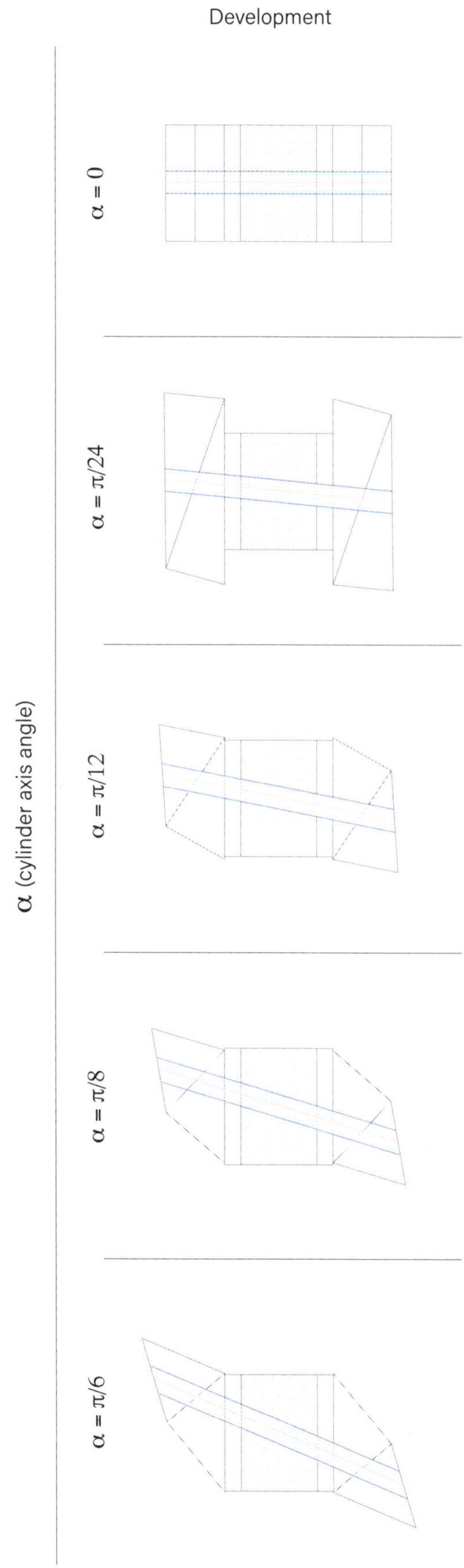

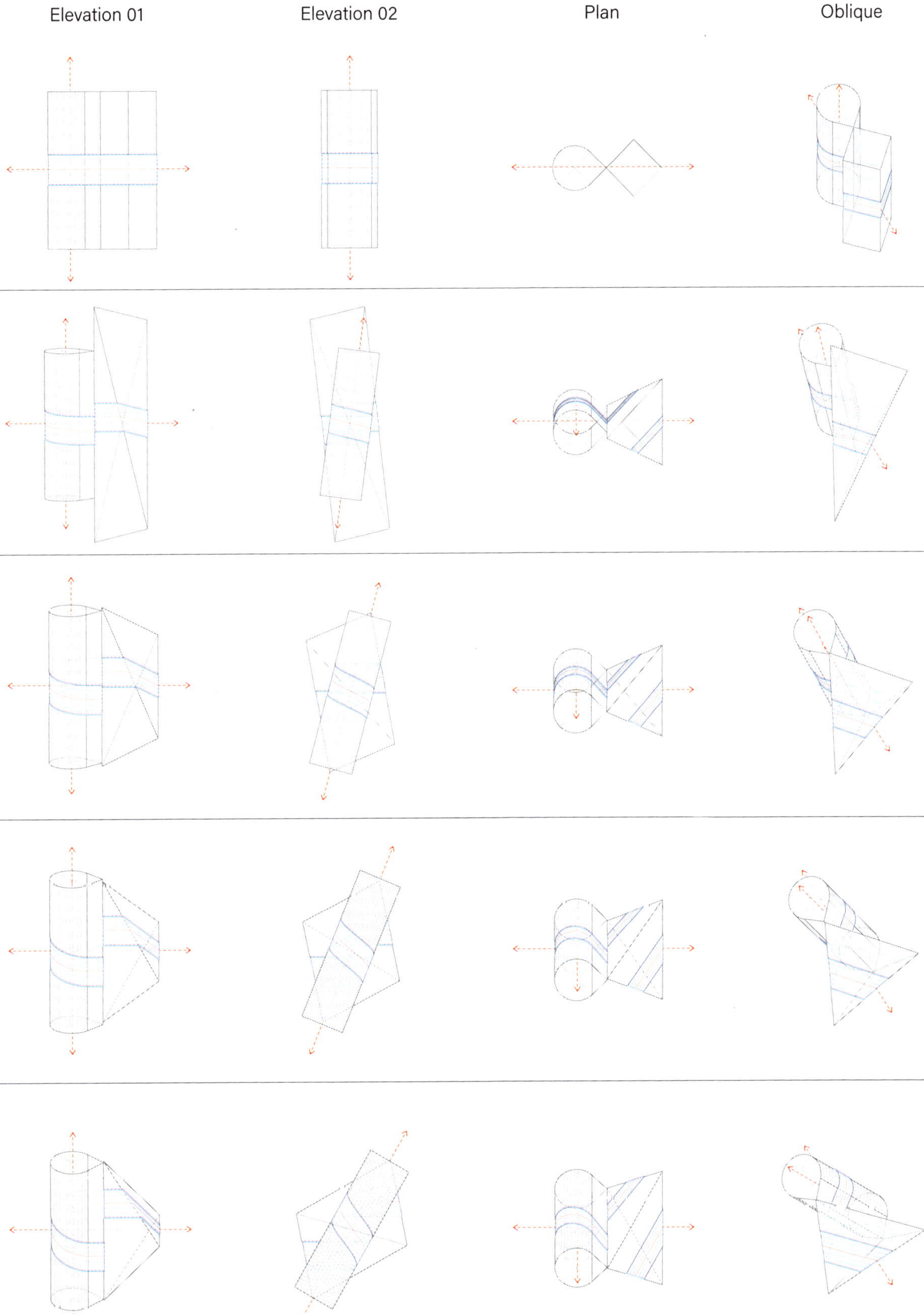

Elevation 01
Elevation 02
Plan
Oblique

HYPAR-HYPERBOLOID CONTINUITY 01 TANGENCY ALONG INTERSECTING RULING LINES

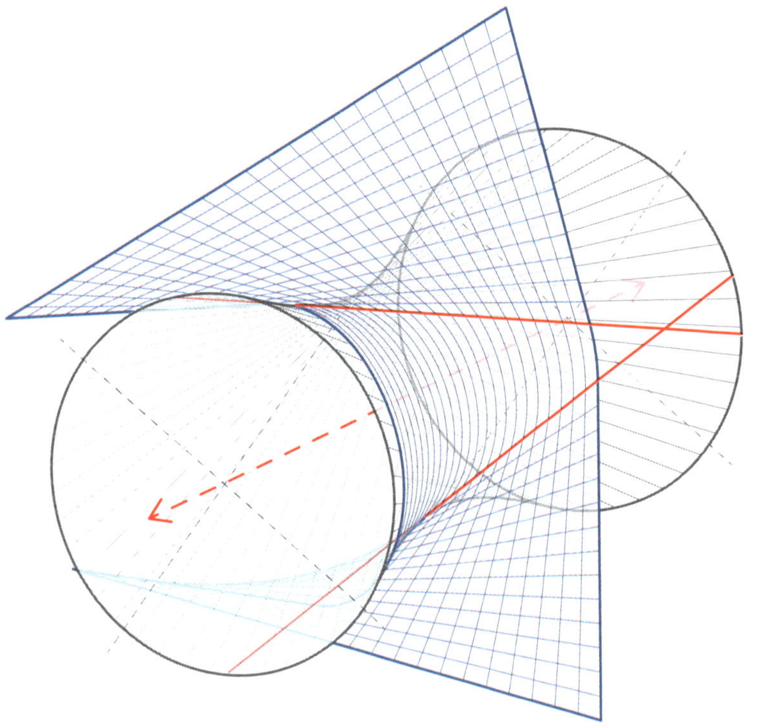

The variations shown here exhibit smooth and piecewise continuous assemblies of two hyperbolic paraboloids (hypars) and a central hyperboloid of revolution. The hyperboloid essentially acts as a continuous “twisted fillet” making a smooth and continous (G1) transition between the flanking doubly ruled hypars. The orthographic projections of ruling line subdivisions of both hypars are constrained to remain orthogonal in plan and in longitudinal elevation. The compound surface thus conveys aesthetic attributes of smooth and unified (curvilinear) envelopes while maintaining projective alignments compatible with any potential orthogonal subdivision. These examples show variations of the hypars tangent along two intersecting ruling lines (from opposite UV curve fields) of the hyperboloid. The resulting compound surface exhibits a bilateral symmetry over a 45-degree axis most discernable in the lateral elevation.

α (hyperboloid axis angle)	Development
α = 0	N/A
α = π/24	N/A
α = π/12	N/A
α = π/8	N/A
α = π/6	N/A

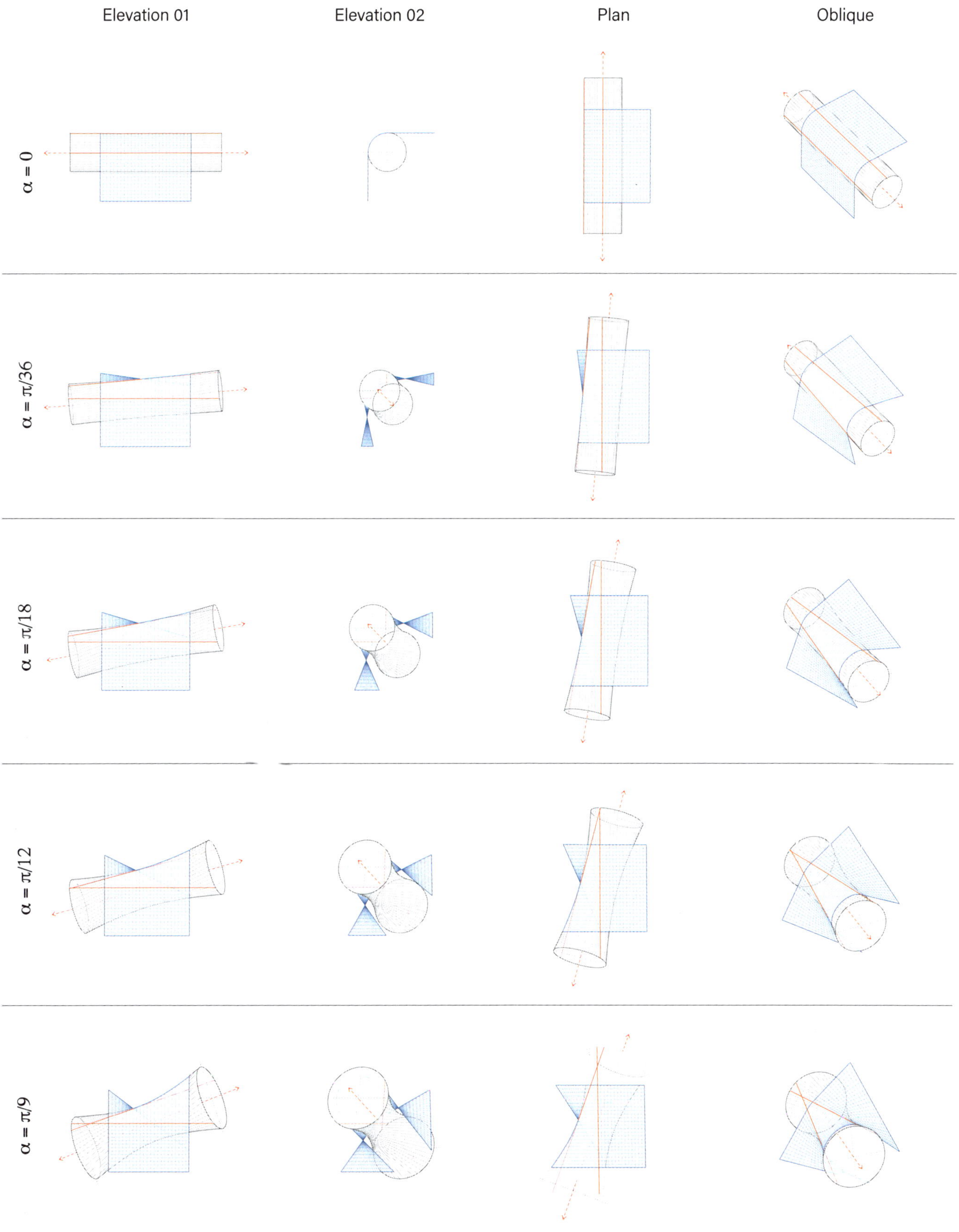
Elevation 01
Elevation 02
Plan
Oblique
α = 0
α = π/36
α = π/18
α = π/12
α = π/9

HYPAR-HYPERBOLOID CONTINUITY 02 TANGENCY ALONG NON-INTERSECTING RULING LINES

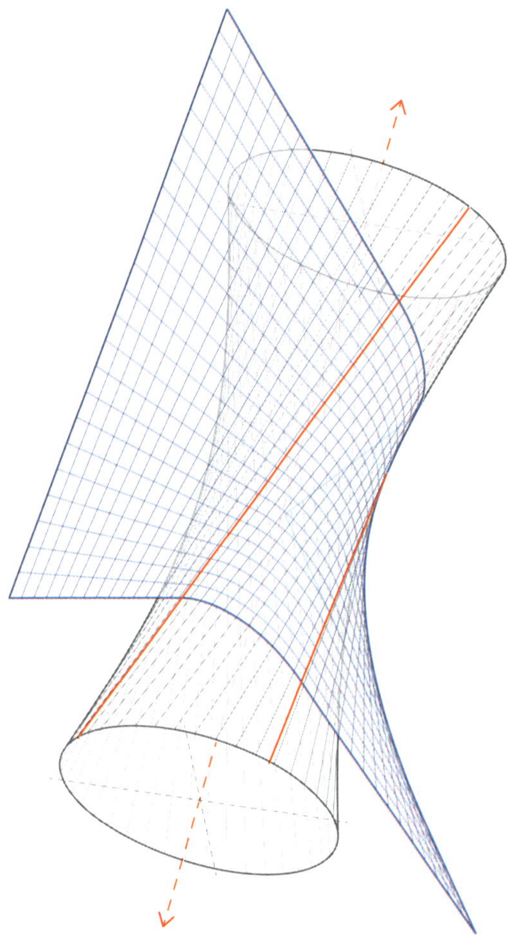

The variations shown here exhibit smooth and piecewise continuous assemblies of two hyperbolic paraboloids (hypars) and a central hyperboloid of revolution. The hyperboloid essentially acts as a continuous "twisted fillet" making a smooth and continous (G1) transition between the flanking doubly ruled hypars. These examples show variations of the hypars tangent along two "parallel" (non-intersecting) ruling lines (from the same UV curve fields) of the hyperboloid. The resulting compound surface exhibits a rotational symmetry about the centroid of the system.

α (hyperboloid axis angle)	Development
$\alpha = 0$	N/A
$\alpha = \pi/24$	N/A
$\alpha = \pi/12$	N/A
$\alpha = \pi/8$	N/A
$\alpha = \pi/6$	N/A

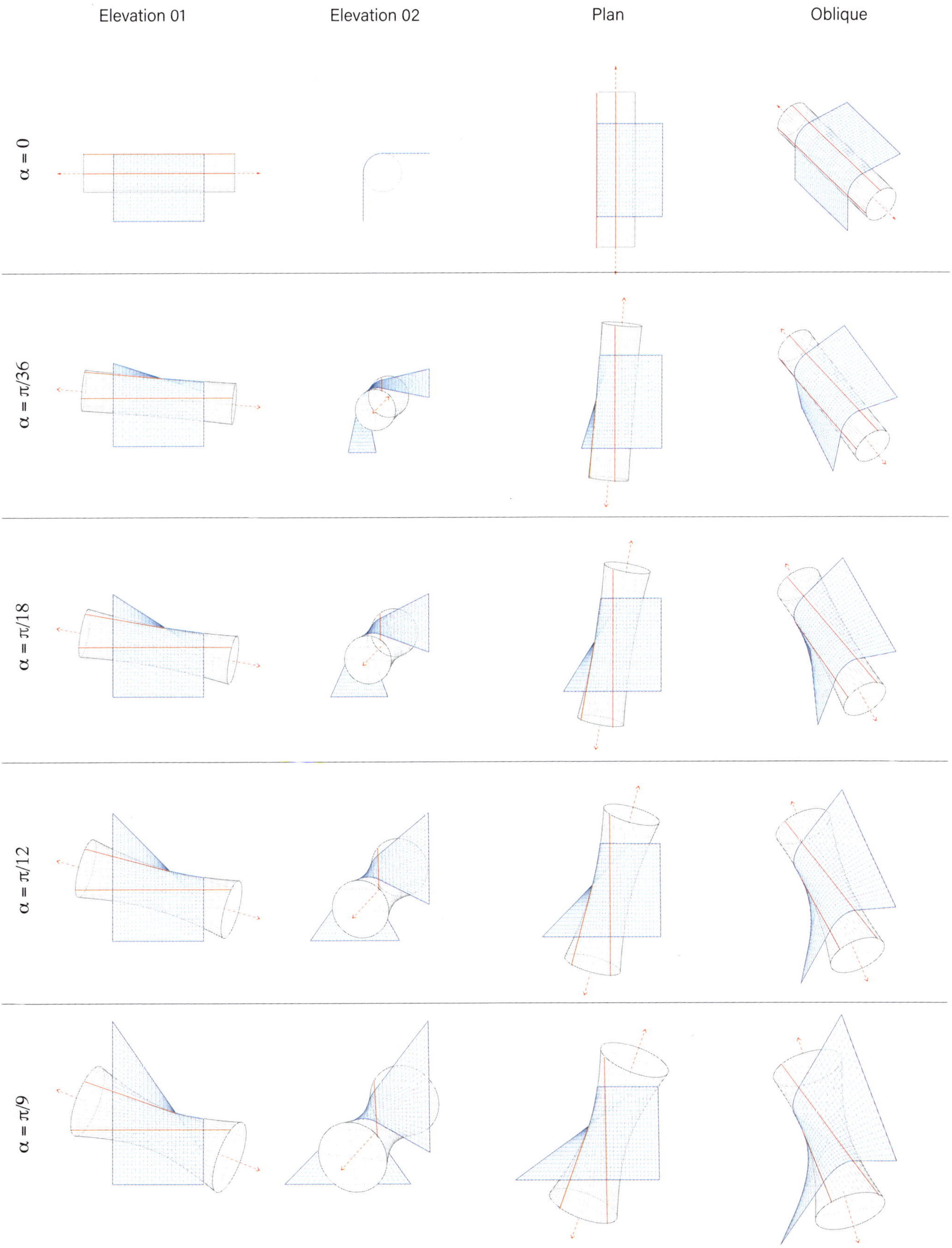
Elevation 01
Elevation 02
Plan
Oblique
α = 0
α = π/36
α = π/18
α = π/12
α = π/9

HYPAR-HYPERBOLOID CONTINUITY 04 CLOSED LOOP (VERTICAL) TANGENCY ALONG INTERSECTING RULING LINES

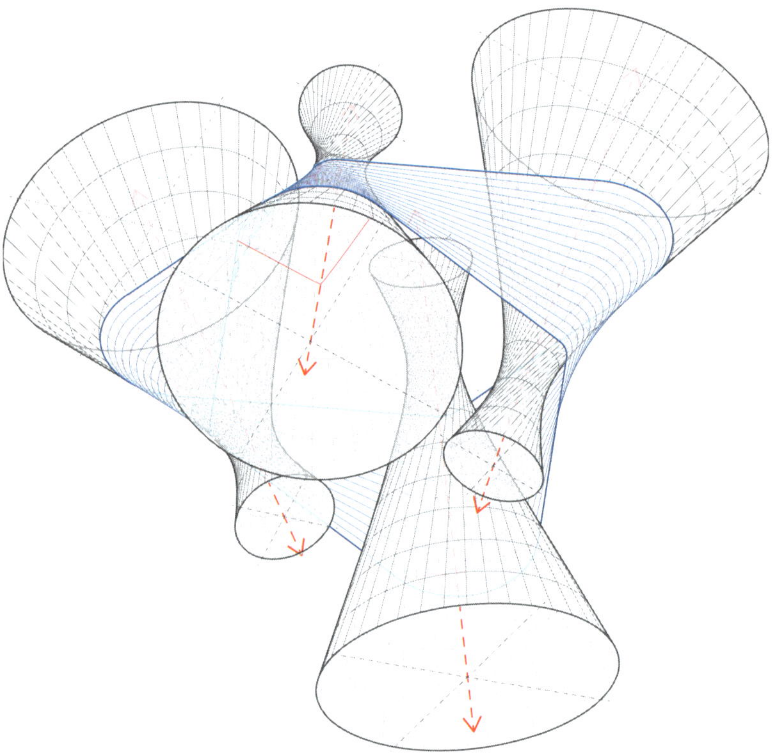

In this vertically oriented version, the orthographic projections of ruling line subdivisions of all hypars are constrained to remain orthogonal in two distinct elevations. The hypars simultaneously comprise much of the continuous curvilinear exterior envelope while maintaining projective aligments with interior orthogonal geometries. The examples here show multiple hypars and hyperboloids which form a continuous oscillating closed loop. The surfaces are tangent along two intersecting ruling lines (from opposite UV curve fields) of the hyperboloid. The resulting compound surface produces two axes of bilateral symmetry in plan.

α (hyperboloid axis angle)	Development
$\alpha = 0$	N/A
$\alpha = \pi/24$	N/A
$\alpha = \pi/12$	N/A
$\alpha = \pi/8$	N/A
$\alpha = \pi/6$	N/A

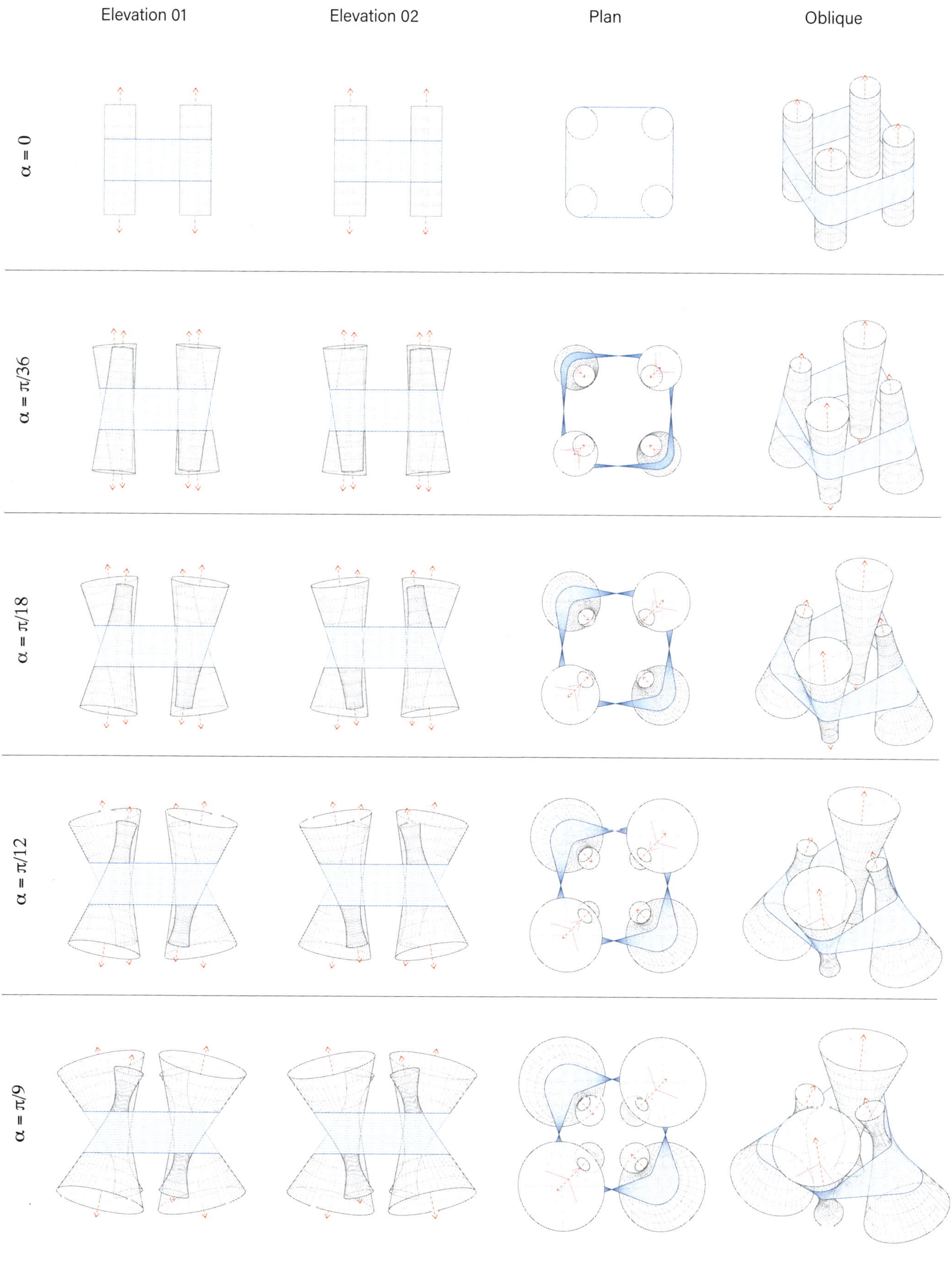
Elevation 01
Elevation 02
Plan
Oblique
α = 0
α = π/36
α = π/18
α = π/12
α = π/9

PROJECTS

01 Exterior view

Geodesic House 02
2014

Geodesic House 02 uses the technique of geodesic leveling to achieve smooth transitions of its façades across zones of sloped circulation paths and level floors. This method allows the exterior surfaces to be constructed with standard planks of siding in curved or planar arrangements. The interior organization consists of a looping volume formed into a continuous three-dimensional figure 8. Living, dining, and kitchen occupy the bottom level, which tapers at both ends to staircases leading to a single loaded corridor connecting both ends on the upper level. The eccentric shape of the unified massing allows for covered entries and access to elevated exterior decks. Reveal lines of the shiplap siding reinforce the properties of the geodesic planks while binding together the tectonic unit of construction, the architectural parti, and the circulatory path of the subject.

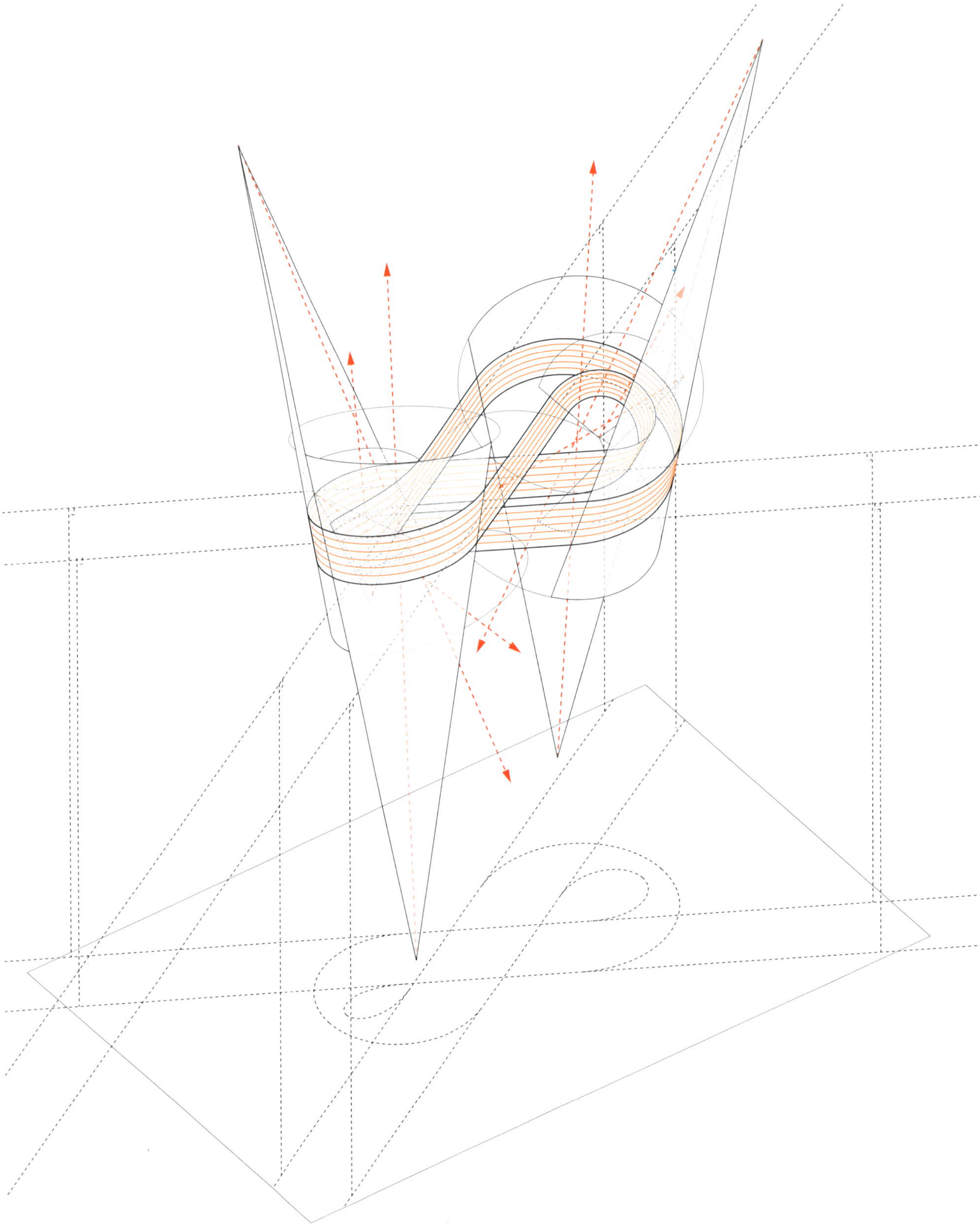

02 3d geodesic leveling

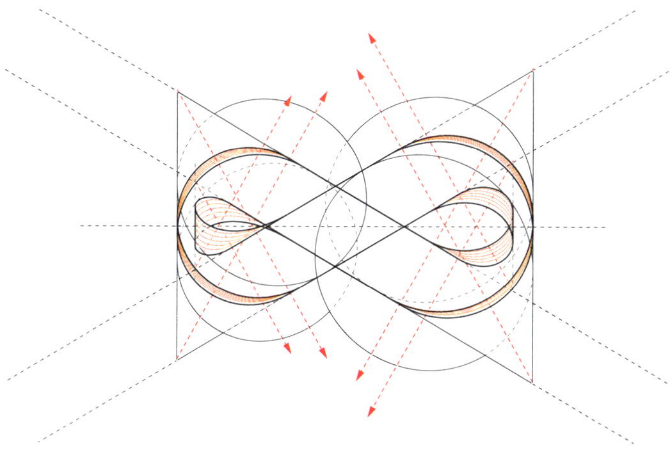

03 Plan of geodesic leveling

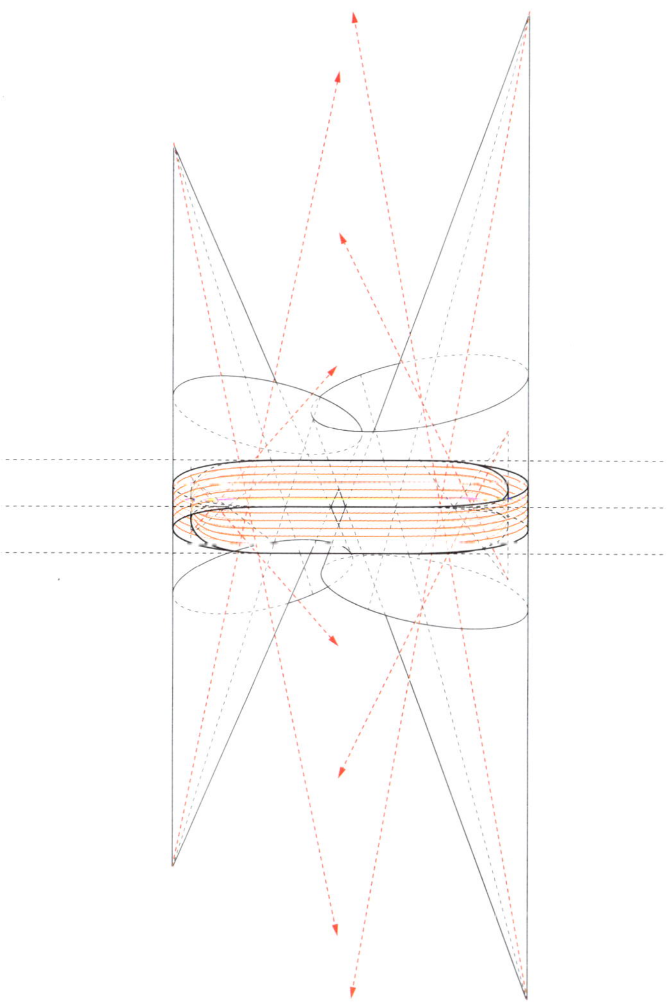

04 Elevation of geodesic leveling

GEODESIC LEVELING

Eight discrete cones trimmed along their ruling line generators are placed tangent to two pairs of plumb plane figures. Two independent looping ribbons defined by geodesic lines/planks taken from these "host" surfaces define a continuous figure 8 volume. The geometries are arranged in specific orientations to produce a constrained range of geodesic inclinations—enabling smooth transitions from horizontal, to sloped, and back to horizontal again. These inclinations are informed by the stair angles, and indicate the trajectory of circulatory movement of the interior.

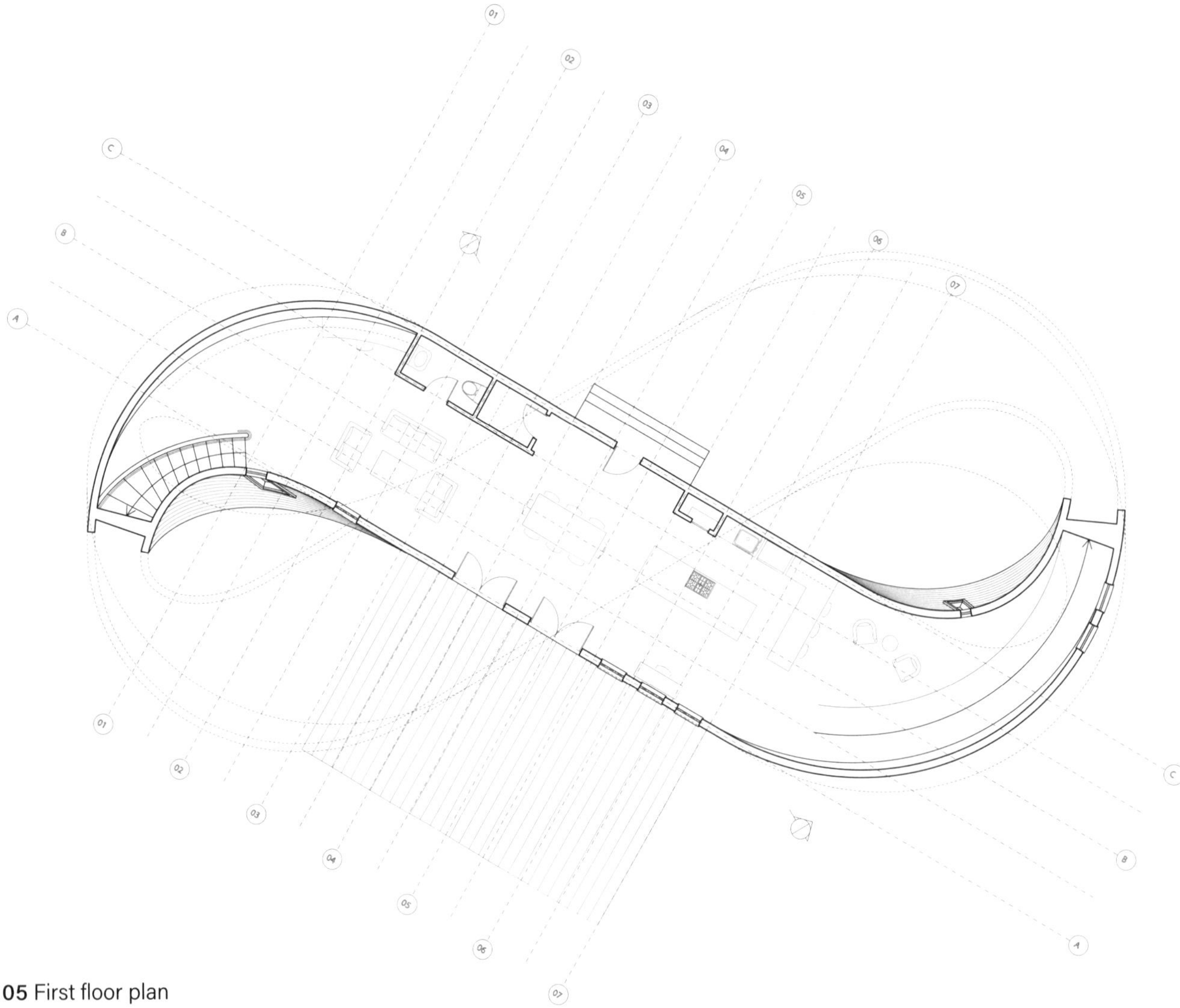

05 First floor plan

DUALISM

The technique of geodesic leveling allows visual dynamism of three-dimensional form in localized areas, while allowing most of the occupiable volume to be well-behaved in plan and elevation. The transverse views are more active and sculptural than the longitudinal elevations.

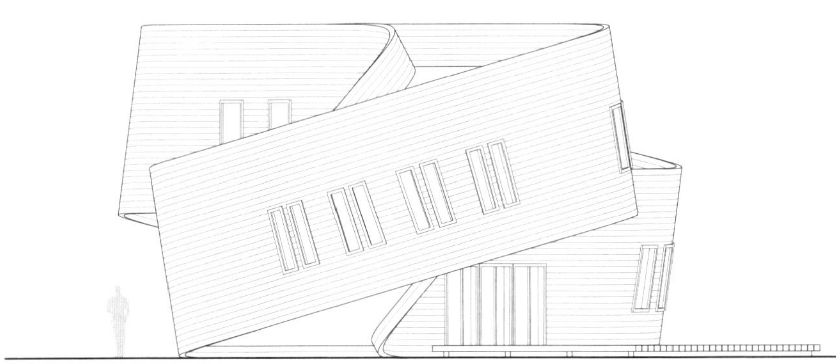

06 Transverse elevation

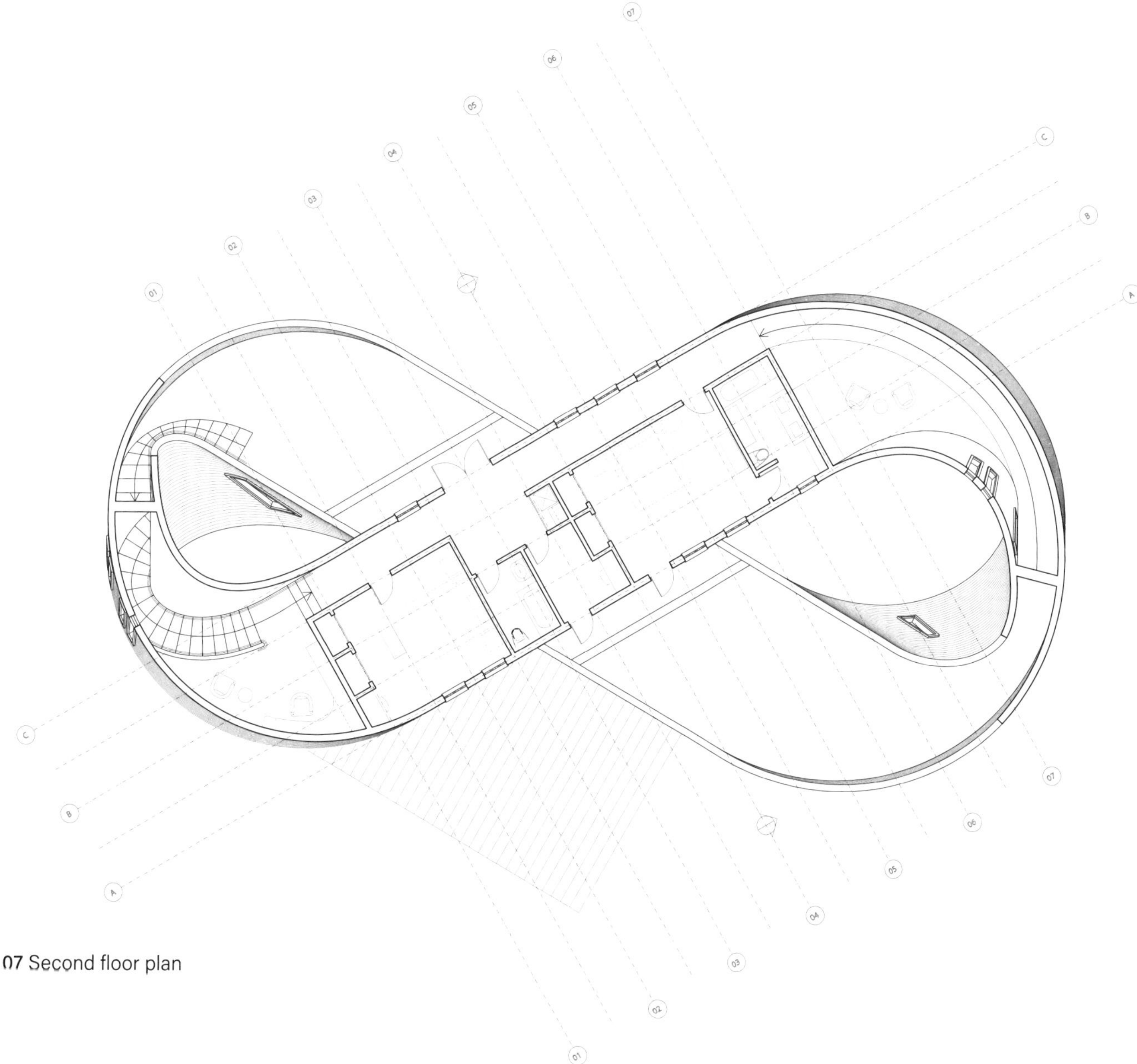

07 Second floor plan

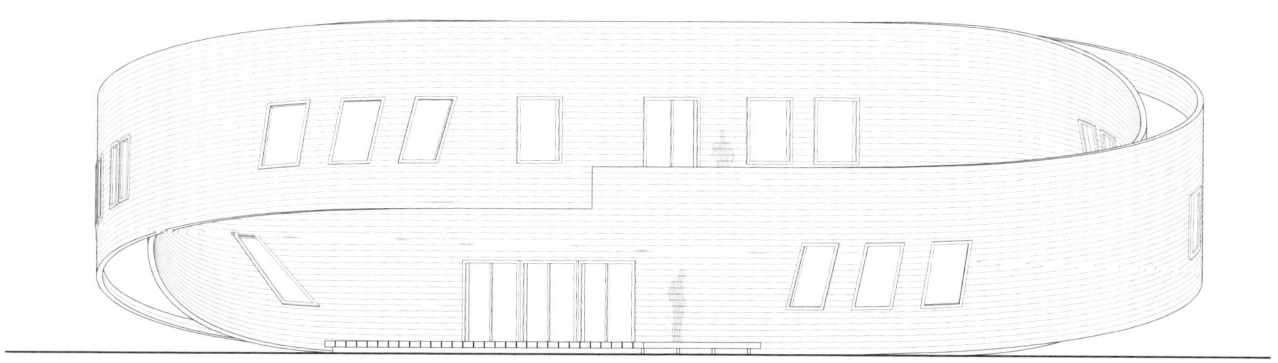

08 Longitudinal elevation

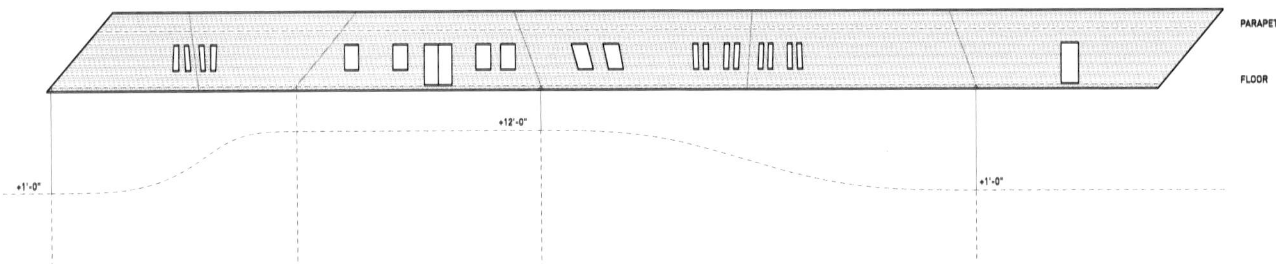

09.1 Developed elevation 01 (with fenestration)

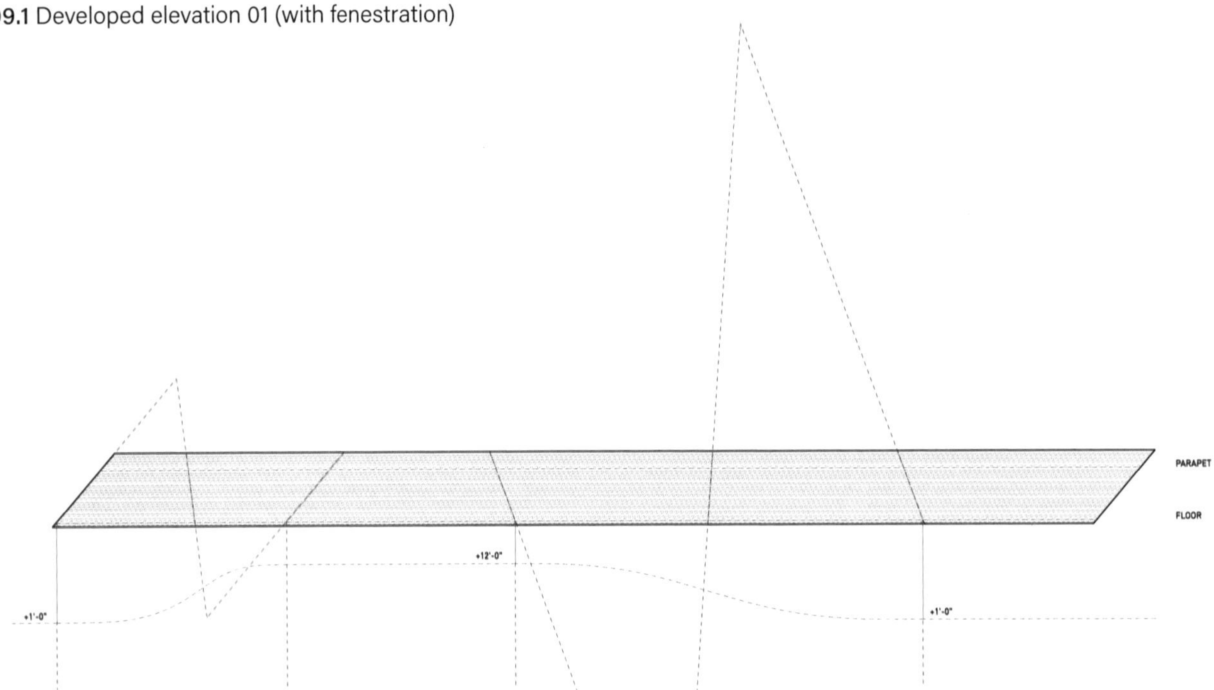

09.2 Developed elevation 01 (untrimmed cones)

DEVELOPED ELEVATIONS

The two exterior elevations unroll to elongated parallelograms. Angled lines of these two-dimensional developed states indicate the contiguous edges between vertical planes and rotationally symmetric cones. These transitions are smooth and continuous in the three-dimensional form. The composition uses two discrete looping ribbons offset from one another to enclose a continuous interior volume. One ribbon serves as the outer limit for one stair and the inner limit for the opposing stair, and vice versa. This inner/outer inversion is evidenced in the disparity of cone sizes of each continuous loop.

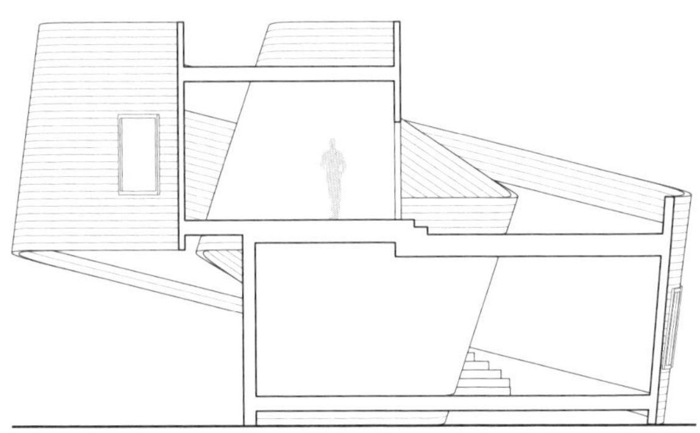

10 Lateral section

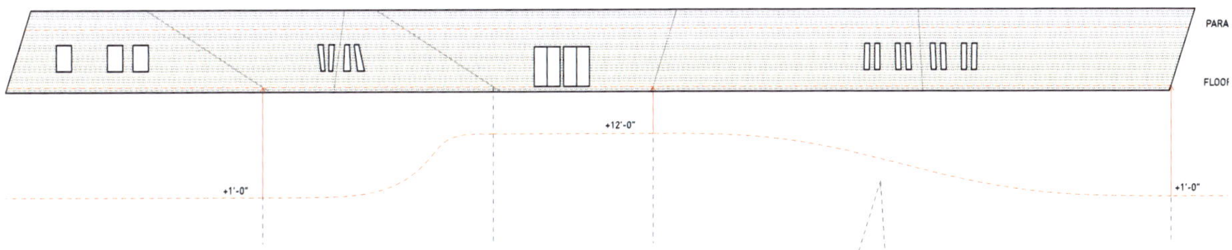

11.1 Developed elevation 02 (with fenestration)

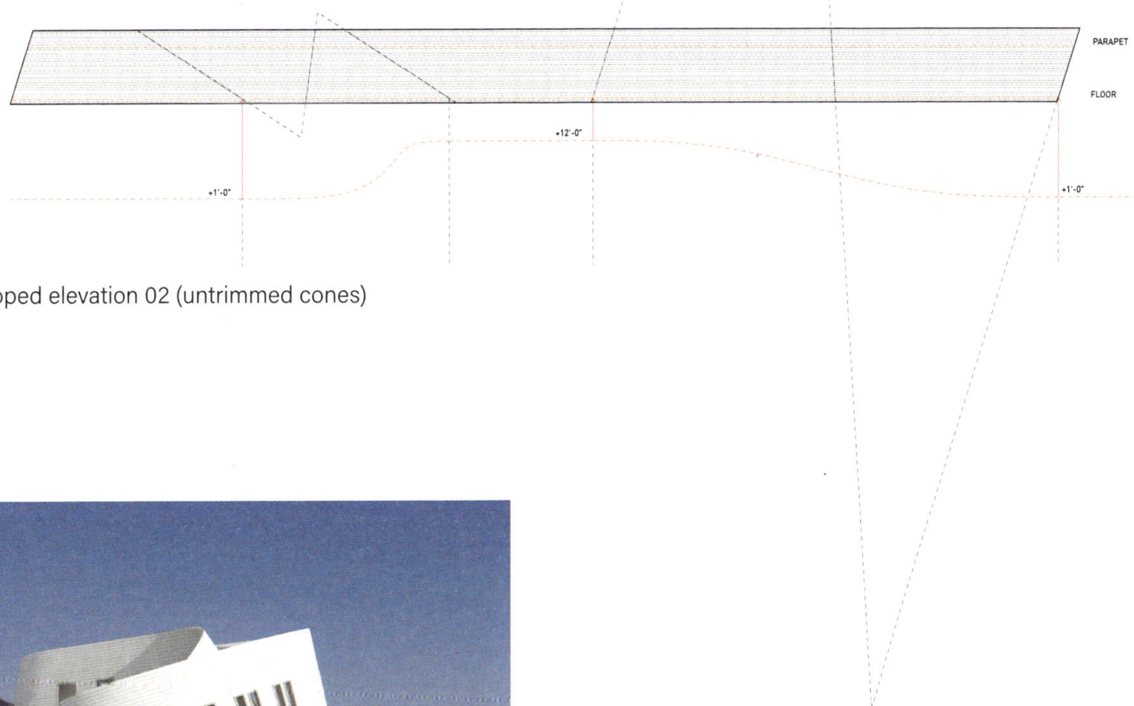

11.2 Developed elevation 02 (untrimmed cones)

12 Exterior view

01 Andrea Palladio. Villa Gazzotti (Bertesina, Italy) 1542
(plan from Scamozzi 1778)

Geodesic House 03
2015

Geodesic House 03 applies the techniques of geodesic leveling and looping exclusively on the corridor and stair circulation form. Departing from plan organizations of certain Palladian villa types, symmetrical stairs escape their traditional confinement within the poché to become exaggerated and externalized, inducing the rotation of the upper floor.

02 Parallel oblique aerial view

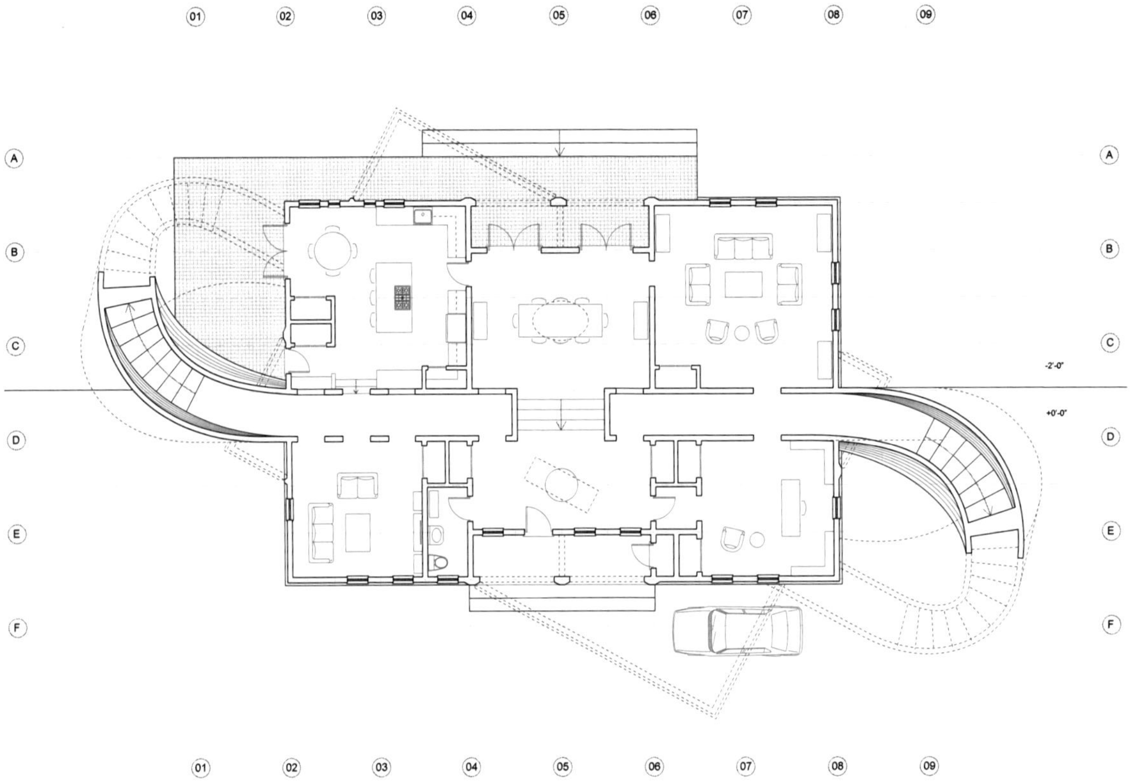

03 First floor plan

BILATERAL / ROTATIONAL

Upon entry, the symmetry of the first floor tripartite plan (**03**) remains essentially undisrupted. The only conspicuous deviations are the rotated overhead aperture in the entry hall ceiling and off-center front door. Grid alignment constraints prohibit having a central bay. Geodesic looping and leveling techniques govern the congruent rotationally symmetrical stairs within acceptable limits of material bending radii. The sheared corridor on the upper floor allows a hierarchy of room dimensions while keeping the centroids of the upper and lower levels aligned in plan. On the entry side, the plan rectangles intersect at the one-third span of the bottom floor (allowing the recessed entry porch to be covered) and at the mid-span of the upper floor. On the back side the situation is reversed, allowing multiple bedrooms to access the exterior deck. The shear of the upper corridor plan produces a single open-ended ribbon, unlike the two discrete closed loops of Geodesic House 02.

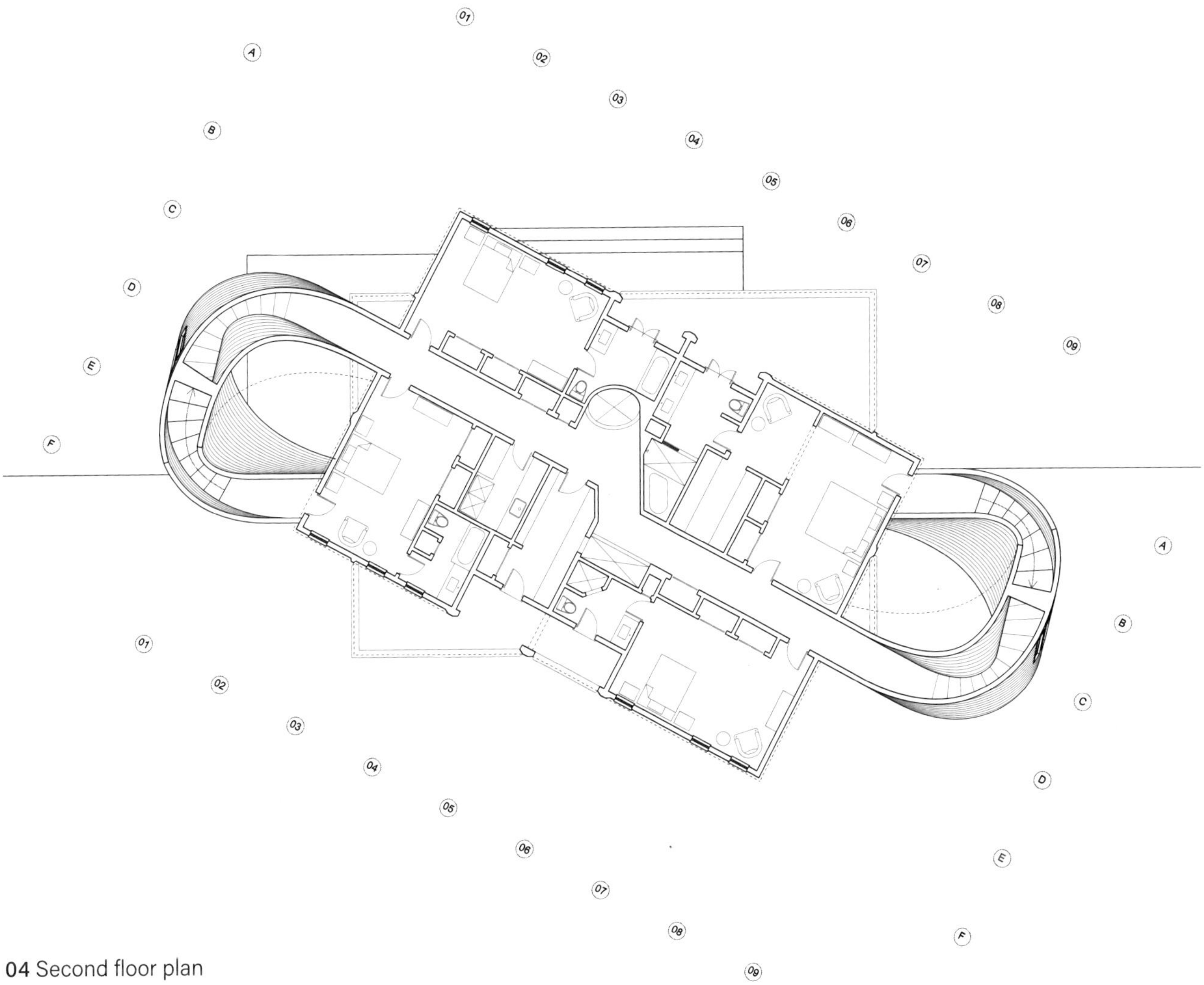

04 Second floor plan

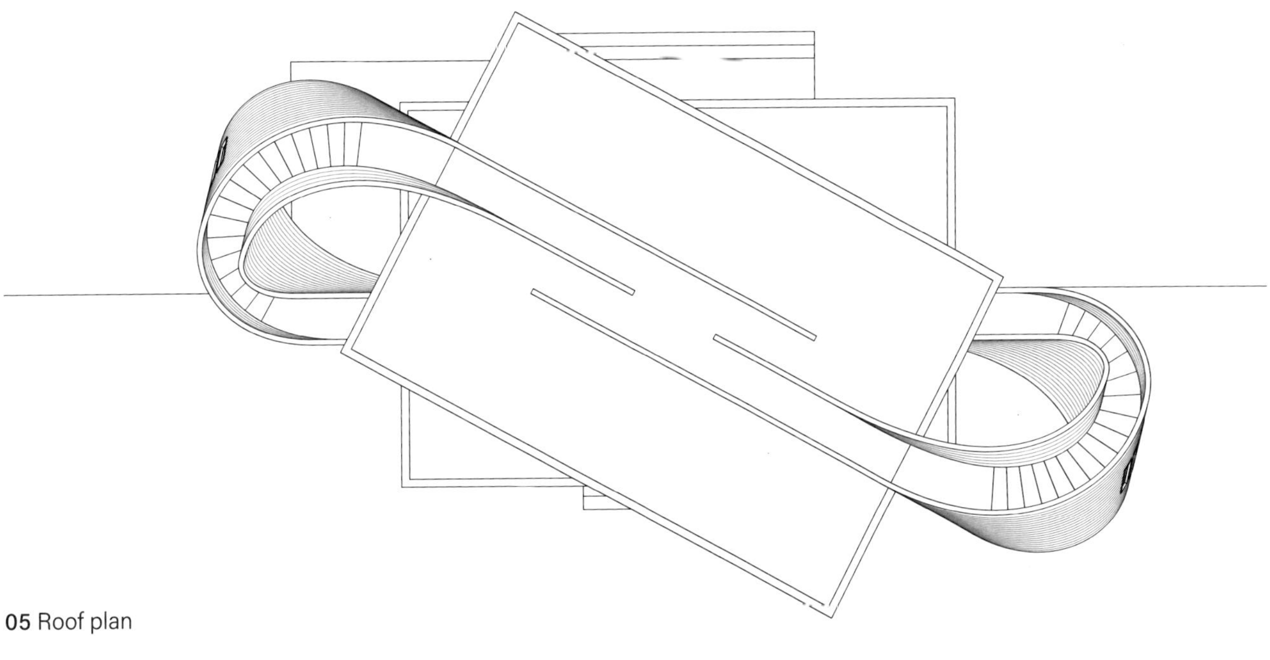

05 Roof plan

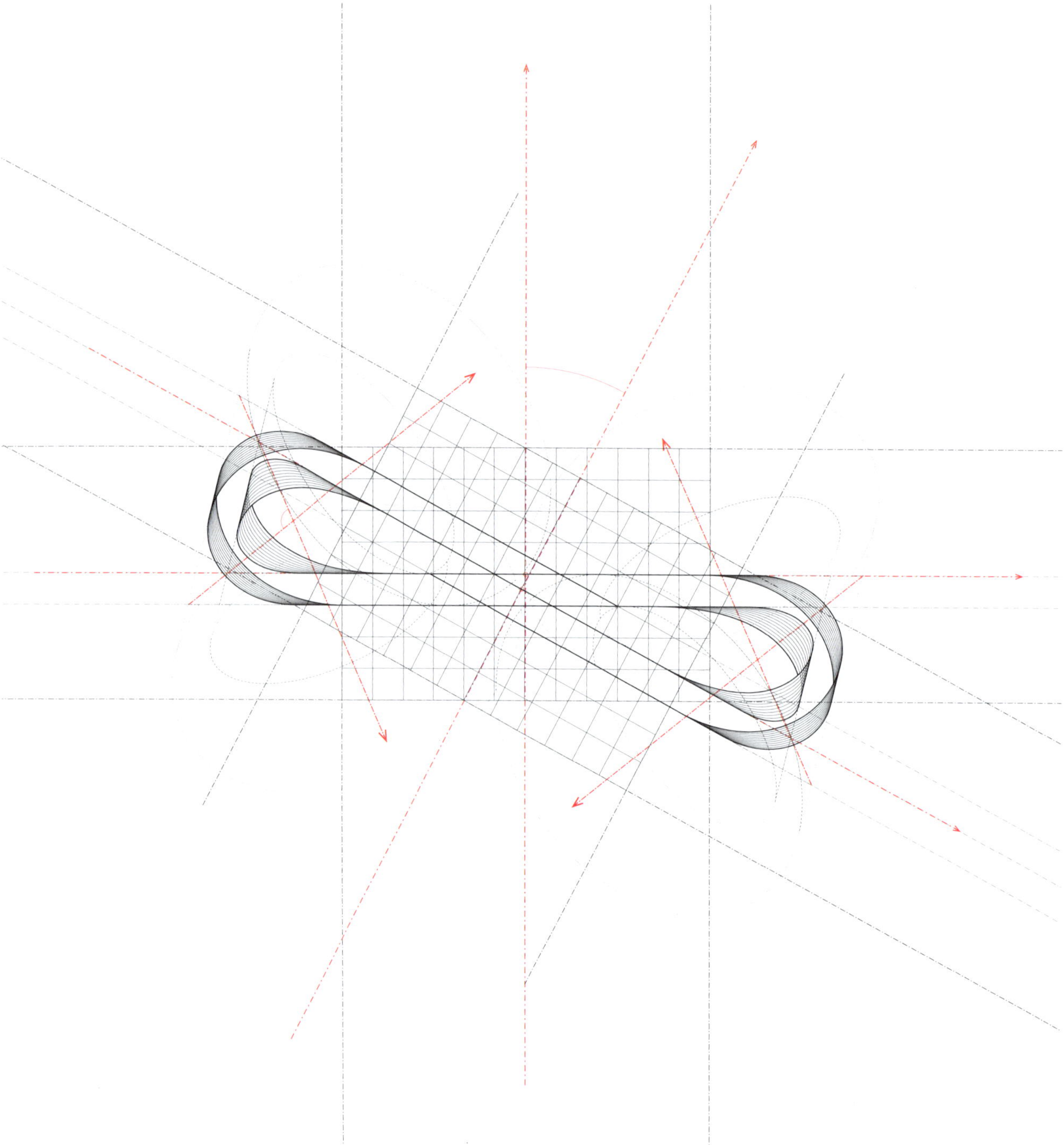

06 Plan of geodesic leveling construction

07 Elevation on approach

VERTICAL BONDING

Vertical pilasters mark the mid-span and third-span of each level. The aspect ratio of the rectangular footprints and structural bay dimensions are calibrated with the geometry of the geodesic looping stairs to achieve these vertical alignments. The mid-span/third-span façade locking between upper and lower levels is reversed on the opposite side.

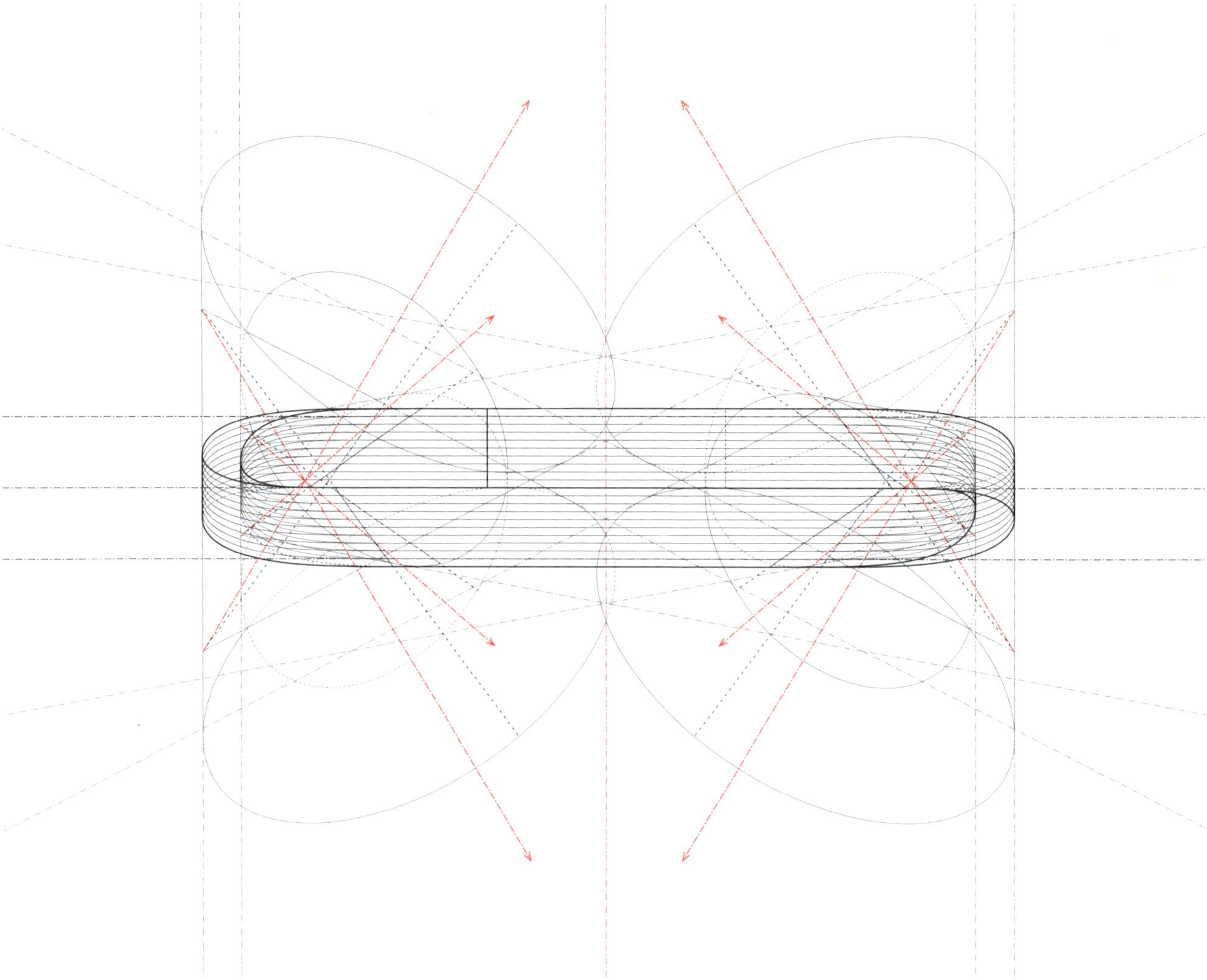

08 Longitudinal elevation of geodesic leveling construction

09 Longitudinal elevation

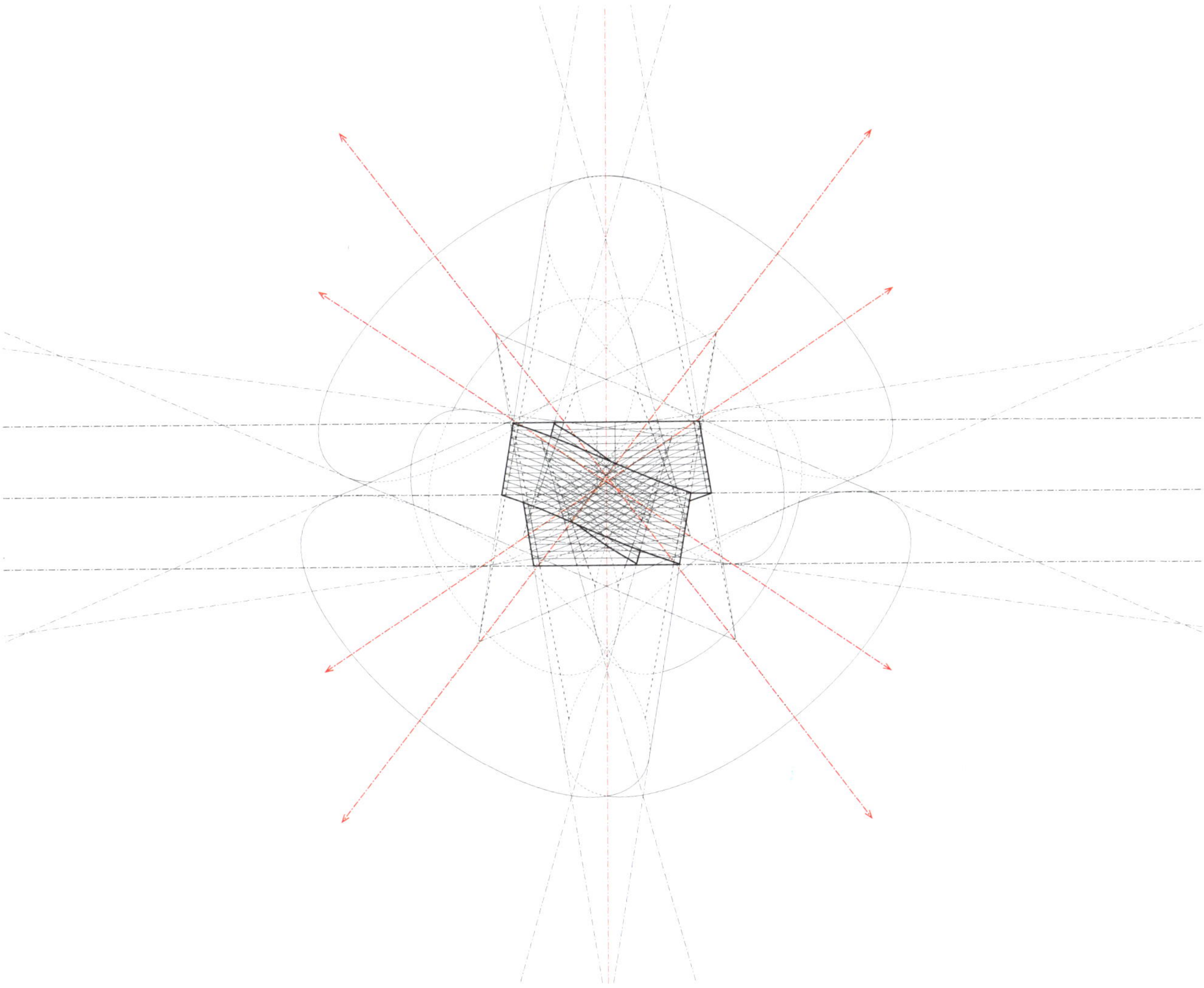

10 Transverse elevation of geodesic looping construction

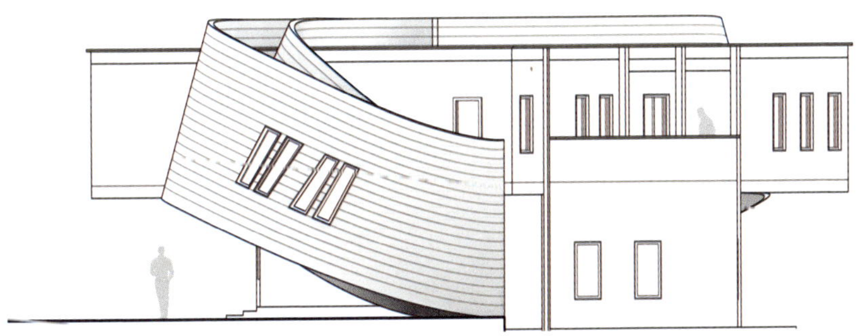

11 Transverse elevation

ROTATIONAL TRANSFORMATION

The two discrete floors of the rectangular massing are dislodged and rotated with respect to each other according to the plan angle prescribed by the extroverted geodesic stairs. The technique of geodesic leveling produces charged moments with small radii of curvature in specific areas, while eventually transitioning to normative and well-behaved planar geometries.

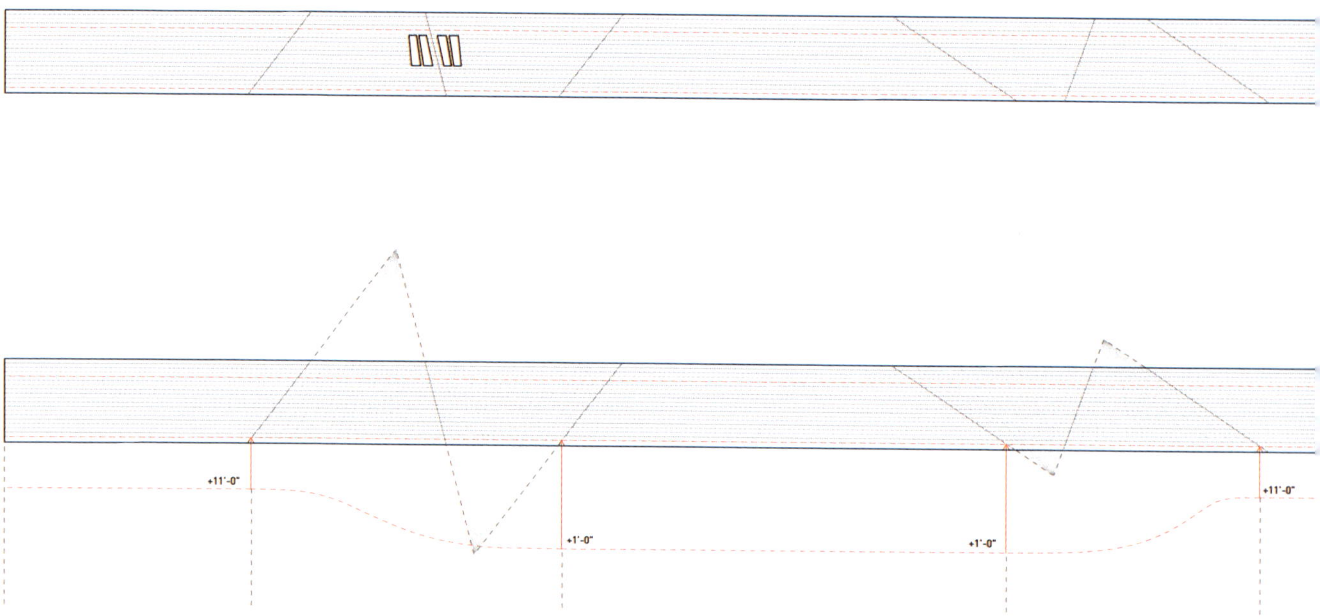

12 Developed elevation of circulation corridor

13 Exterior view

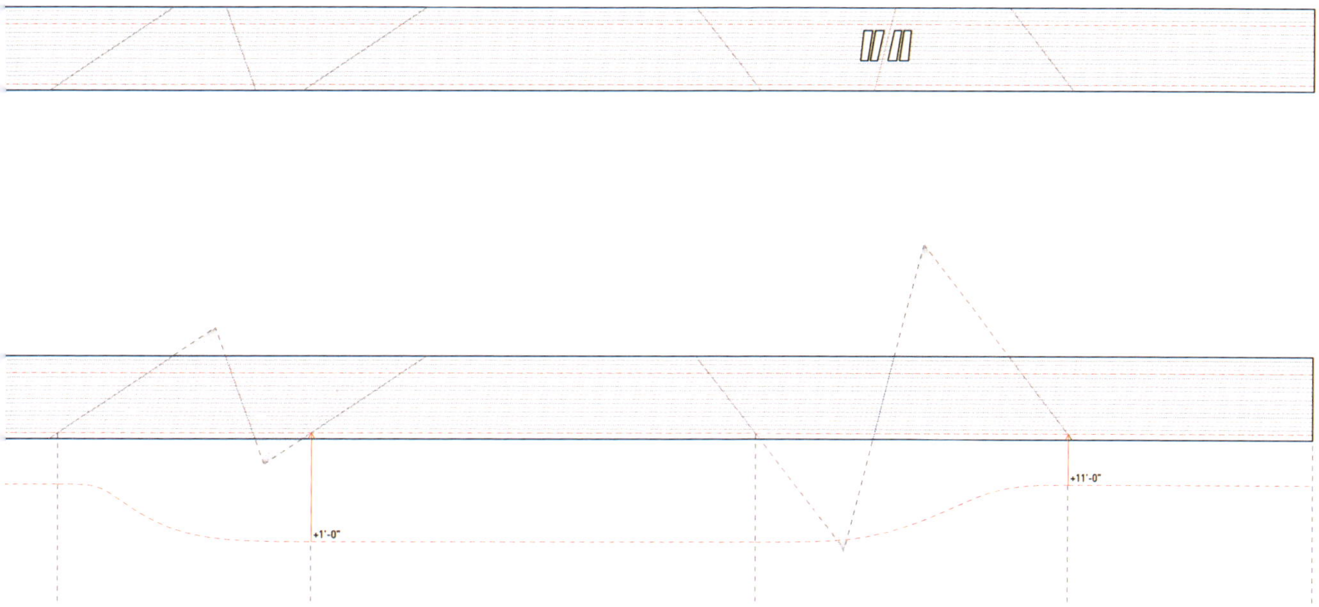

14 Inner loop of stair

DEVELOPED ELEVATION OF CORRIDOR

The hall offset of the upper level allows the corridor wall surface to unroll as a single elongated rectangle that traces the figure 8 twice (unlike the two offset ribbons of Geodesic House 02). Angled lines of the developed elevation show the contiguous edges between vertical planes and rotationally symmetric cones—transitions which are smooth and continuous in the three-dimensional form. The floor-to-floor rise occurs in a small plan area and produces tight radii of curvature (**14**).

Coney Inland

MoMA PS1 Young Architects Program
Long Island City, New York
2012

For generations of New Yorkers, Coney Island has served as the quintessential local retreat from the city. Unfettered access to sky, land, and sea makes it a welcome contrast to the urban metropolis, drawing crowds in search of spatial and social release. Through the architectural translation of qualities inherent to this ocean-side precedent, CONEY INLAND imports the culture of casual beach leisure into the courtyard at MoMA PS1.

Colorful cabana/boardwalk hybrids provide longitudinal subdivision of the courtyard space. These boardwalks are deployed as programmed spaces modulating the circulation patterns rather than being the path of travel. Latticework parasols overhead provide extensive spatial coverage in addition to considerable and necessary shade. These dynamic conical forms recreate a sensation of suspension between sky, land, and sea. Recalling observation decks with soaring views, elevated sun decks allow one to rise above the canopy and survey the courtyard and all of its colorful activity. Shallow pools, sand pits, and play courts provide leisurely activities reminiscent of various seaside past-times and boardwalk life.

01 Gridshell canopies and cabana sleds modulate the MoMA PS1 courtyard

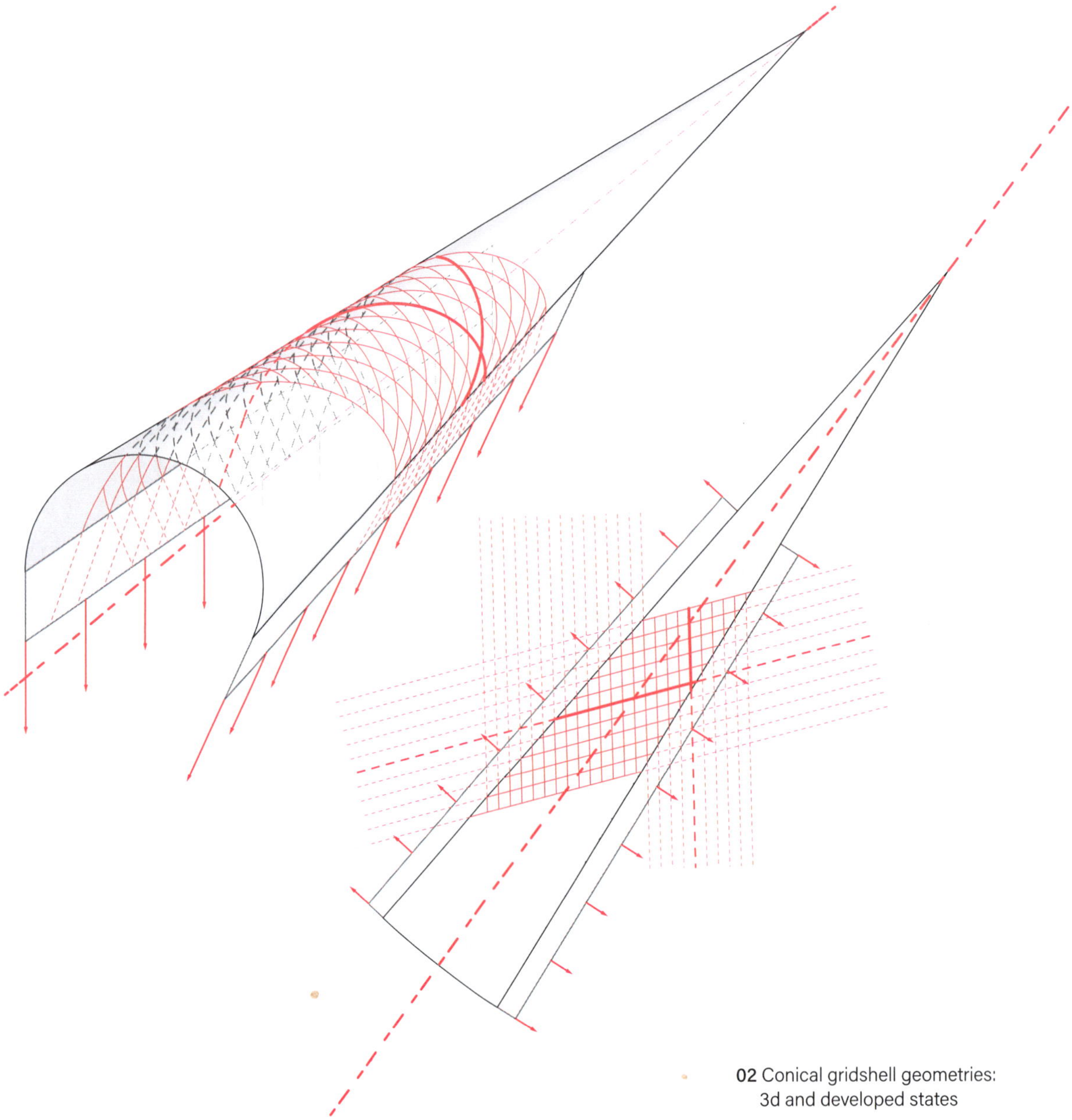

02 Conical gridshell geometries: 3d and developed states

CANOPY FORM AND SUBDIVISION

The canopy structures, developed in collaboration with Schlaich Bergermann Partner, use geodesic lines of conical and cylindrical surfaces to minimize twisting of the structural gridshell elements. The resulting strips of wide geodesic planks are calibrated to allow cladding material to be identical when unrolled, shown by equally spaced parallel lines in the developed state (**02**). The uniform width of material minimizes cost and waste. Due to the nature of the developable surfaces, the orientations of structural elements at the edge beams (which lie in plumb planes) are all identical and details can be standardized.

03 Aerial view

04 Elevated platform above the canopies

VIEW FROM ABOVE

Taking its spatial and experiential cues from the environs of the seaside precedent, Coney Inland aspires to reproduce visceral effects beyond mere form and geometry. Multiple elevated platforms and sun decks (**04**) allow one to rise above the canopy and survey the courtyard and all of its colorful activity below—a place of suspension between sky and sea.

05 Cylindrical vault in the side courtyard

ON THE BOARDWALK

The more serene environment of PS1 Coney Inland during the daytime hours is characterized by quiet and repose. Shallow pools, sand pits, and play courts provide leisurely activities reminiscent of various seaside pastimes and boardwalk life.

06 The dense crowd at MoMA PS1 Warm-Up! series

IN THE CURL

During the weekend MoMA PS1 Warm Up! series, seas of people will flow unimpeded through the courtyard and into the concert space. Colorful cabana sleds house concession services and choreograph movement around the courtyard, while the illuminated gridshell canopies serve as a lively backdrop for the weekly summer gatherings.

07 MoMA PS1 Warm-Up! poster mock-up

GRAPHIC IDENTITY

Concepts for graphic design and merchandising were developed according to the Coney Inland theme. Logo design showing PS1 Warm-Up! gathering with scalar hybridization of conical gridshell geometries served to inspire the menu of snow cones for summer refreshment.

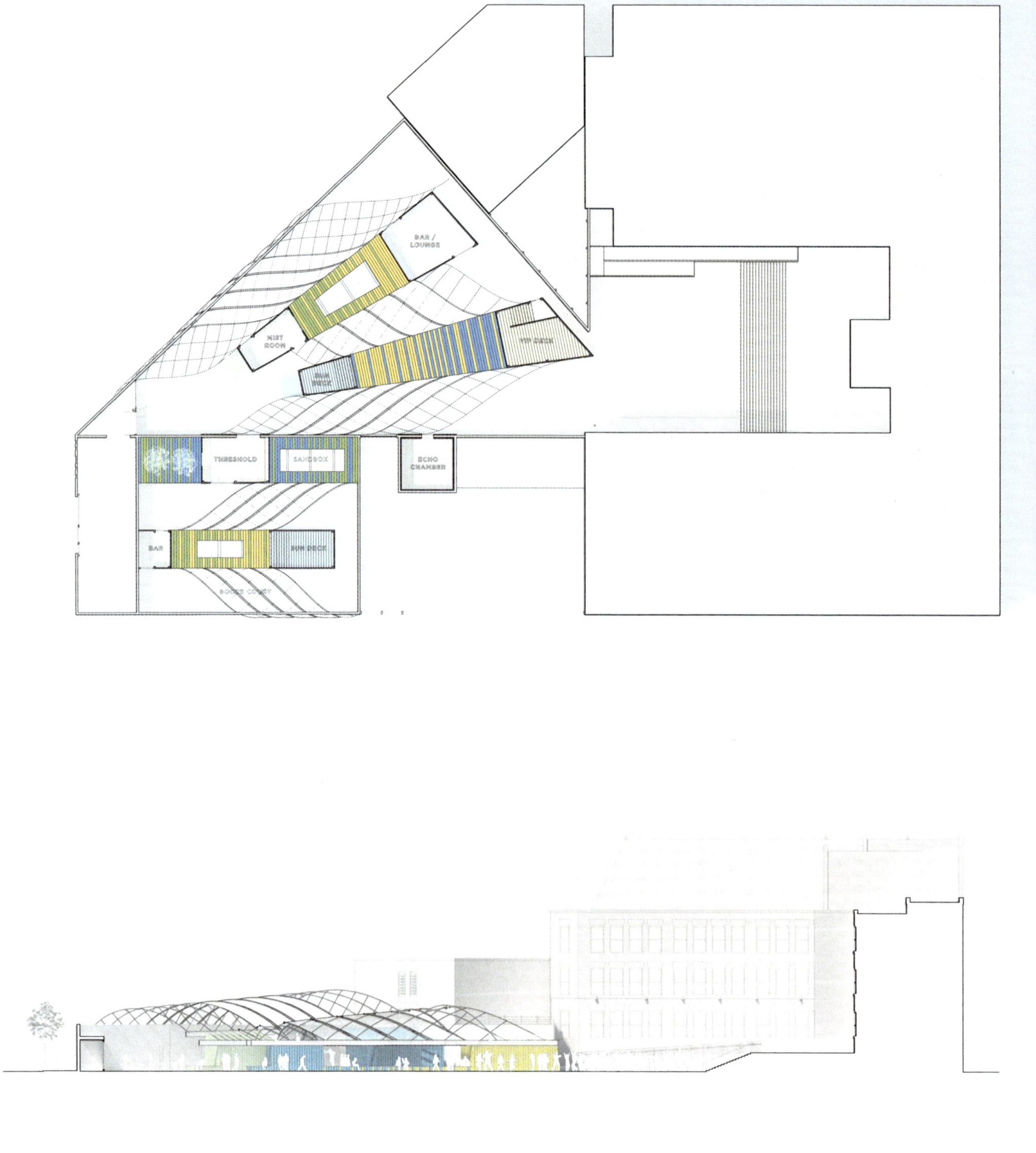

08 Plan and section

09 Detail view of canopy tectonic elements

TAPERED SITE RESPONSE

Coney Inland is an architectural strategy which formally unifies the challenging MoMA PS1 courtyard site. A series of developable surfaces (cones and cylinders) and their base structures normalize the contingencies of scale and shape of the three courtyard spaces, while their legible transformations register the idiosyncratic nature of the overall site geometry.

10 Nighttime aerial view

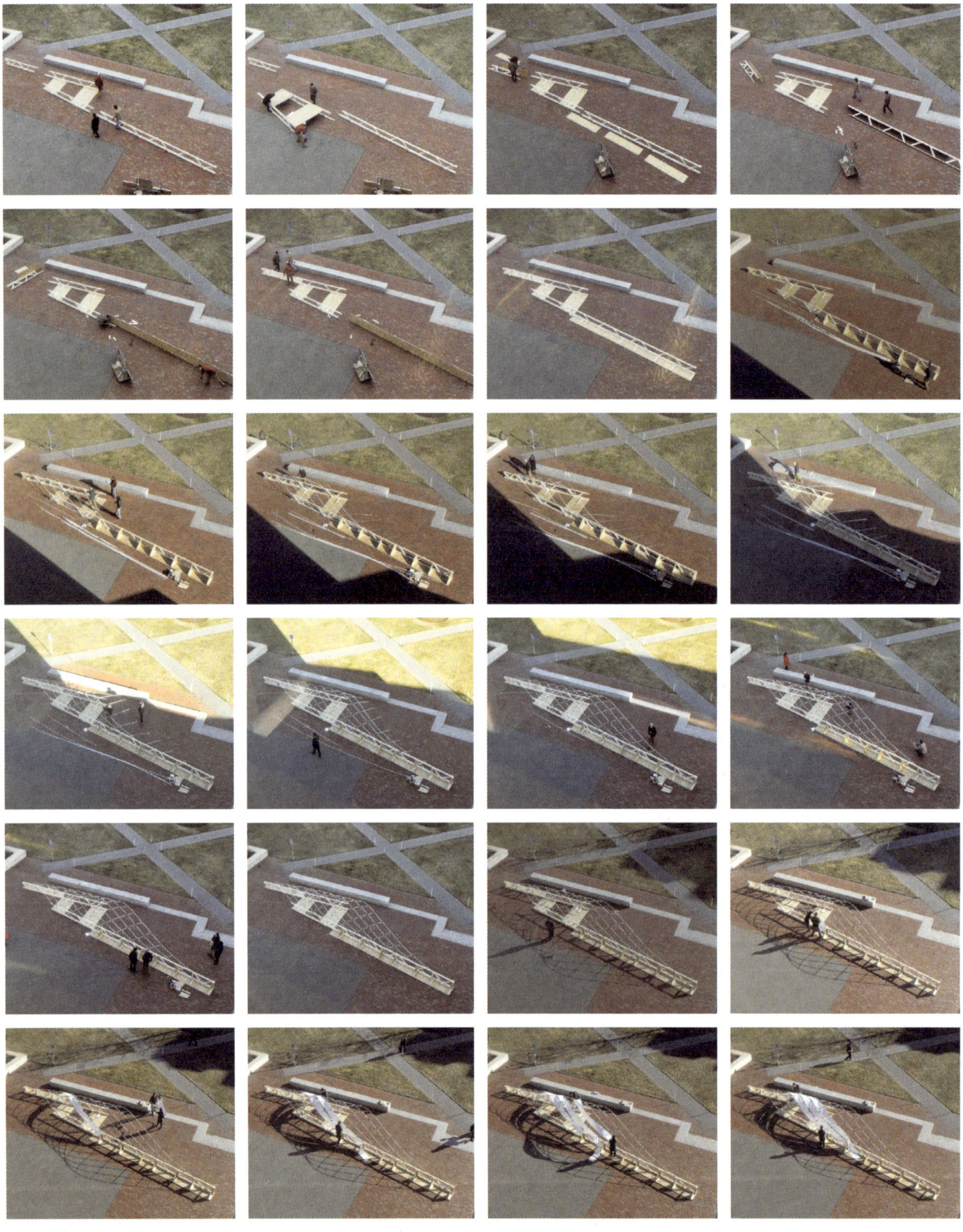

11 Mock-up construction sequence

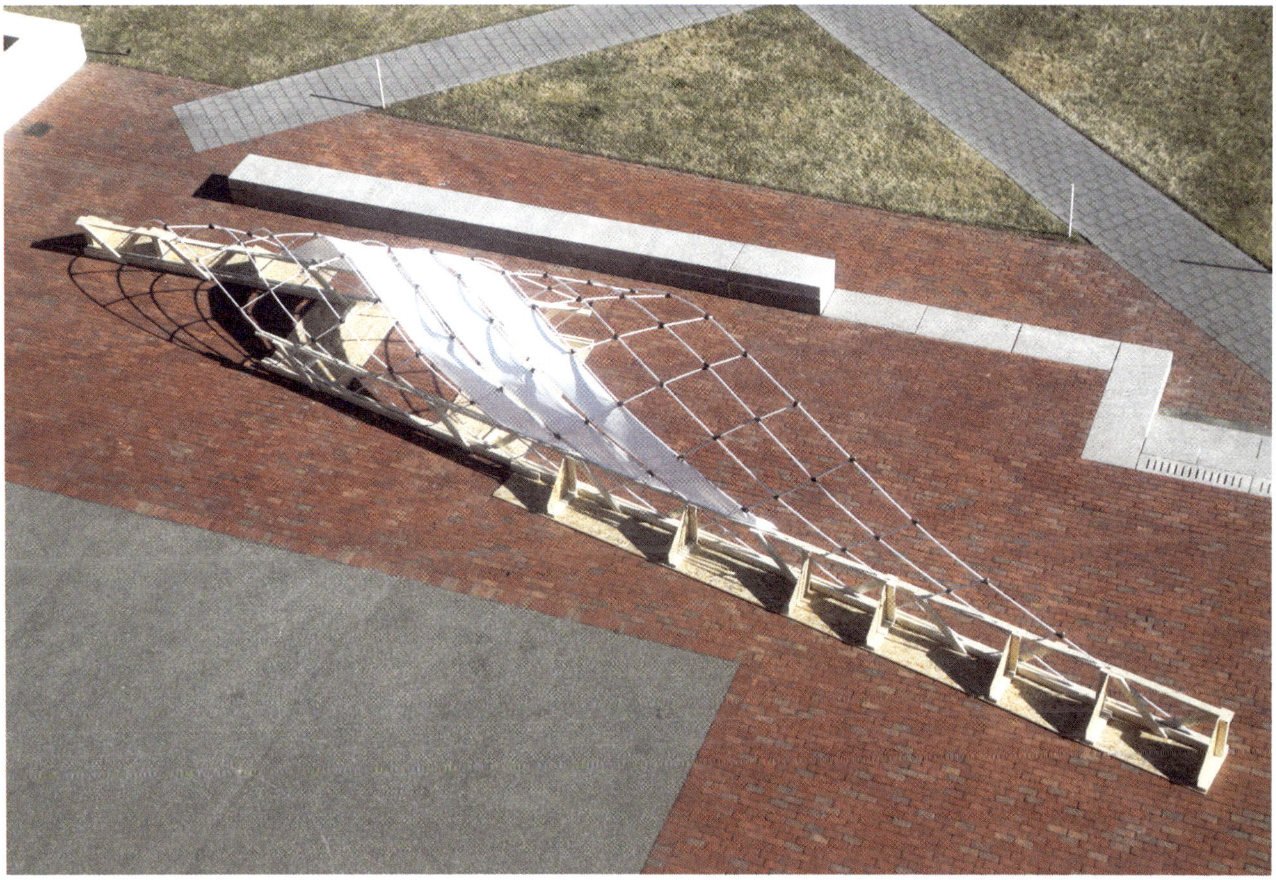

12 1:2 scale prototype

1:2 SCALE PROTOTYPE

A half-scale mock-up was constructed as a proof of concept for the conical gridshells. Lengths of 1" PVC were joined for the longest spanning members. Plumb base wall assemblies were prefabricated and intersection nodes pre-determined for expedient assembly.

13 Model

MODEL

1/8″ = 1′-0″ physical model shows overhead views of the idiosyncratic MoMA PS1 courtyard. Both gridshell members and shade cladding were constructed from paper, a benefit of the developable surface geometry.

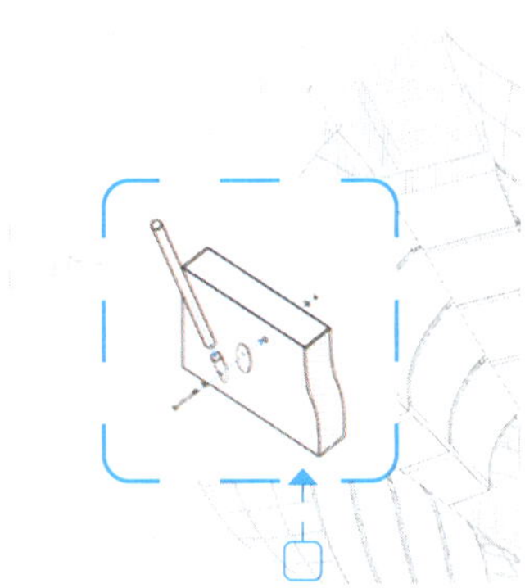

14.1 Connection detail of gridshell members to exterior courtyard wall

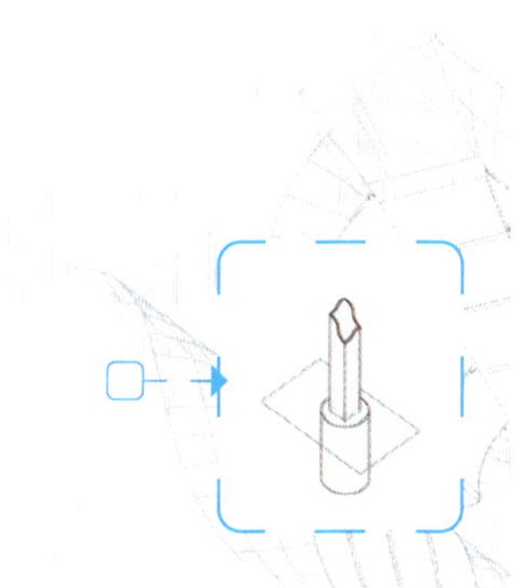

14.2 Post foundation detail

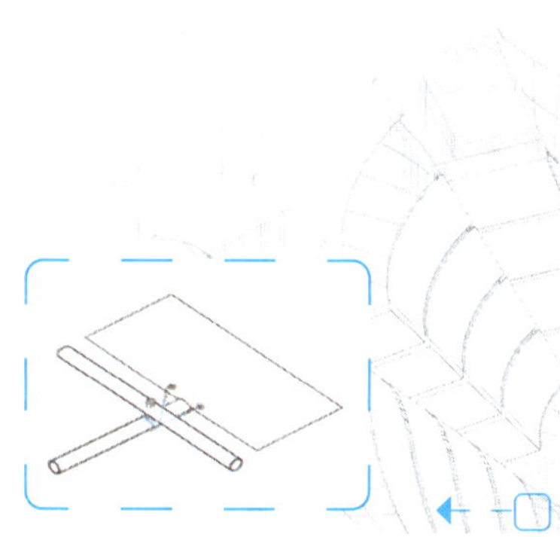

14.3 Lashing and grommet detail for Tyvek cladding

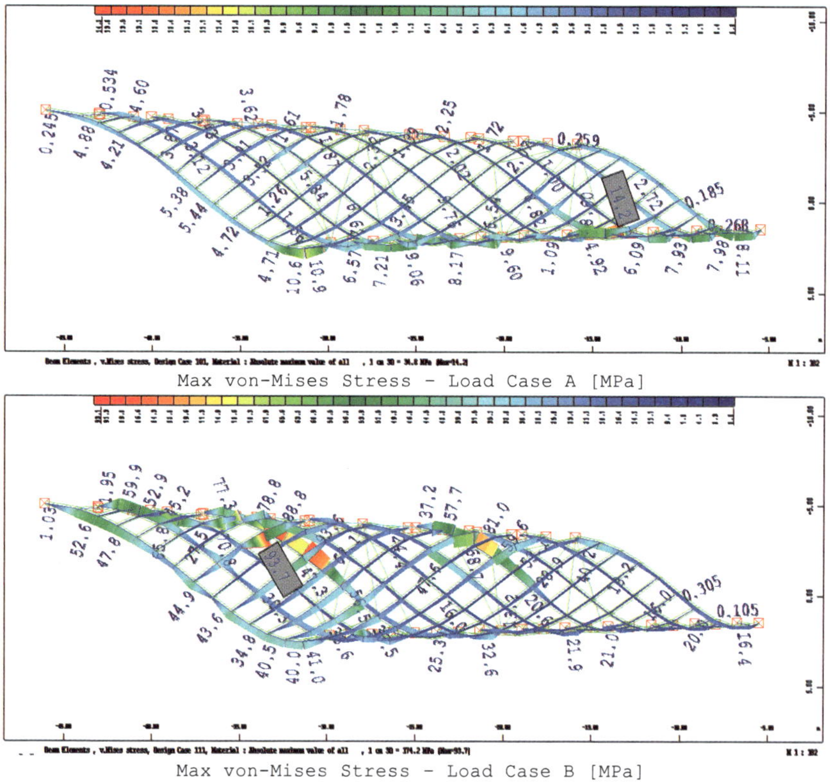

15 Stress diagrams

STRUCTURAL ANALYSIS

Preliminary analyses (**15**) provided an overall understanding of the structural behavior of the canopies. Various concepts were simulated to improve the performance of the tubular elements, including cable truss system, membrane elements, and multiple layers of tubular elements.

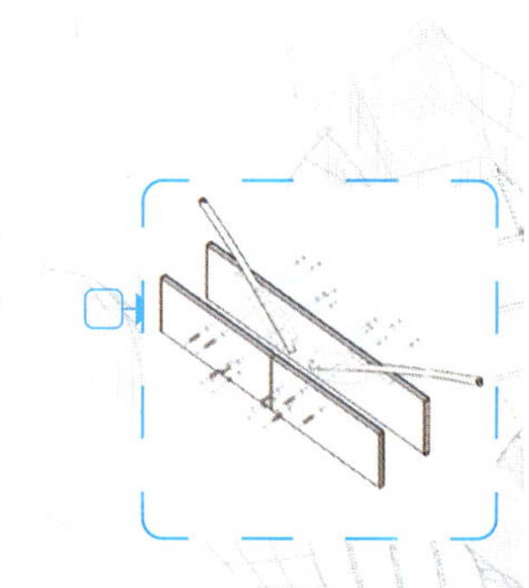

14.4 Carriage bolt assembly for gridshell-to-LVL beam connection

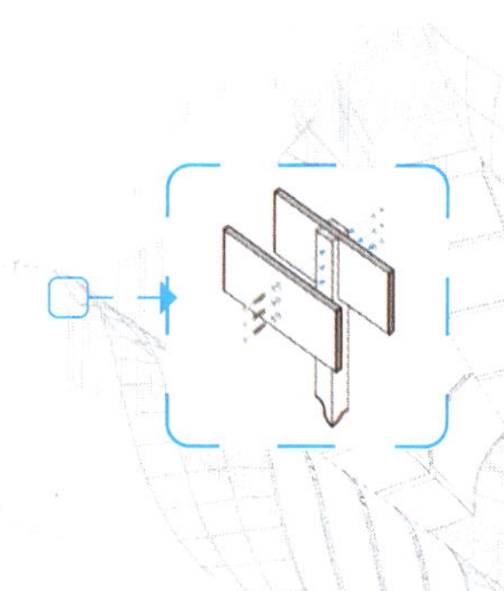

14.5 Post-to-LVL beam connection

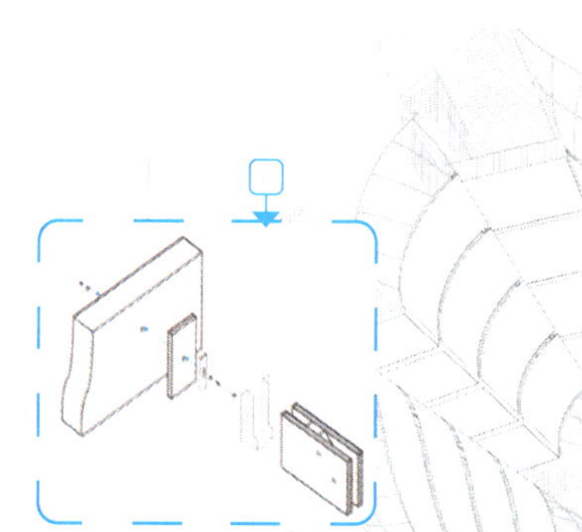

14.6 LVL beam connection to interior courtyard wall

Chrysalis

Ragdale ring proposal
2016

Chrysalis deploys flat-to-form geometric techniques of developable surfaces to produce a figural, cocoon-like stage. The linear expression of the central angular truss and oblique support members serves as the formal opposition to the continuous, hand-crafted nature of the curvilinear skin. The developable properties of the geodesic planks comprising the bending surface allow the use of conventional shiplap siding. As a striking aesthetic icon located amid the bucolic backdrop of the campus, Chrysalis provides a sheltered venue for speakers, artists, and equipment for live performances and serves as a focal point of the outdoor gathering space for artists-in-residence and visitors.

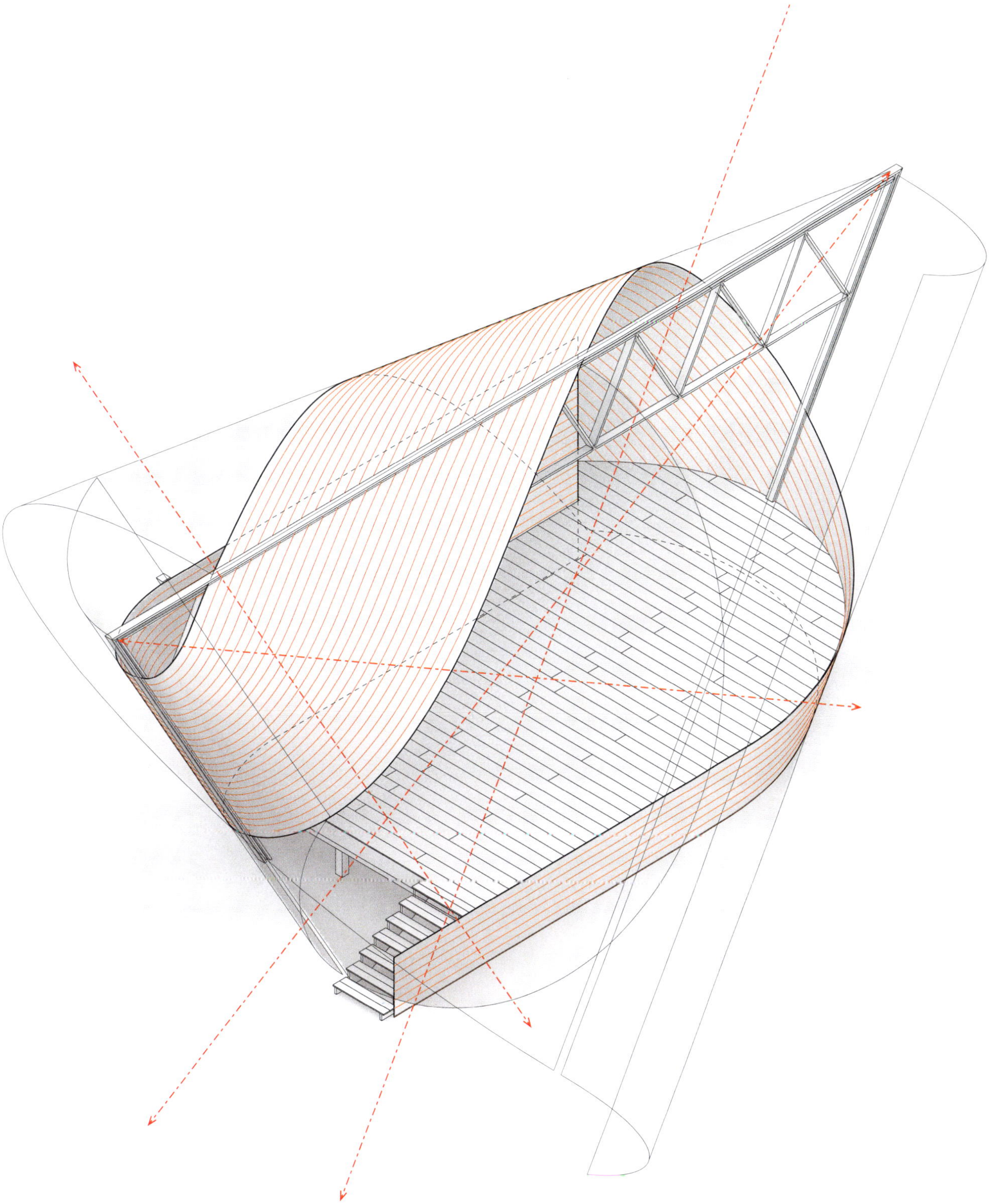

01 Geometric construction using cones, cylinders, and planes

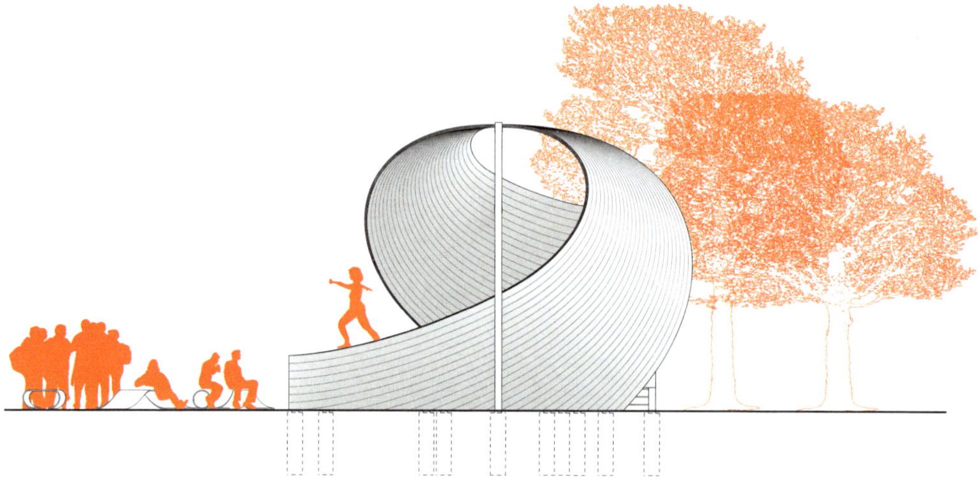

02 Right elevation

03 Front elevation

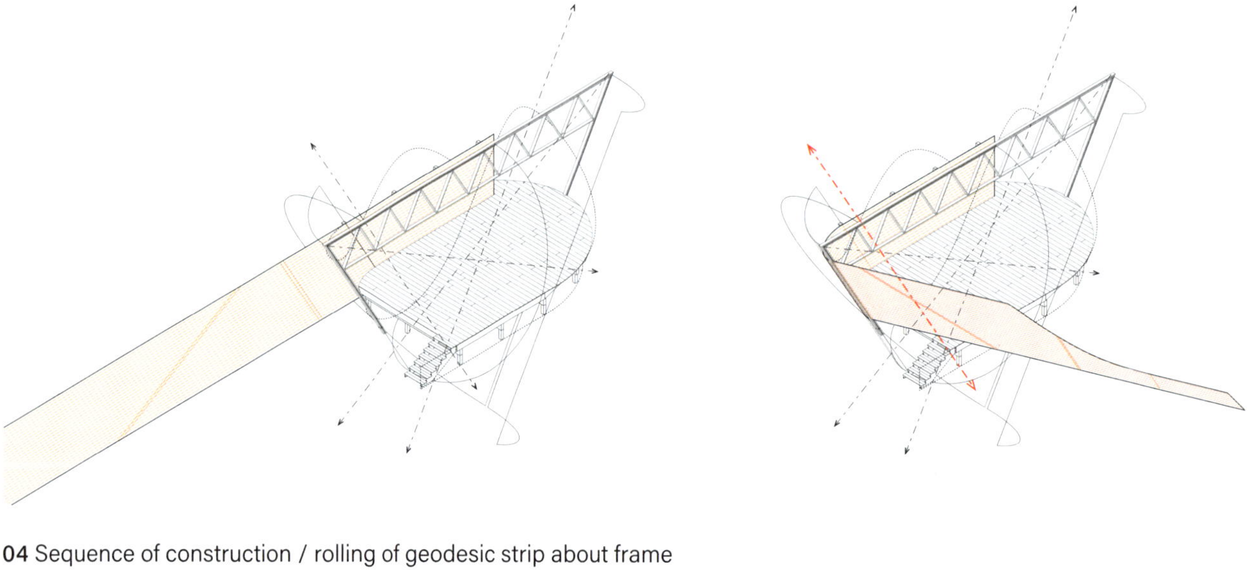

04 Sequence of construction / rolling of geodesic strip about frame

05 Aerial view

DISCRETE PARTS

The composition uses cones, cylinders, and planes trimmed along straight ruling lines and placed tangently to each other to define a compound "host" surface (**04**). Geodesic lines drawn on this compound surface subdivide it into geodesic planks which become straight and parallel when unrolled to a plane. A raised platform (with front and back-stage stairs) benefits from the cover provided by the curving surface overhead. Various smaller-scale incarnations of geodesic planking serve as playful seating for audiences (**05**).

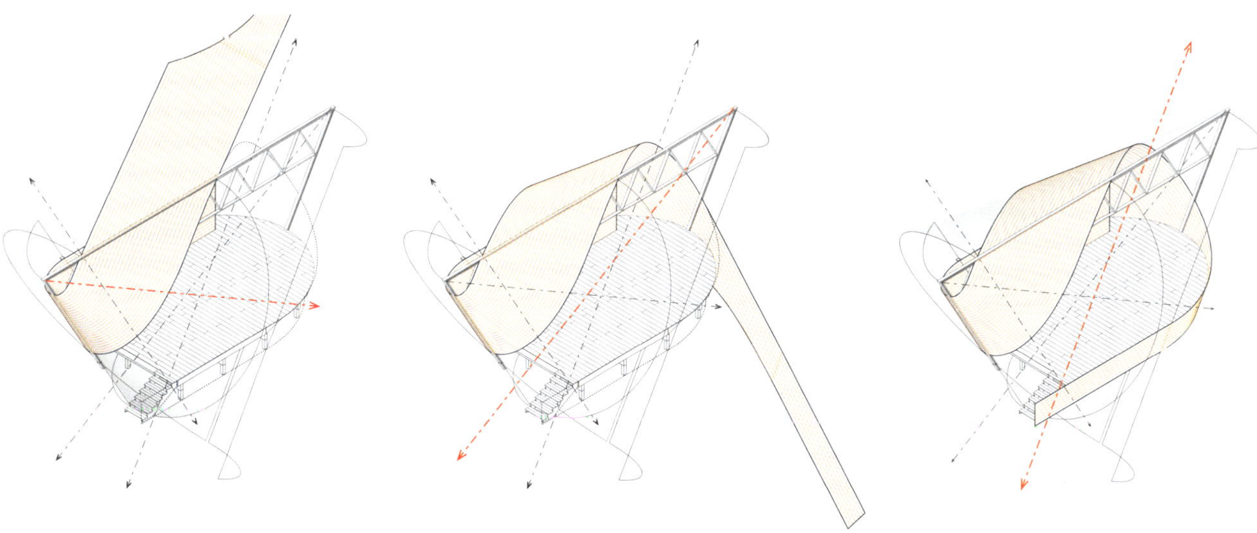

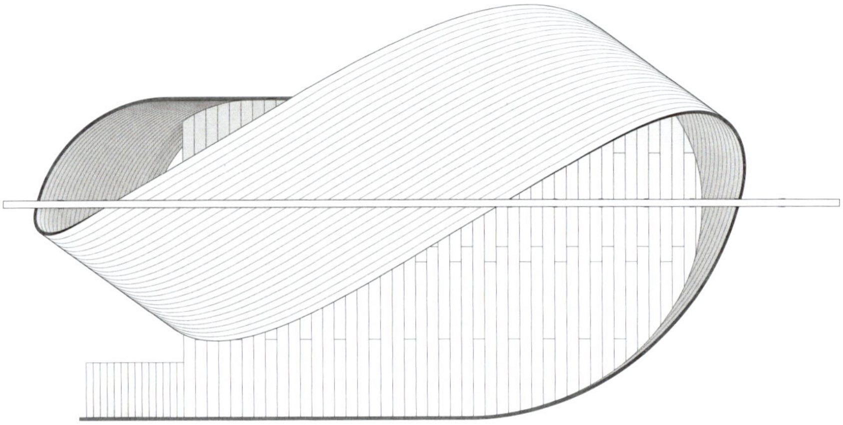

06 Roof plan

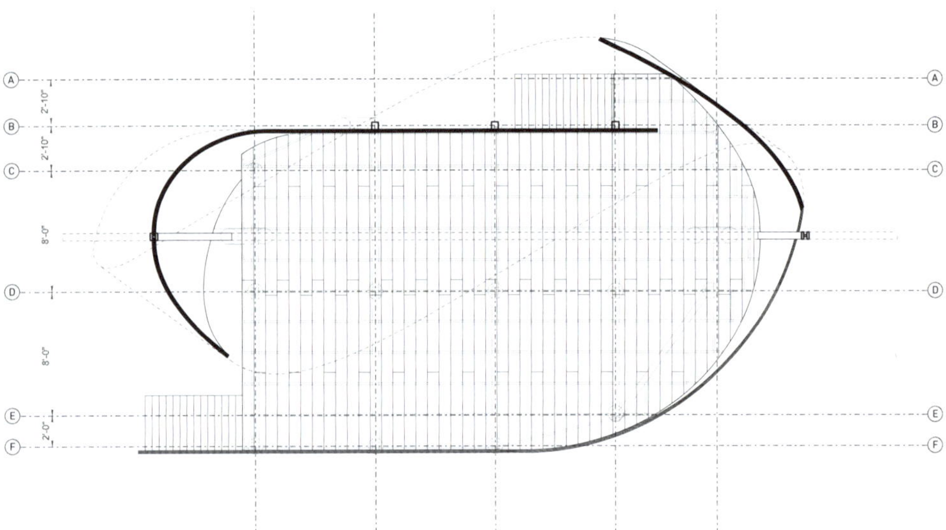

07 Stage plan

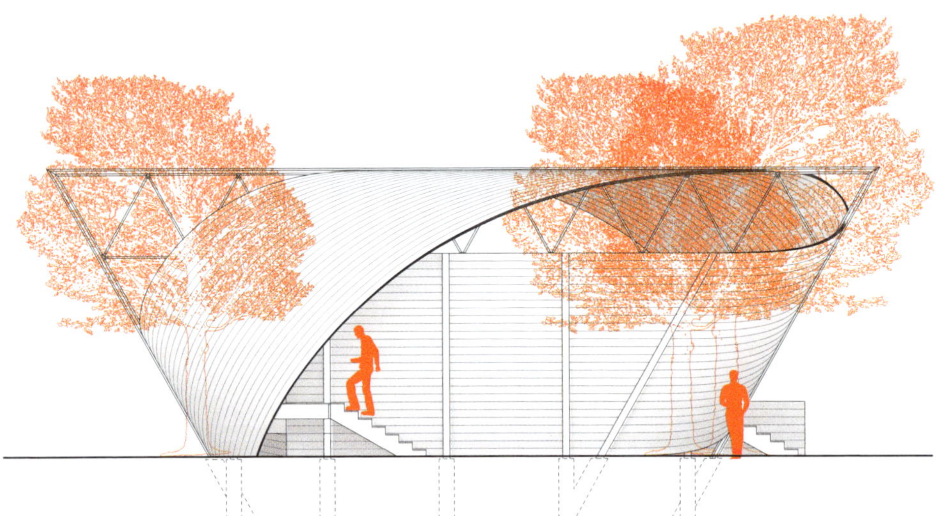

08 Back elevation

09 Perspective view of stage and seating

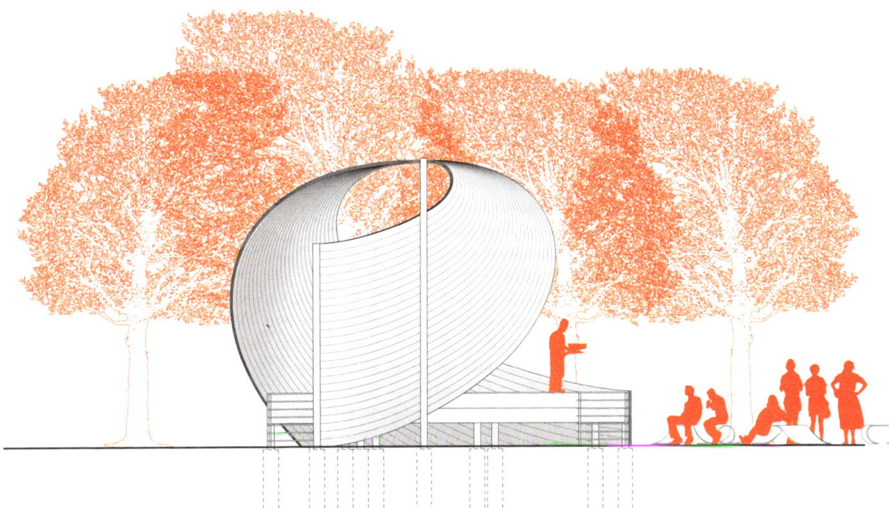

10 Left elevation

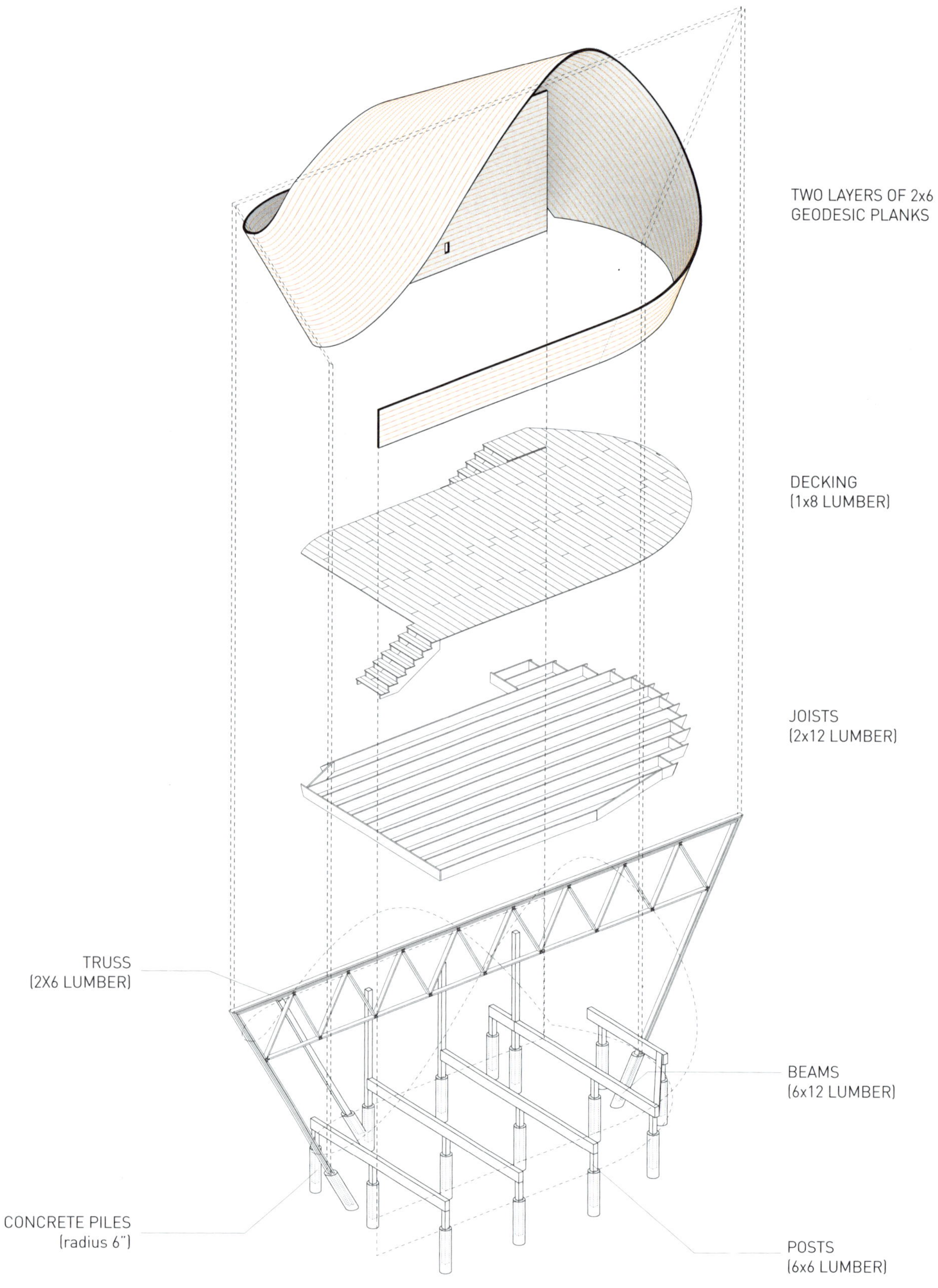

11 Exploded axonometric / structural make-up

ISOMETRY

The isometry between the two-dimensional unrolled state and the three-dimensional form of developable surfaces does not distort linear dimensions of the material. The geodesic plank subdivisions can thus be fabricated from conventional lumber, metal, plastic, or other flat stock to produce various families of smooth and piecewise continuous form. The linear members of the truss structure are coincident with the ruling line seams between the cones, cylinders, and planes for ease of attachment at the structural support (**14**).

12 Study model

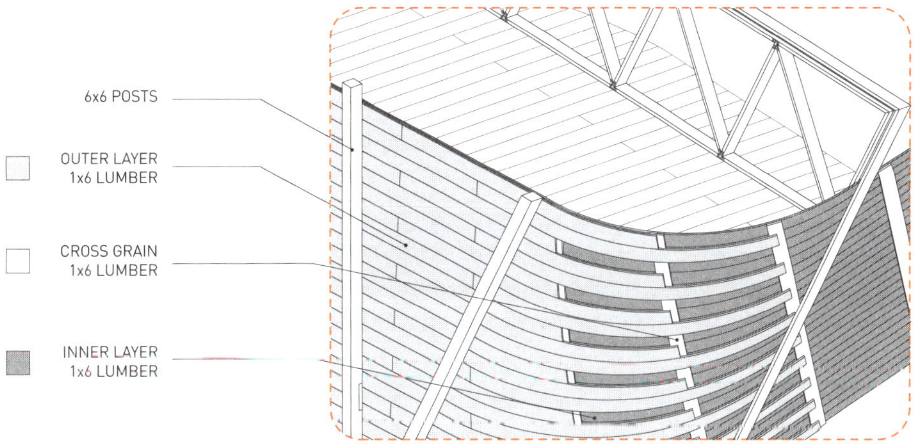

13 Construction detail of planking layers

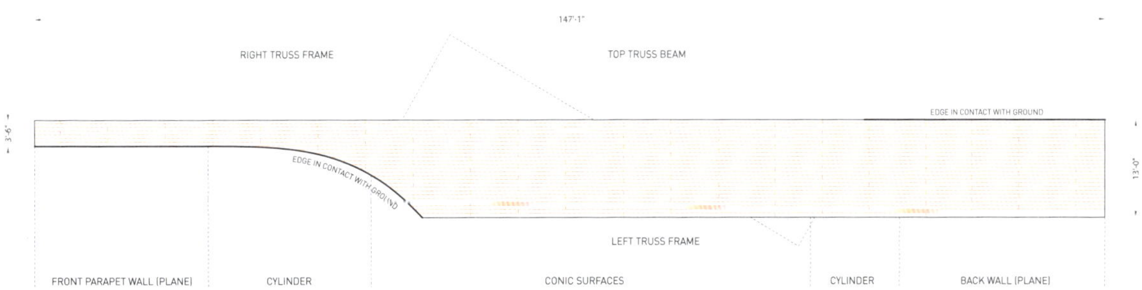

14 Developed geodesic plank surface

Atlanta History Center Competition

2011

The Atlanta History Center (AHC) is one of the largest museums of its kind, requiring a spatial strategy to address its heterogeneous curatorial requirements. The museum's fragmented organization of galleries, event spaces, and circulatory corridors betrays an institution that has expanded in a provisional manner over time, responding to various disparate initiatives. A dearth of immediate connections between galleries, event spaces, and educational facilities frustrates efforts to promote the institution's scholastic and curatorial work during social events.

The AHC would benefit from a well-defined circulation zone that better utilizes the two existing axes, allowing increased access to flexible gallery spaces and multiple connections between them. Such a zone will ensure direct visual access to the galleries from all peripheral spaces, creating a mixing chamber at the heart of the museum, and enabling multiple curatorial narratives to be organized and cross-referenced. This scheme deploys a two-way matrix of intersecting conical vaults to produce a flexible and open circulation network that negotiates multiple axes of movement.

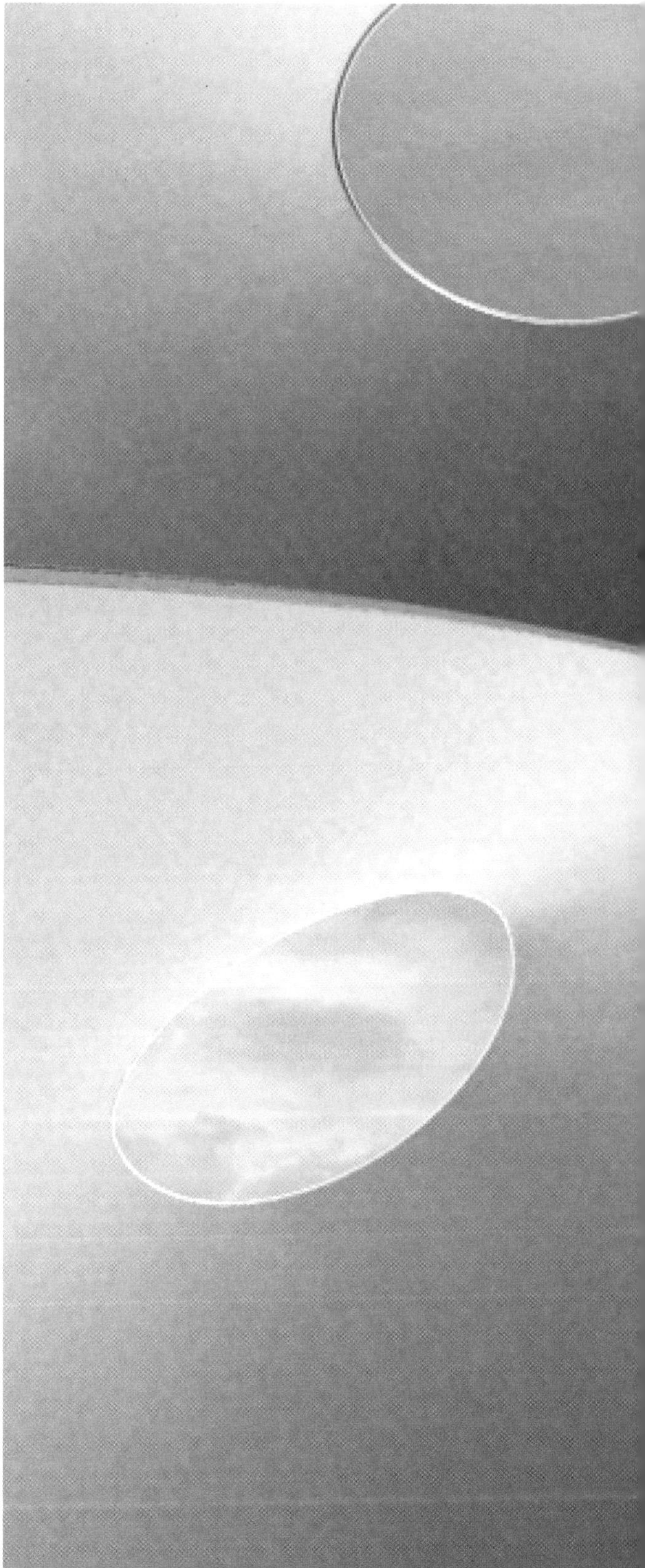

01 Interior view of New Allen Atrium

CONICAL VAULTS

The proposal redefines the organization of the interior through the insertion of a system of conical vaults. Each spatial module of this system comprises two large cones, carefully positioned to mutually intersect one another. The apexes of each cone are truncated to produce oculi covered with glazed skylights. The aggregation and subsequent clipping of these twin-cone modules produces supple curvilinear arches. The rotationally symmetrical deployment of the vaulted circulation zone guides the visitors seamlessly to and from galleries and event spaces while the multiple oculi evenly distribute natural light to the spaces within—even those deep within the interior. By limiting the distribution of the vaults to the newly defined circulation zones, the galleries remain largely neutral and undisrupted.

While cones and their curving intersection lines offer a provocative visual aesthetic, their developable geometric form offers some key fabrication and construction advantages. The formwork required to fabricate the glass-fiber reinforced gypsum (GFRG) panels for the interior vaults would be more expedient and repeatable than any other curvilinear form.

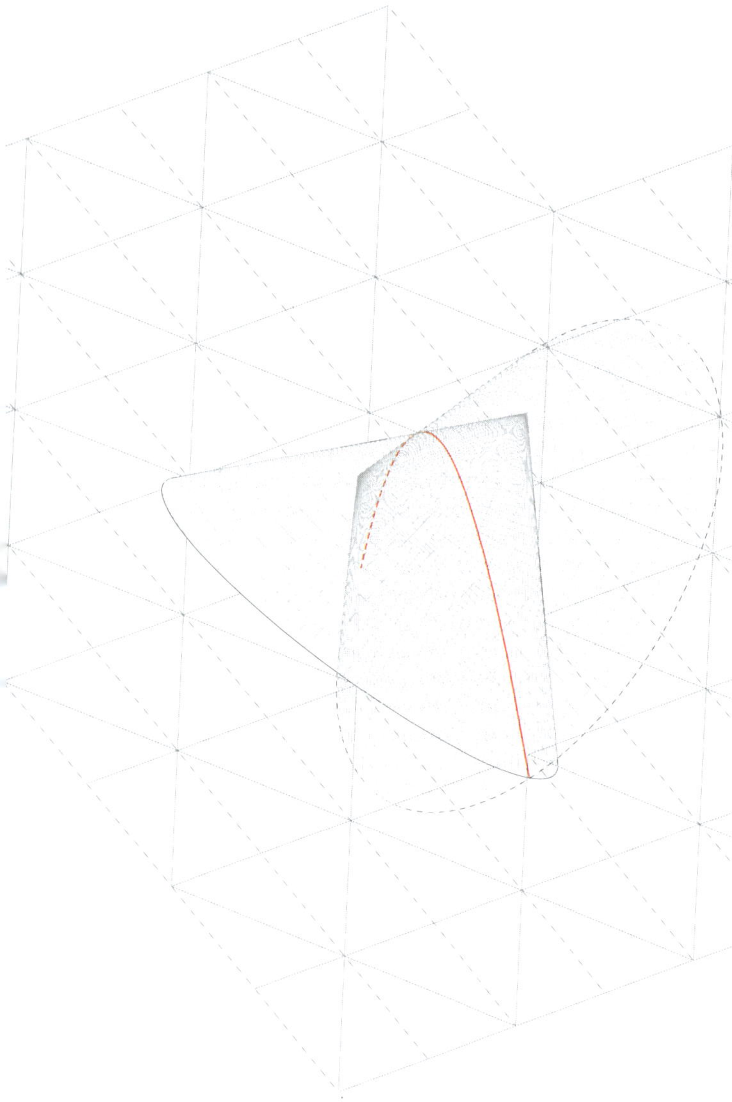

02.1 Module from conic intersection

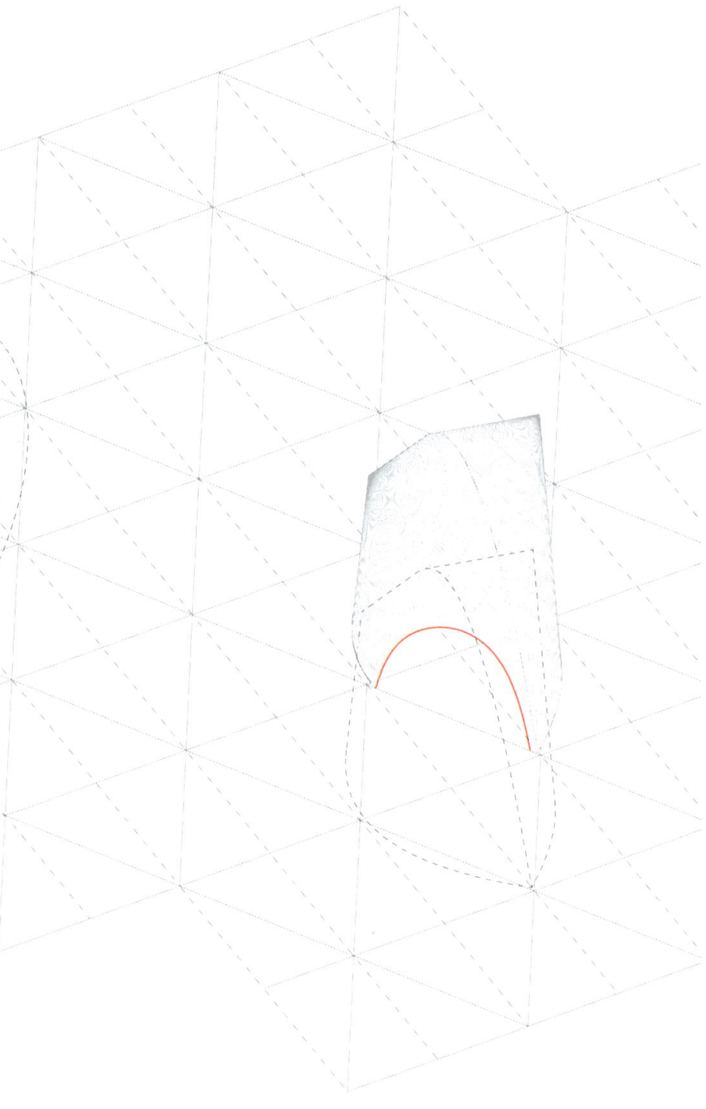

02.2 Arch intersection of two modules

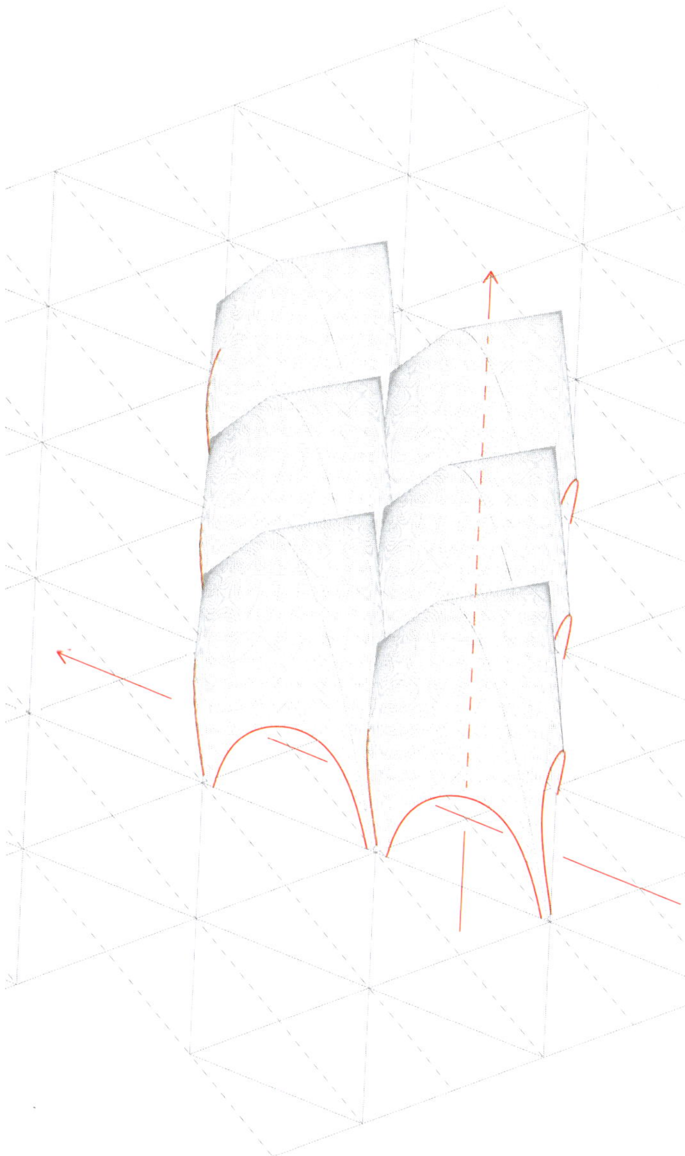

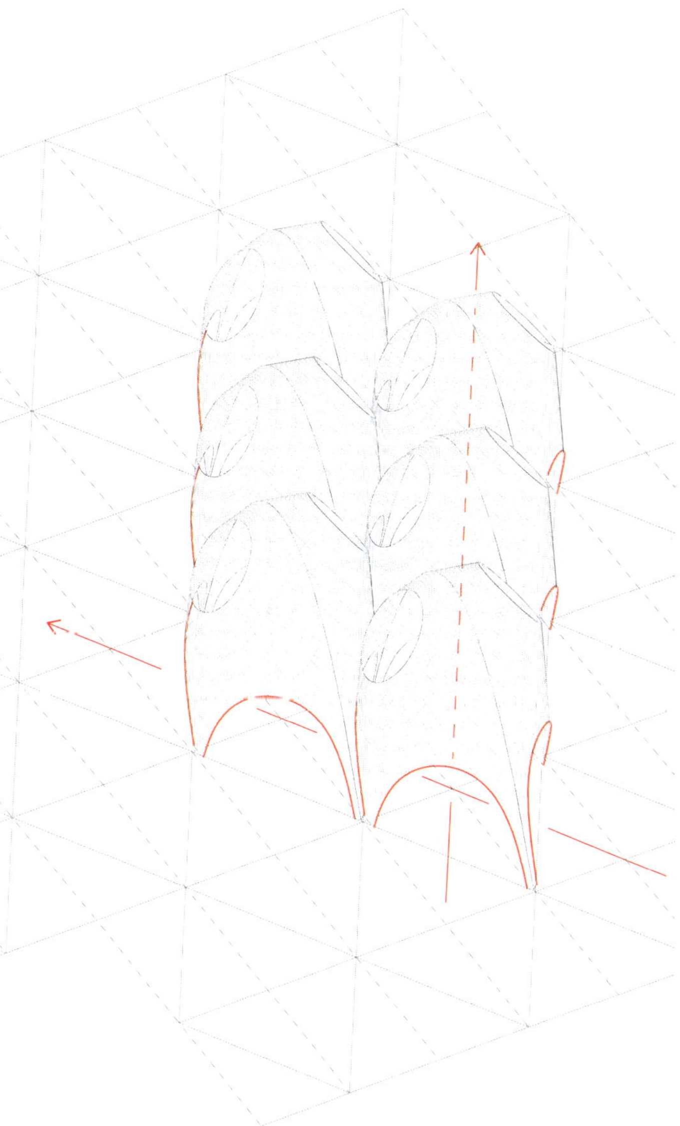

02.3 Aggregation of modules

02.4 Oculi via truncation

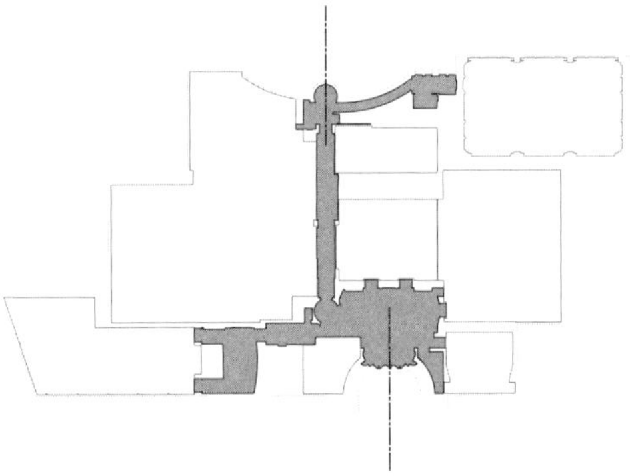

03.1 Existing circulation

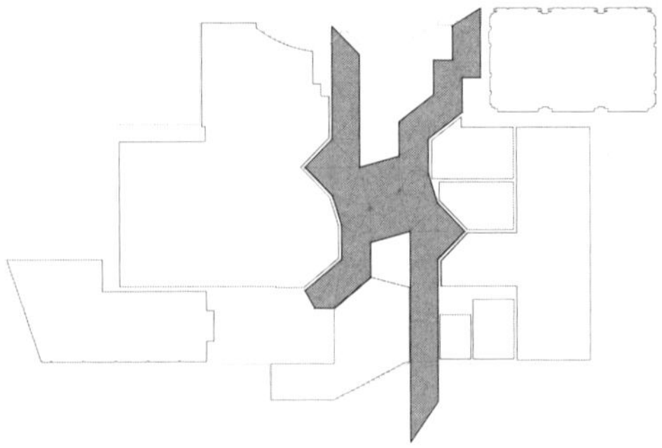

03.2 Proposed circulation

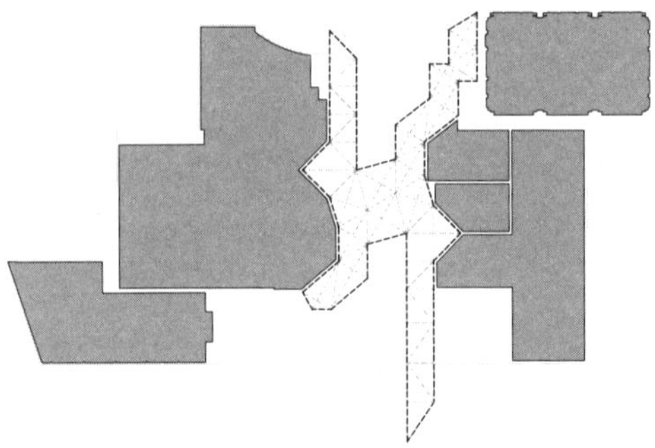

03.3 Proposed galleries

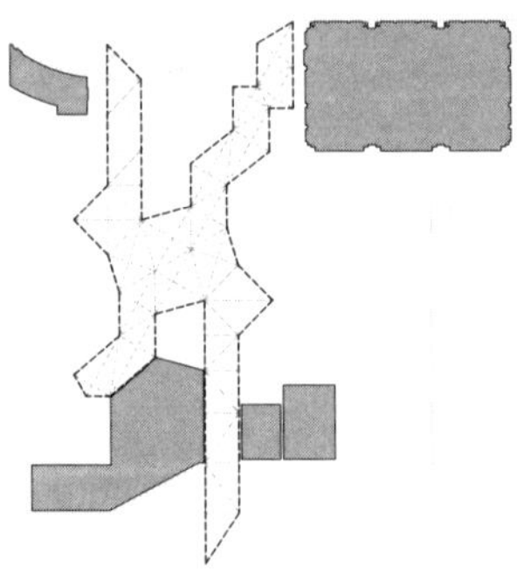

03.4 Proposed event space

NEW CIRCULATION ROUTES

The museum's most notable urban feature is a pair of parallel axes on site (**03.1**), which orient the building to multiple exterior points of reference. The front axis corresponds to the main street entrance, marking the location of the museum from the city, while the rear axis aligns to the Reeder Amphitheater, historic Quarry Garden, and Swan House beyond. The potential for these lines to organize interior space remains largely unexploited because the connection between the two axial corridors is singular and abrupt. Additionally, there is another diagonal axis defined by two major programs within the museum's interior—the Grand Overlook Ballroom and the Olympic Gallery—placing even greater demand on the plan to satisfy additional circulatory needs. A newly defined entry and circulation zone would better utilize the two existing axes (**03.2**), while allowing increased access to flexible gallery spaces and connections between them. The aspect ratios of the proposed twin cone vaulted bays are variable, allowing them to individually adjust and aggregate in plan to accommodate multiple directions of movement.

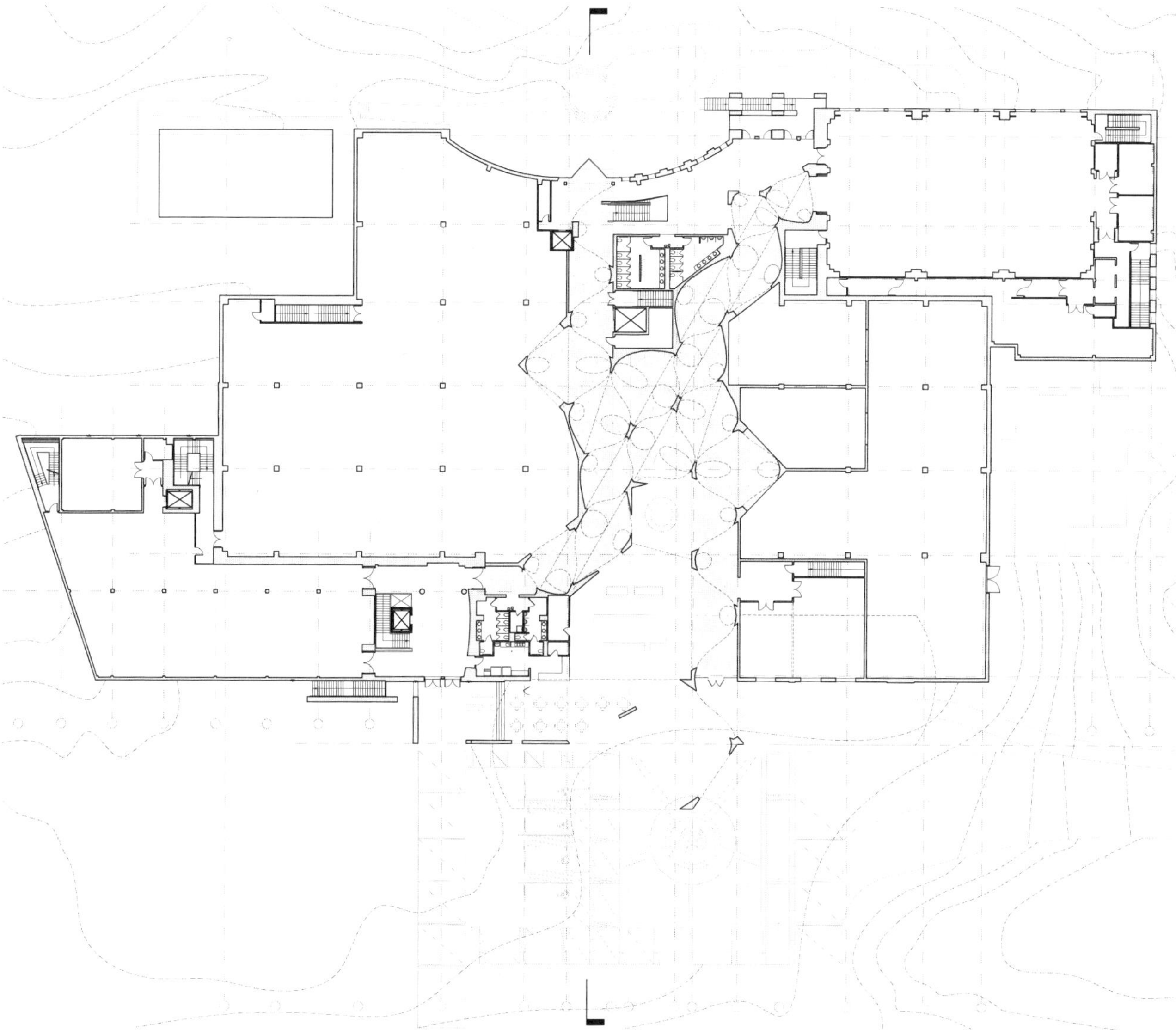

04 First floor plan

05 View of entry from parking

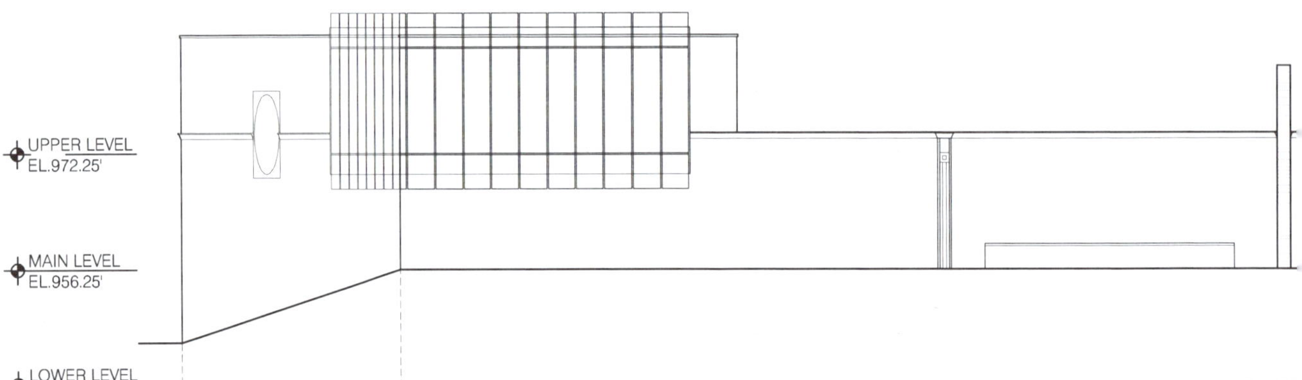

06 Proposed elevation at entrance

07 Exterior view at entrance

UPDATED IDENTITY

Upon arrival at the Center, one is immediately presented with a variation of the vaulting system which leaves the front pair of cones untrimmed. These larger exterior conic surfaces achieve a grander institutional scale, redefining the image of the museum from the street. One serves as a canopy for vehicular drop-off while the other guides pedestrians walking across the new façade from the nearby parking garage (**05**). An enhanced open-plan retail space and a new café occupy prominent positions at the front of the museum, both of which can be accessed by non-ticketed visitors (**09**).

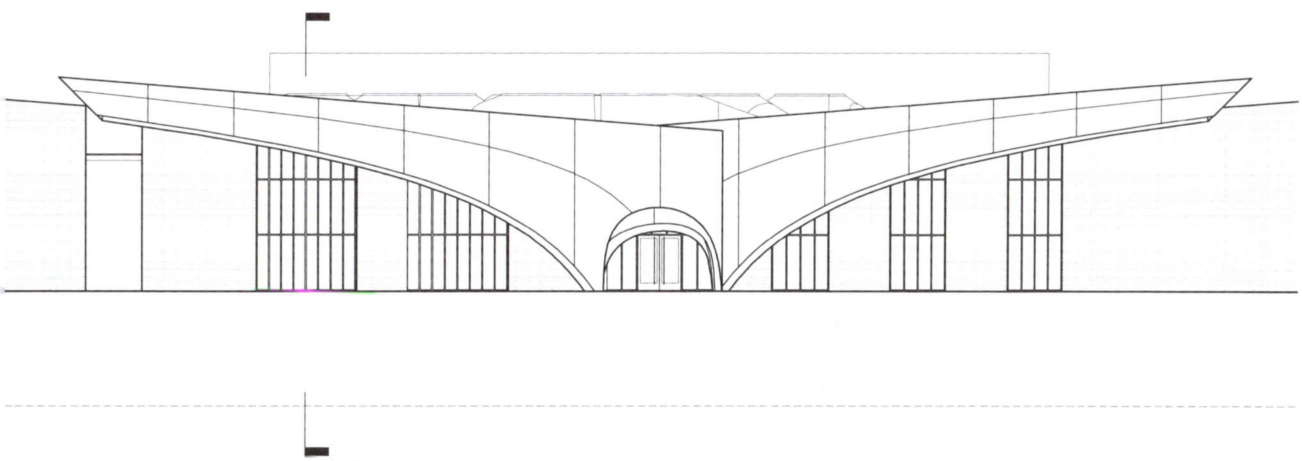

08 Interior view at New Allen Atrium

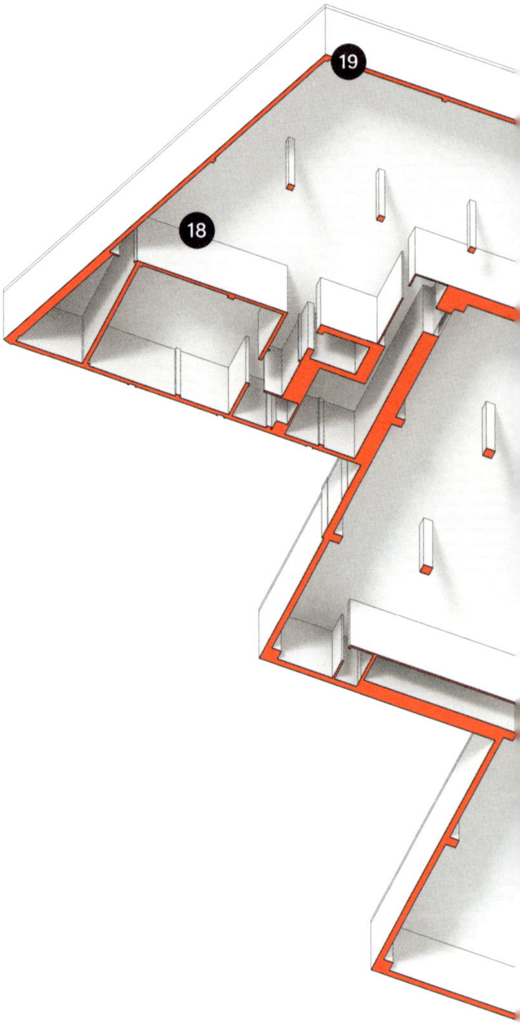

FLEXIBLE WAYFINDING

The vaulted concourse leads down the entry axis to the information and ticket desk, which precedes the New Allen Atrium—the spatial and circulatory hub of the new museum. The soaring ceiling of the atrium (**01**) covers a commodious pre-function space (**08**) directly connected to the Grand Overlook Ballroom. Galleries are accessed via apse-like foyers which flank the atrium, serving as a spatial buffer between those entering and exiting exhibitions from the main circulation flow. The New Allen Atrium deftly absorbs the diagonal axis connecting the Olympic Gallery and the Overlook Ballroom with its expanded South Foyer. Classrooms have been moved to the front of the museum gallery level, allowing increased accessibility and expanded storage capacity below.

1. Forecourt
2. Lobby
3. Cafe
4. Bookstore
5. Covered Drop-Off
6. Entry
7. Classrooms
8. Information / Ticketing
9. New Allen Atrium
10. Atlanta's Story
11. Metropolitan Frontiers
12. Rotating Gallery
13. Rotating Gallery 1
14. Ballroom
15. South Foyer
16. New Overlook
17. Dubose, Goizueta, and Bobby Jones Gallery
18. Mechanical
19. Olympic Gallery

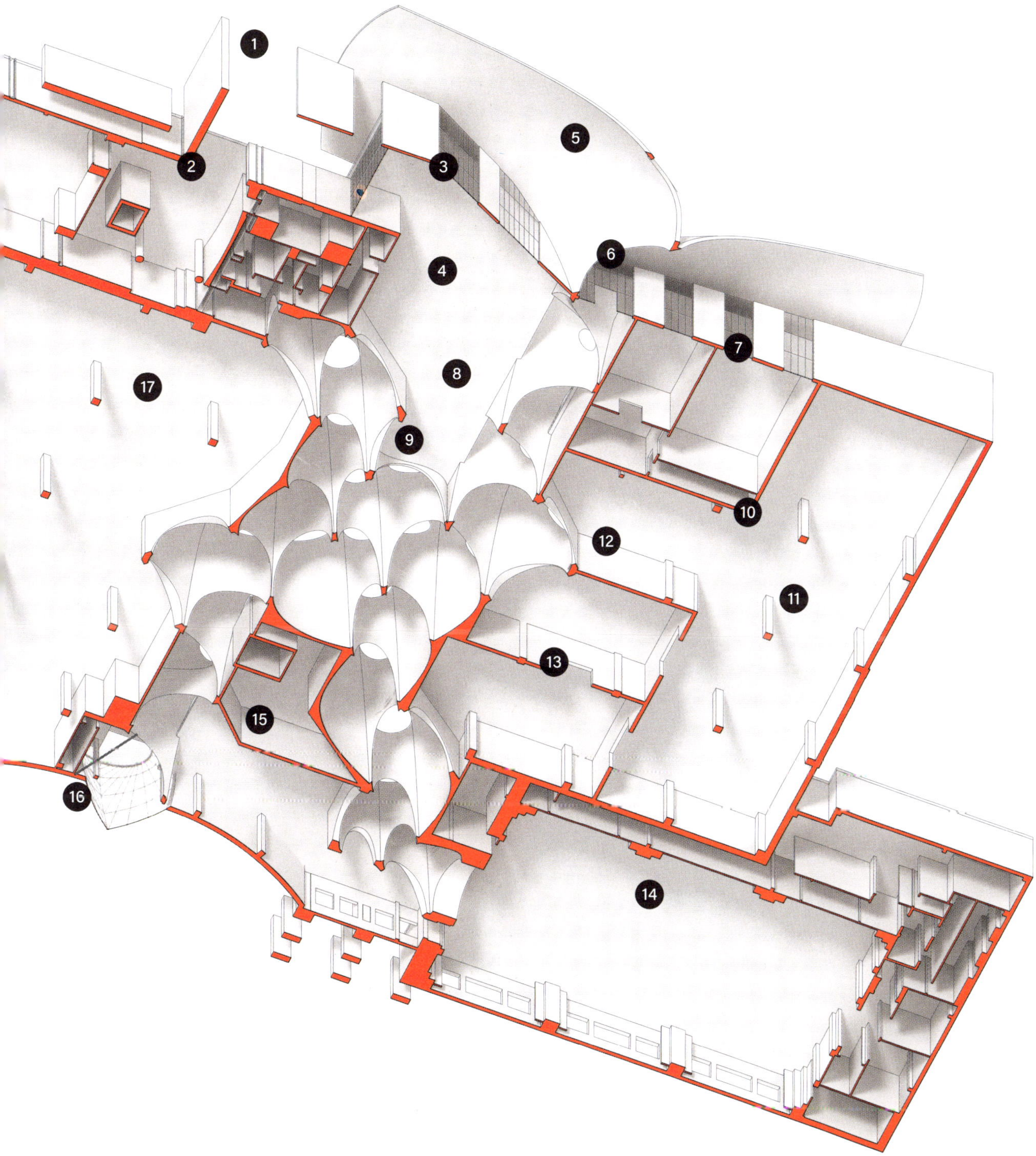

09 Worms eye view of museum organization from below

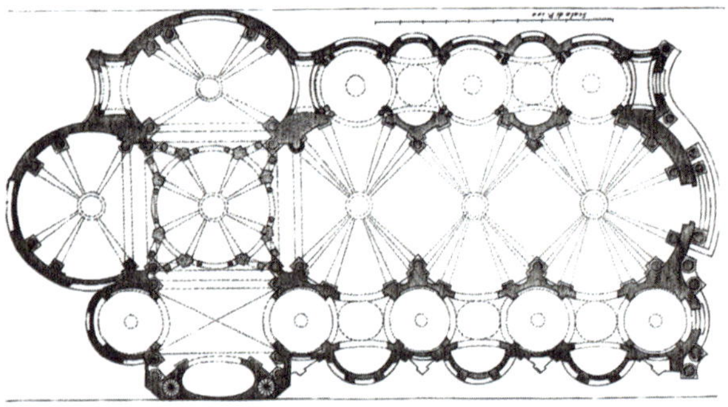

01 Guarino Guarini (1624-1683) *"Unnamed Church" from Architettura Civile (1737)*

Notre Dame de l'Assomption Cathedral Competition

Port Au Prince, Haiti
2012

The cathedral persisted as a stable architectural type for centuries, able to withstand the cultural and technological frictions between evolving historical styles and canonical forms of organization. The cruciform plan, vertically attenuated nave, flanking side aisles, rose windows, and choir terminus have largely endured, irrespective of the cultural and stylistic trends of their time and geography. However, contemporary tendencies to exhibit strict allegiances to specific historical styles often lead to poor reproductions of architectural idioms ill-suited for their day. This scheme for the new Notre Dame rejects such historicist inclinations, opting instead to express contemporaneity with novel geometries within the established formal organization of the cathedral type.

02 Interior view of reconstructed nave

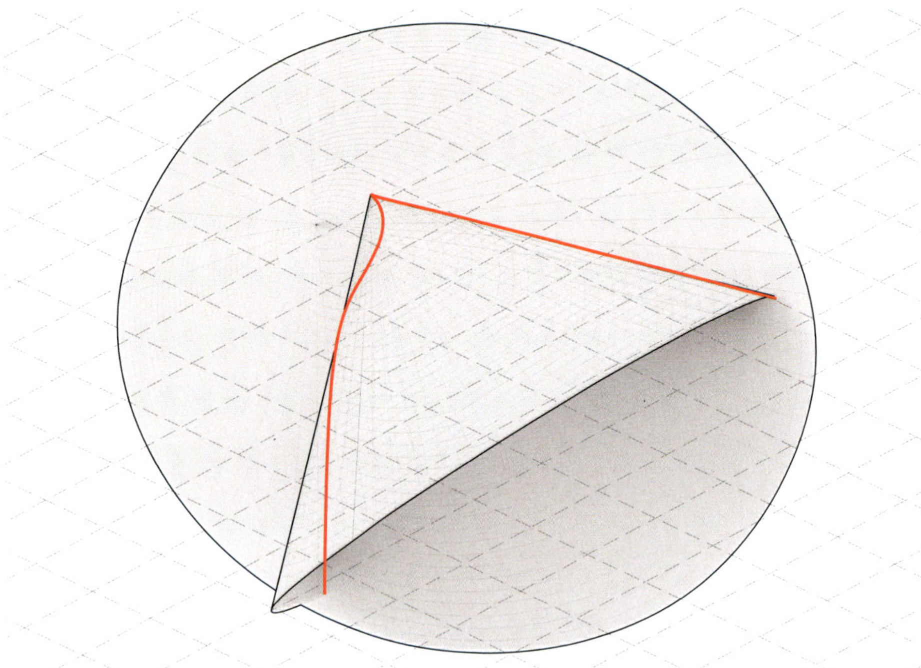

03.1 Two right cones intersected

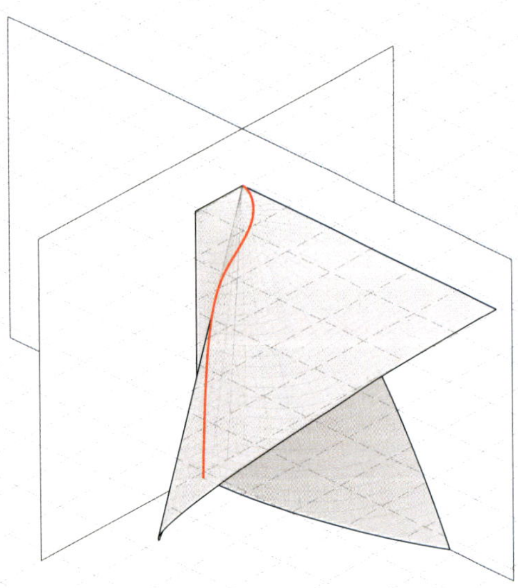

03.2 Cones trimmed with intersection line and perpendicular planes along ruling line generators

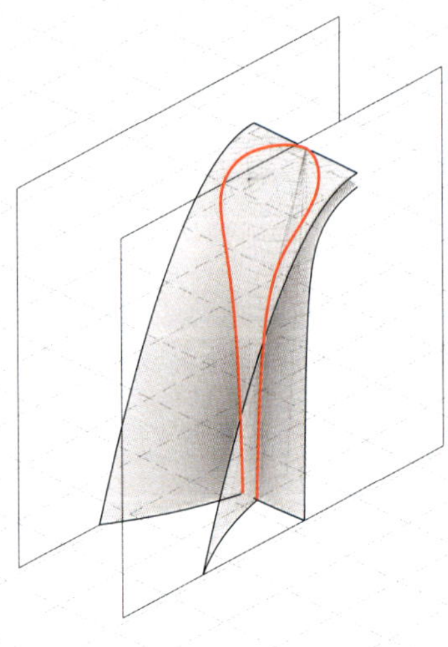

03.3 Partial cones mirrored and trimmed with parallel planes according to existing bay dimensions

CONE GRAMMAR

The periodic vaulted bays are composed of concrete shells of intersecting conical surfaces. Right circular cones are arranged in perpendicular relationships, mutually clipping each other and resulting in surfaces whose intersections form expressive curves that terminate in oculus windows lining the nave and transept (**03.1-03.4**). This particular arrangement of conic surfaces allows for differentiation in the plan, while maintaining "well-behaved" lines of intersection which govern the boundaries of each bay (**03.5**). The regular and repetitive developable geometry is ideal for casting limited sets of identical modules on site to be installed via tilt-up construction sequence.

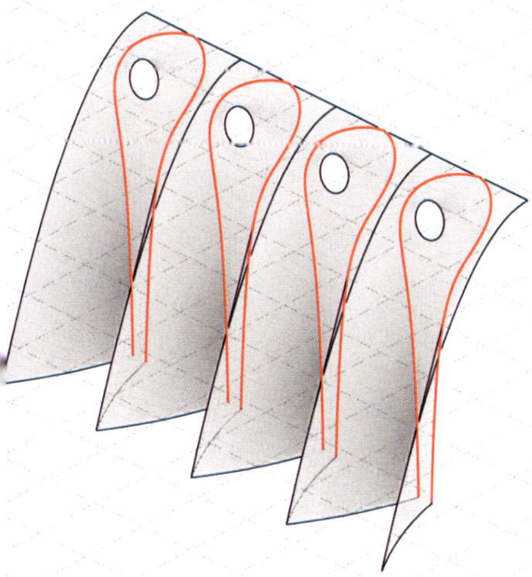

03.4 Serial aggregation of two-cone bay units with oculus truncation

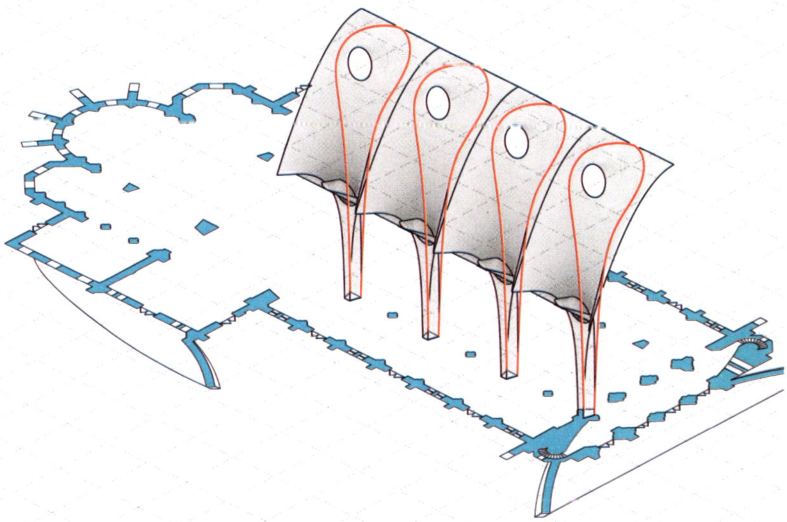

03.5 Addition of secondary aisle geometry and superimposition on plan

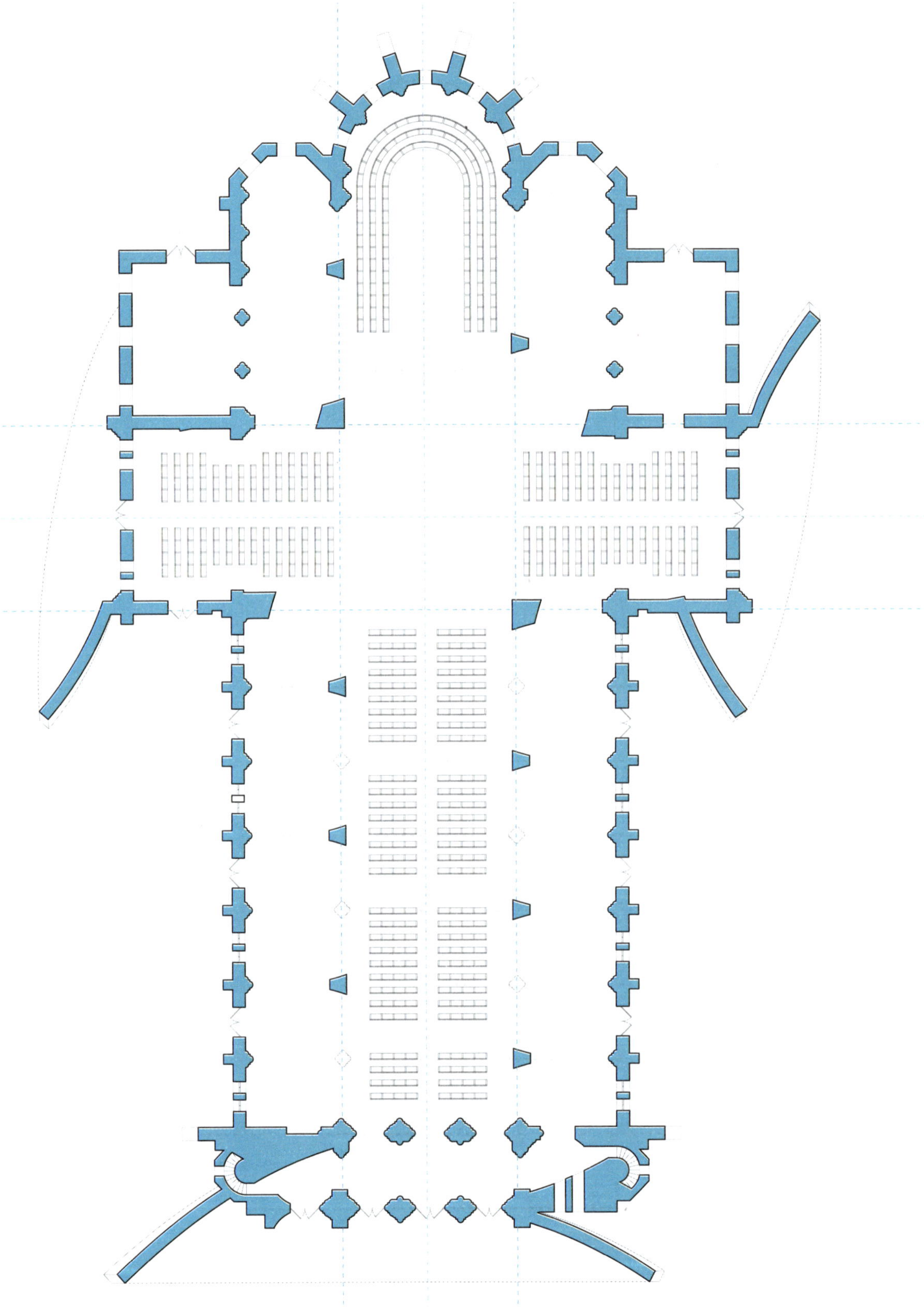

04 Floor plan

BALANCED ASYMMETRY

Inspired by Guarino Guarini's asymmetrical "Unnamed Church" (**01**) the proposal is a study of the negotiation between bilateral and serial/rotational systems. Allegiance is dutifully paid to the original column grid, yet the new bays are offset and staggered in plan, challenging the normative condition of bilateral symmetry. The paradoxical presence of both symmetrical cruciform plan and asymmetric bay slippage produces provocative and unexpected outcomes—alignments with existing site conditions (**05**), new notions of centrality, and decentered axes of movement.

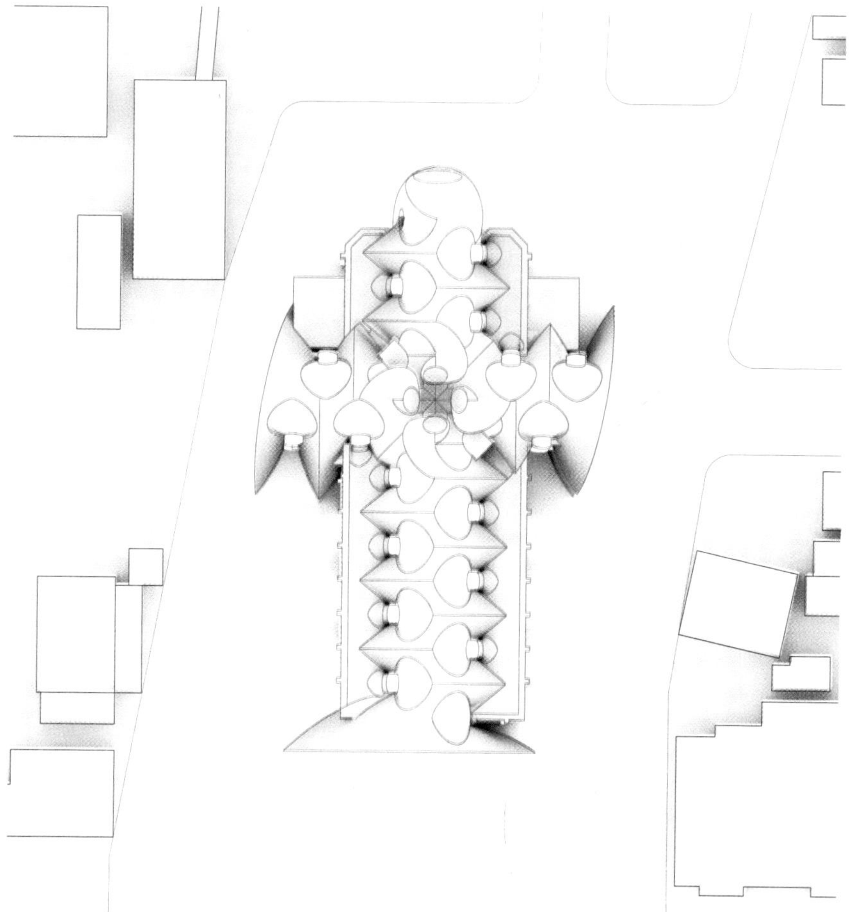

05 Site plan

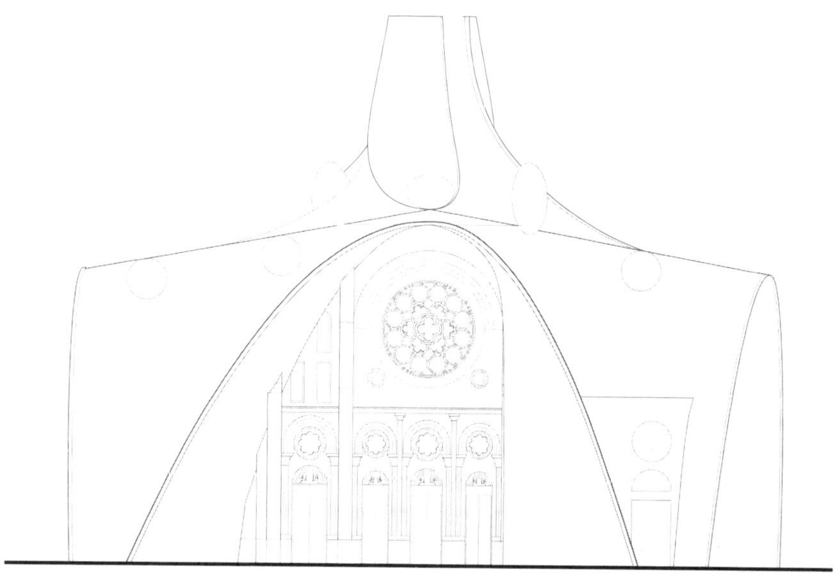

06 West elevation

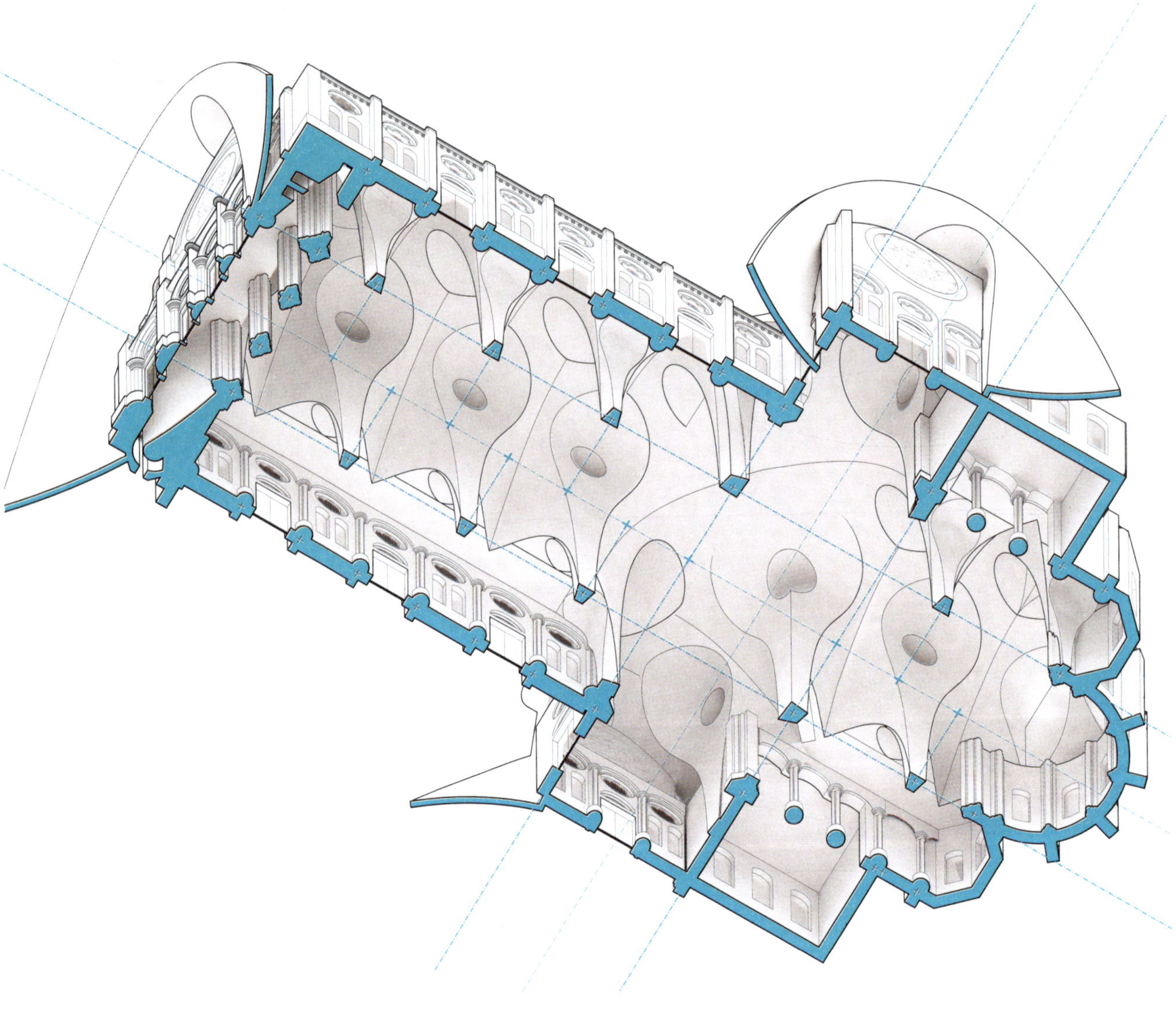

07 Worms eye view of vaulted interior

VOLUMETRIC EXPRESSION

The exterior of the cathedral shows the convex side of the periodic conical vaults and cruciform figuration grafted to the surviving walls of the original building. The western façade/narthex and the transept arms leave the outermost cones unclipped. These larger exterior conic surfaces with a parabolic edge achieve a grander institutional scale, redefining the image of the cathedral from the city (**06, 08**). The lineaments of the plaza paving are hyperbolas (a different conic section) produced by intersecting the infinite cone geometries of the nave and aisle vaults with the ground plane, thereby extending the serial bay pattern to the exterior.

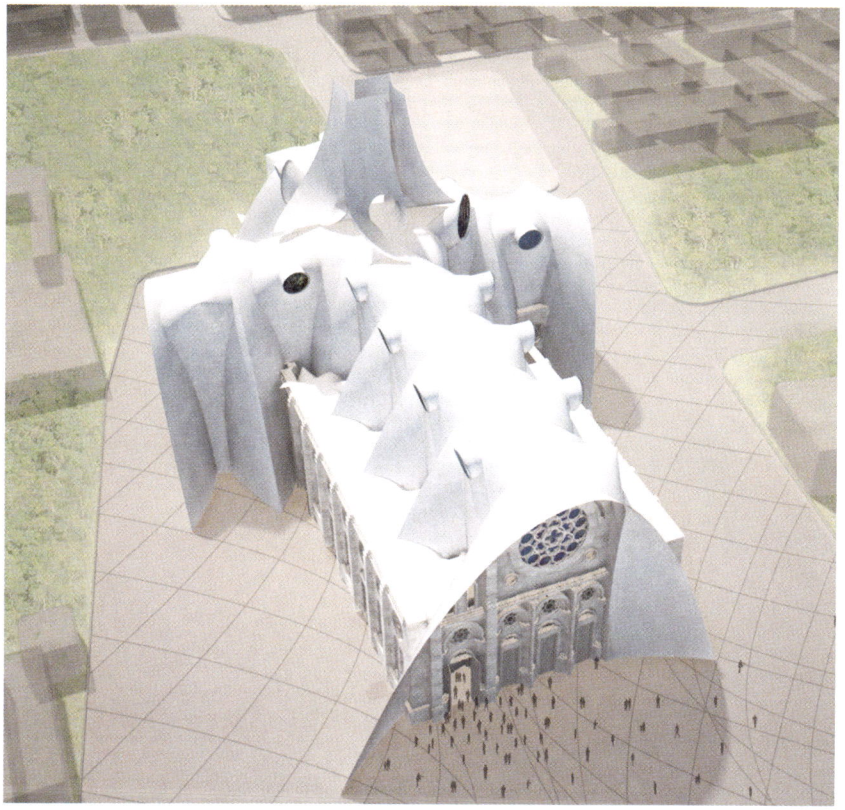

08 Aerial view of cathedral plaza

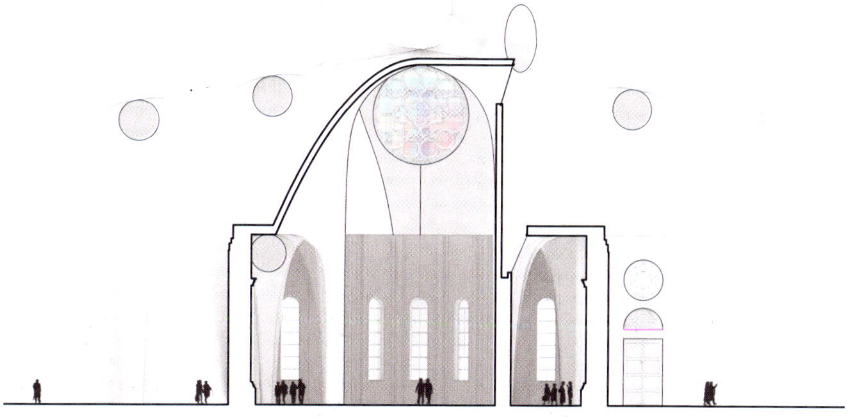

09 Transverse section

10 Interior view

11 South elevation

12 Longitudinal section

SERIAL REPETITION

Exterior walls of the original design are reconstructed (up to the triforium) on the cathedral plaza, providing a tactile presence of the cathedral's history and connection to the community. Set within this perimeter, contemporary geometries rise aloft, producing curving lines of intersection among the unadorned conical vault surfaces. Existing rose windows of the narthex and transept are restored, inset with an abstract pattern of pixelated stained glass. Carefully calibrated and repetitive forms convey formal exuberance while the strategic reduction of geometric difference fosters economic advantages for cost and construction. The geometric properties of cones as developable surfaces provides significant advantages for reusable formwork and fabrication.

Geodesic house 06
2017

Geodesic House 06 is similar in form and concept to Geodesic House 02, except the full figure 8 of the latter is truncated, producing cross-sectional end façades of the bar. These short façades reveal the orthogonal disposition of the planar portions of the massing (**01**). Two inverted cones are also used here to achieve the geodesic leveling effect, leading to the slight canting of the curved exterior walls which connect the two orthogonal ends (**09**). The organization is a single-loaded corridor transformed with 3/4 helical turn, indicative of the interior spiral stair which motivates the overall massing. Reveal lines of the shiplap siding reinforce the properties of the geodesic planks while binding together the tectonic unit of construction, the architectural parti, and the circulatory path of the subject.

01 Exterior view

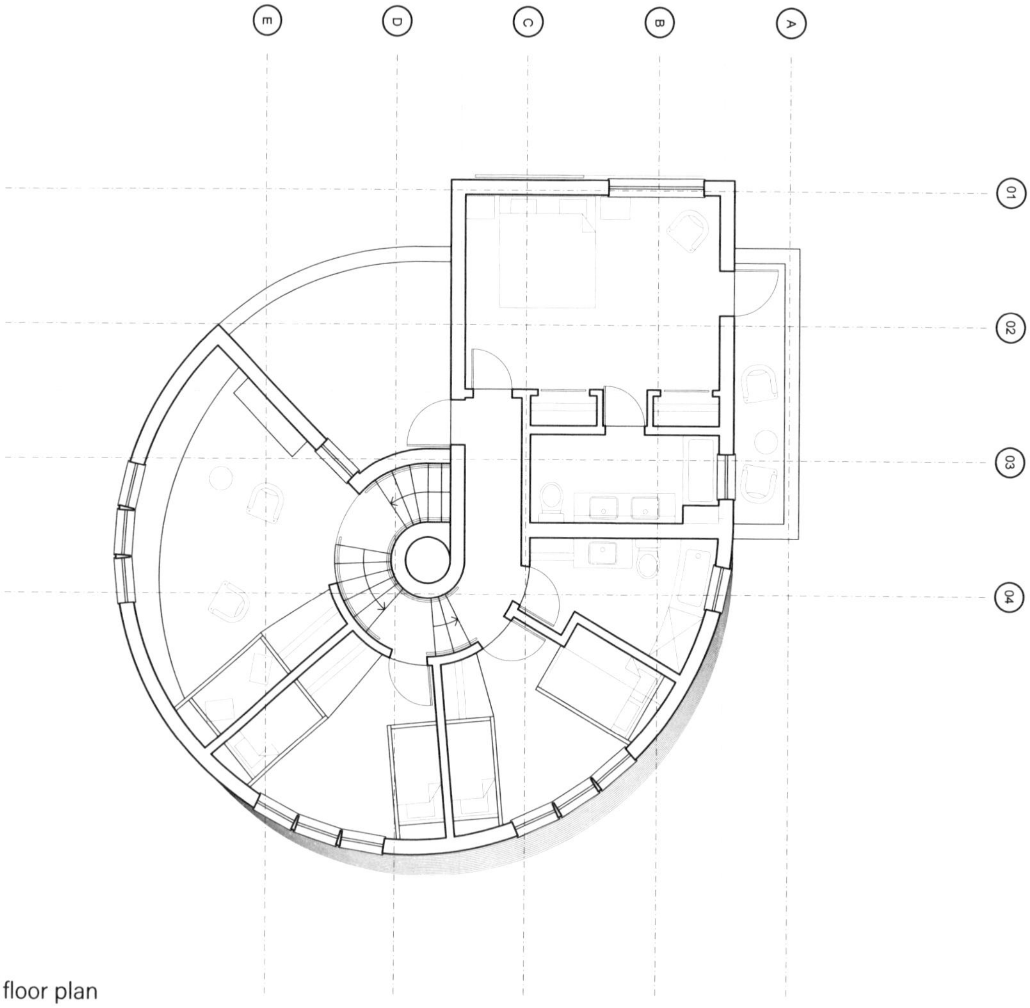

02 Ground floor plan

03 North elevation

FORM AND ORGANIZATION

The parti is a single-loaded corridor bending 270° while simultaneously rising such that one end of the bar rests on the other (**01**). The two orthogonal ends sit comfortably overlapped; the lower volume containing the dining and living room while the upper volume accommodates the primary bedroom. The dimension by which each volume extends beyond the other defines the size of a balcony for the primary bedroom as well as the depth of the covered entry (**05**). A cascade of wedge-shaped spaces are accessed from stair landings, including the kitchen, informal family room, bunk rooms, and bathroom.

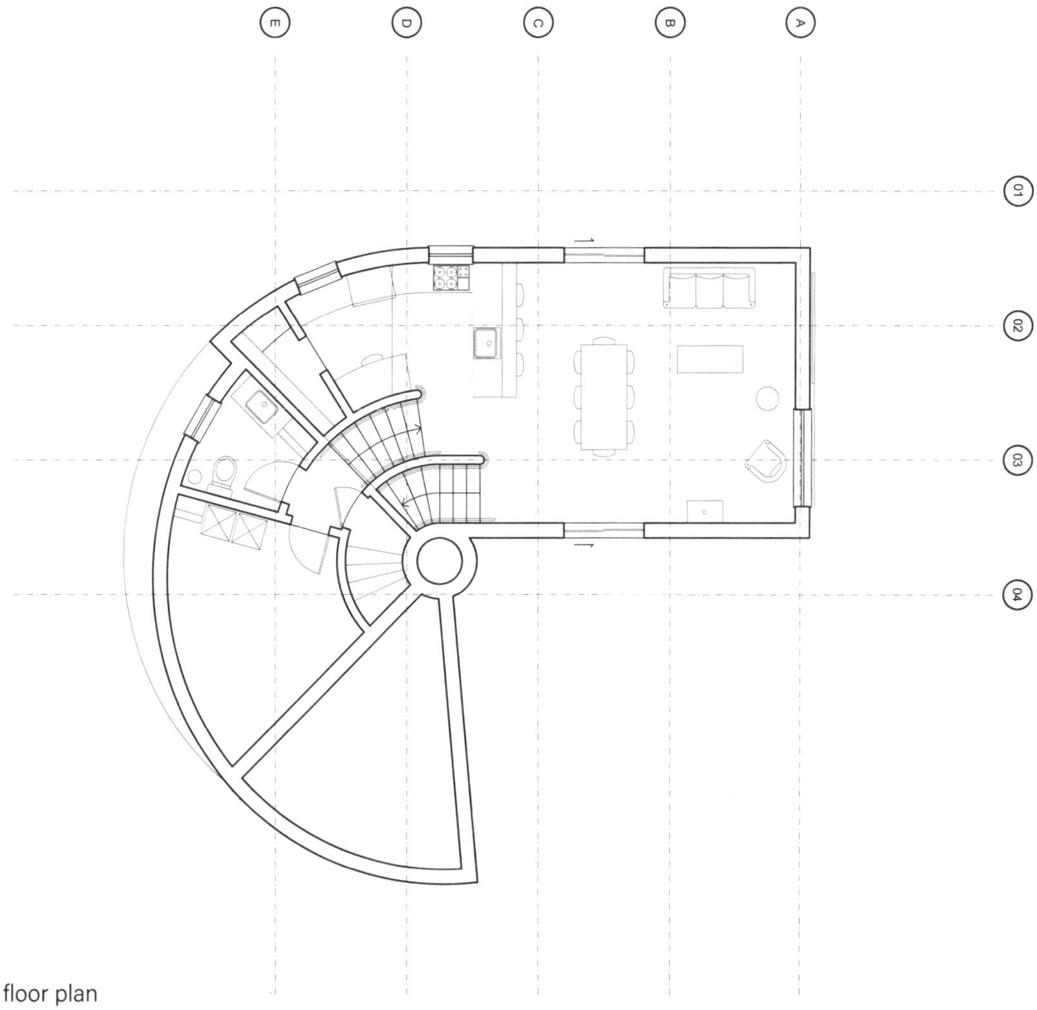

04 Upper floor plan

05 Exterior View

COMPACT SERIALITY

The level of privacy increases as one rises through the linear arrangement of spaces. The dashed profile on the developed section (**07**) shows the actual location of the primary bedroom (end of sequence) atop the living room (beginning of sequence), indicating the relative compactness of the plan. The technique of geodesic leveling allows visual complexity of three-dimensional form in localized areas (**03**), while allowing much of the occupiable volume to be well-behaved in section and elevation (**08**).

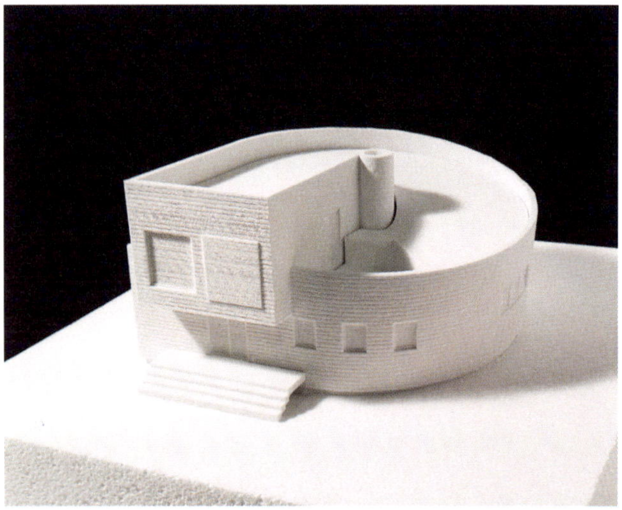

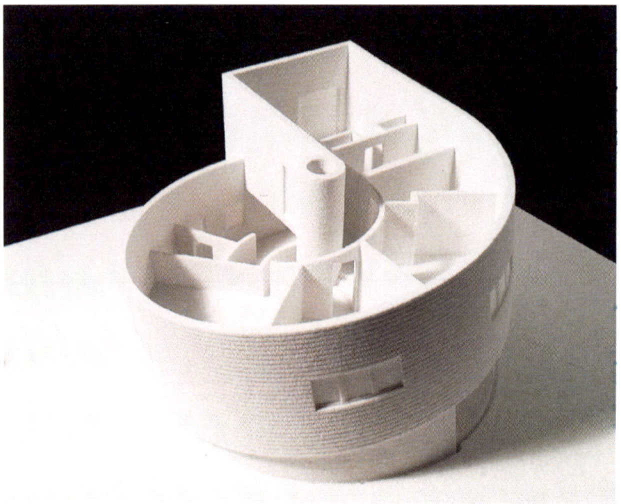

06 Model

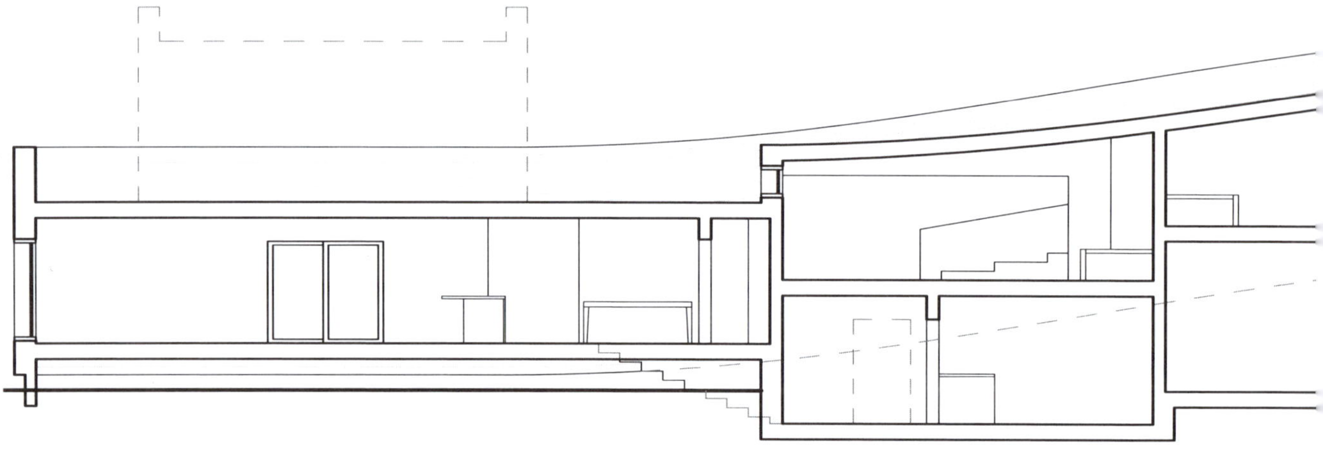

07 Developed section

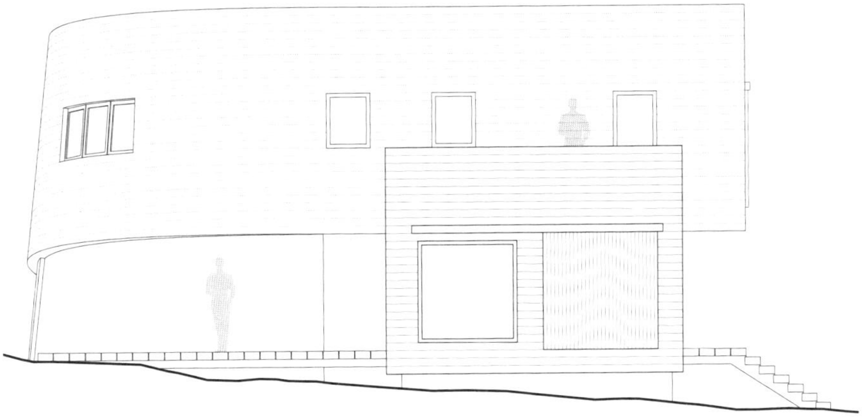

08 West elevation

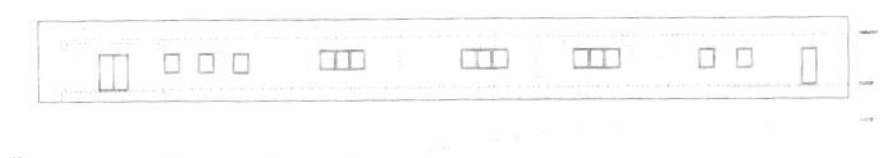

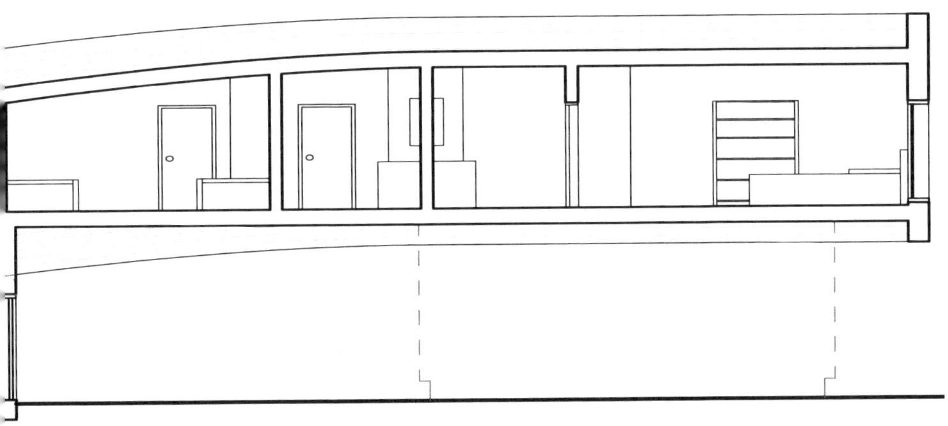

09 Developed elevation

Geodesic house 07

2017

In Geodesic House 07, cylinders enable smooth and continuous transitions between perpendicular orientations of geodesic plank siding. The main 3-story rectilinear mass is clad with a vertical grain of shiplap siding. A cylinder oriented at a 45° slope negotiates the transition between vertical grain of the main volume and the horizontal grain of the wraparound deck. In doing so, the cladding surface peels away and inverts its orientation, producing a topologically ambiguous wrapper covering an otherwise orthogonal volume. A second vertical cylinder defines a conventional fillet between horizontal planks bounding the L-shaped walkway and deck. The orientation and radii of curvature of the cylinders are linked to the dimensions of the interior, producing imbricated relationships between the seemingly independent facade and the contents it encloses.

01 Exterior view

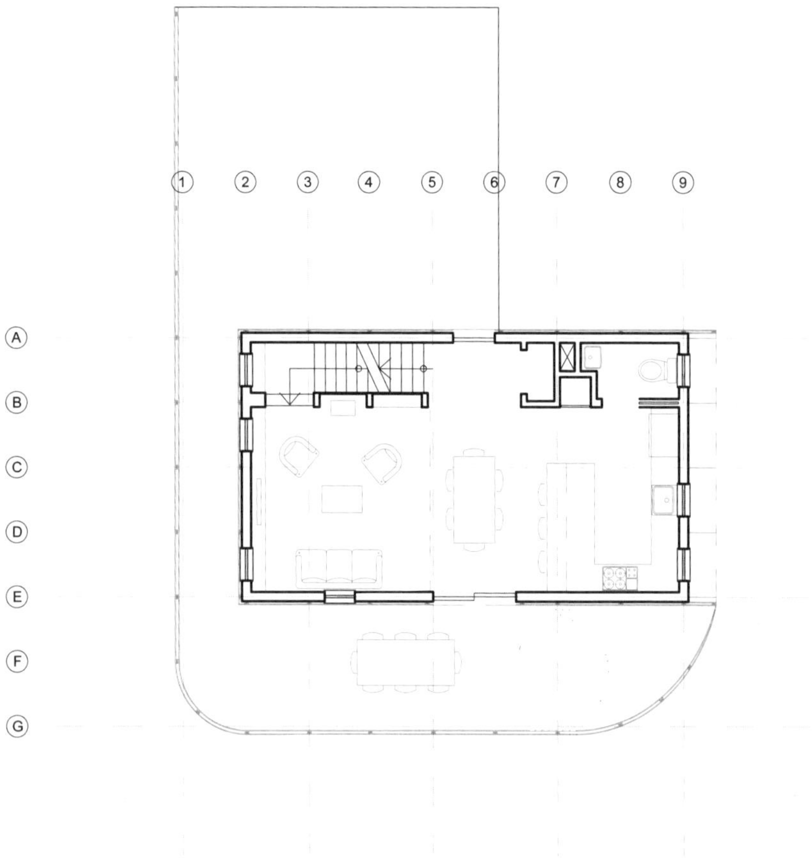

02 MId-level plan

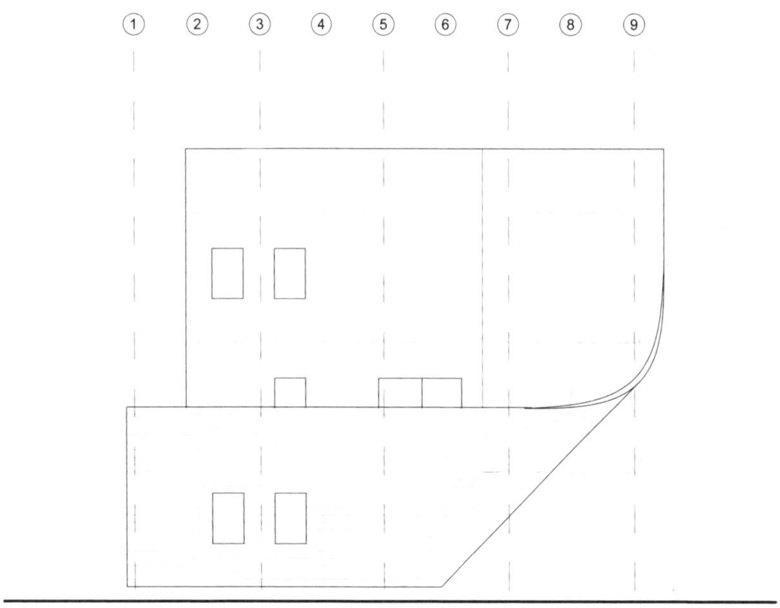

03 Ground floor plan

PERPENDICULAR UNION

The orientation of the siding reinforces the proportional character of the volumes underneath–vertical seams for the tall central volume and horizontal seams for the low surrounding volume. The curving geodesic planks of the inclined cylinder unify these perpendicular orientations into a continuous expression.

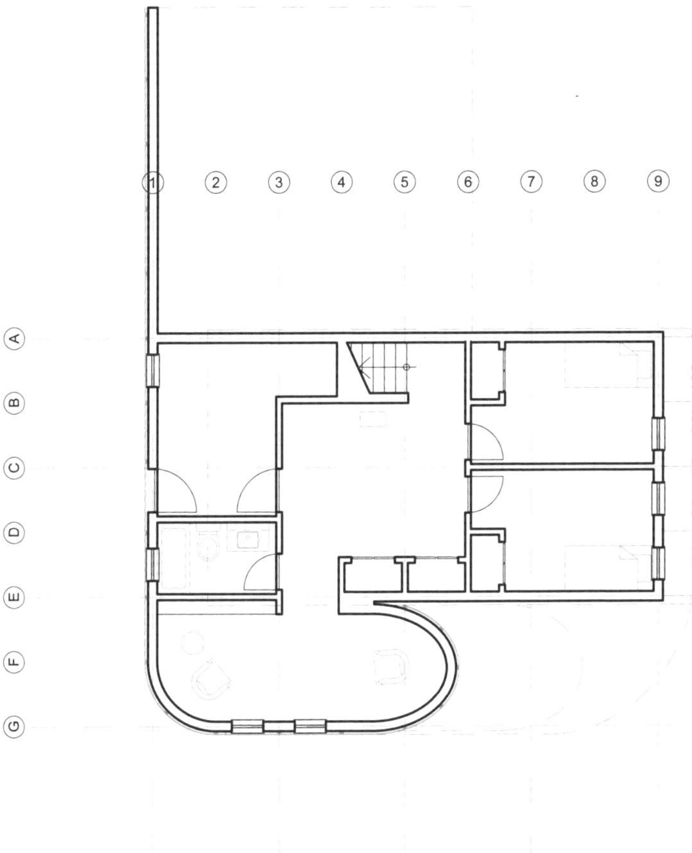

04 Lower-level plan

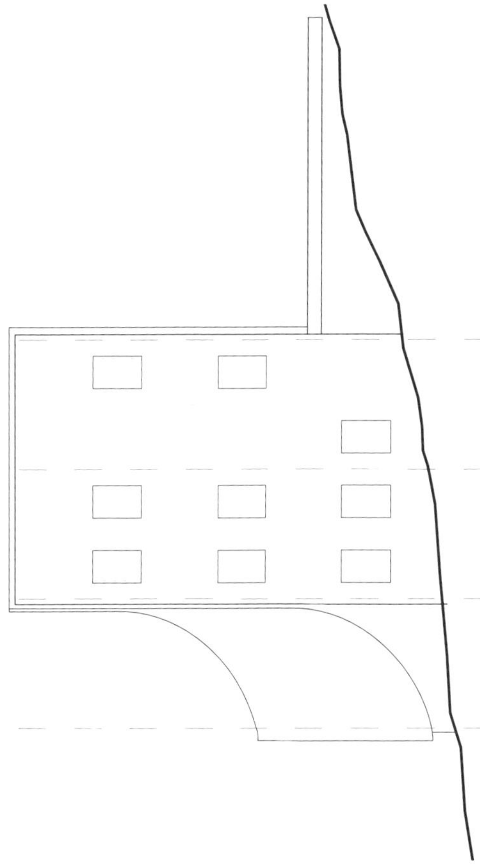

05 East elevation

06 Model

SURFACE TOPOLOGY

The lower level room produced by the cladding surface inversion introduces topological issues of enclosure (**04**). This discrete oblong space remains discernably outside the boundary of the main rectilinear volume while the double wall threshold evidences the independence of the geodesic plank skin.

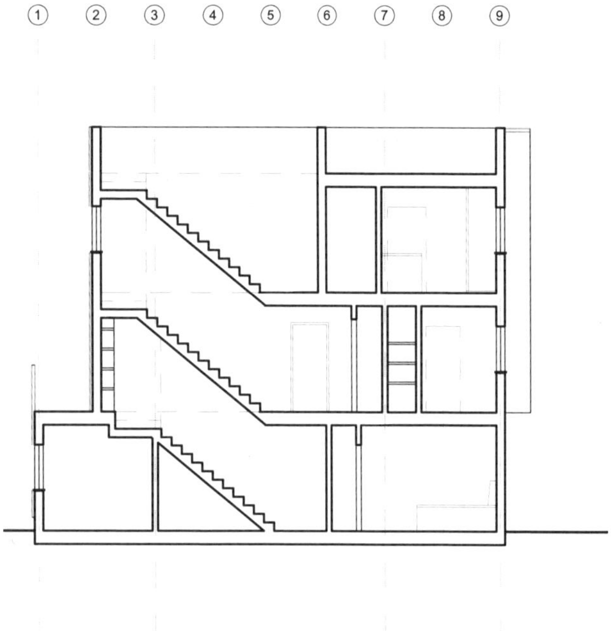

07 Longitudinal section

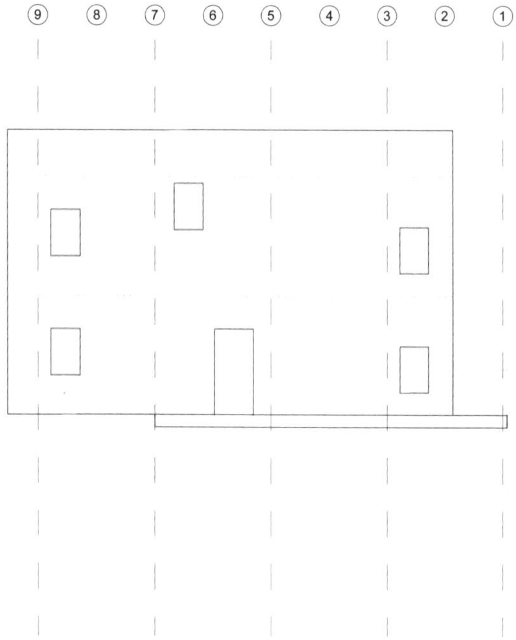

08 North elevation

09 Exterior view

STACKED EFFICIENCY

The vertical organization of the house is efficient and compact in plan, relegating the geometric interest to the perimeter.

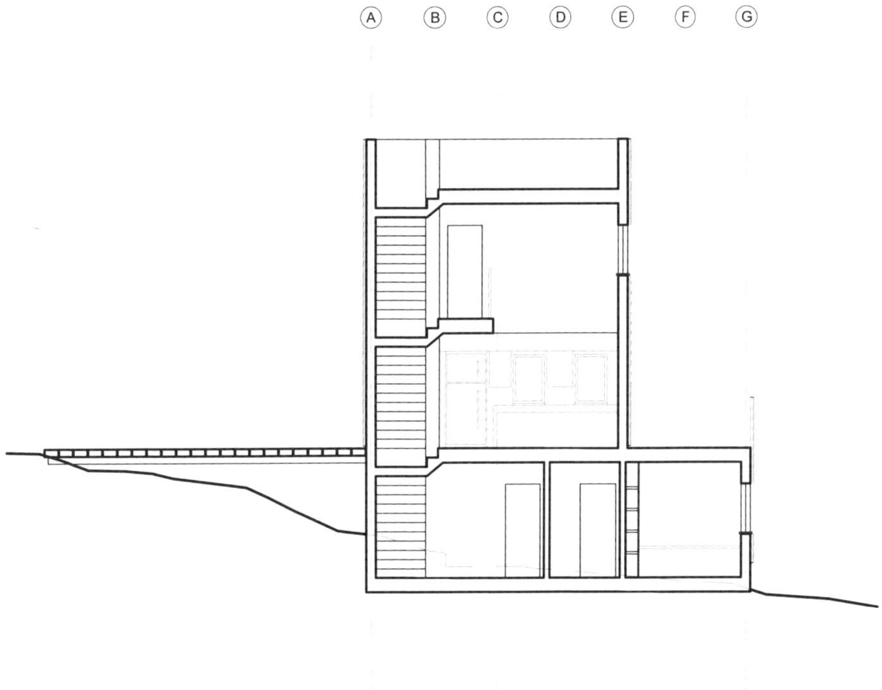

10 Transverse section

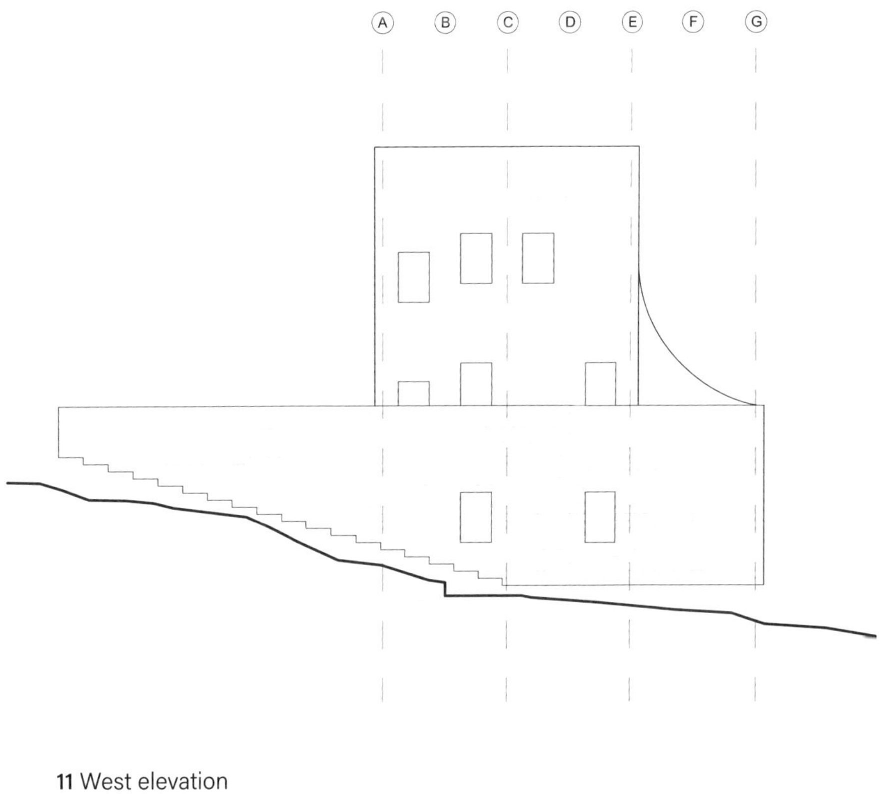

11 West elevation

01 H. H. Richardson. The Stoughton House (Cambridge, MA) 1880

Epker house (Geodesic house 01)

Concord, MA
2014-2015

Shingle Style residential types can be formally interpreted as assemblies of discrete volumes unified beneath a smooth and continuous skin. This is apparent when observing local conditions where concave fillets convey tensile qualities of a shrink-wrapped surface that transitions between prismatic volumes, cylinders, and cones. The diminutive scale of the individual shake allows the Shingle Style to manifest a broad range of geometric surface classes in its exterior roofs and façades, including those exhibiting double curvature. The relative size and construction tolerance of small shakes in comparison to the radii of curvature of its forms allows exterior surfaces to bend in two axes. When using clapboard or shiplap siding in geodesic plank configurations, however, curvature can only occur in one direction, necessitating the use of singly-ruled developable surfaces.

Mediating between the vernacular precedents and more contemporary geometric and material aesthetics, Epker house deploys calibrated cone geodesics to express wrappings around its figurative corners using steam-bent shiplap siding. Unlike the pixelated cladding of the shingle style, the linear plank siding requires specific profile angles and radii of curvature of its cones to achieve precision of its varied geodesic orientations. This calibration allows critical alignments to be achieved between horizontality, roof slopes, and stair slopes.

02 Detail of conical corner

03 Model

GEODESIC ORIENTATION

The main conical corner is calibrated with a profile angle and axial tilt to produce a constrained range of geodesic inclinations that choreograph transitions of siding seams from horizontal (level lines) to the slope of the entry stair, and from the gable slope to the inclined header of the covered entry.

Multiple orientations of geodesic lines may be drawn on a single surface. This allows one discrete geometric primitive to be associated with multiple slopes and alignments while producing a layered tectonic effect.

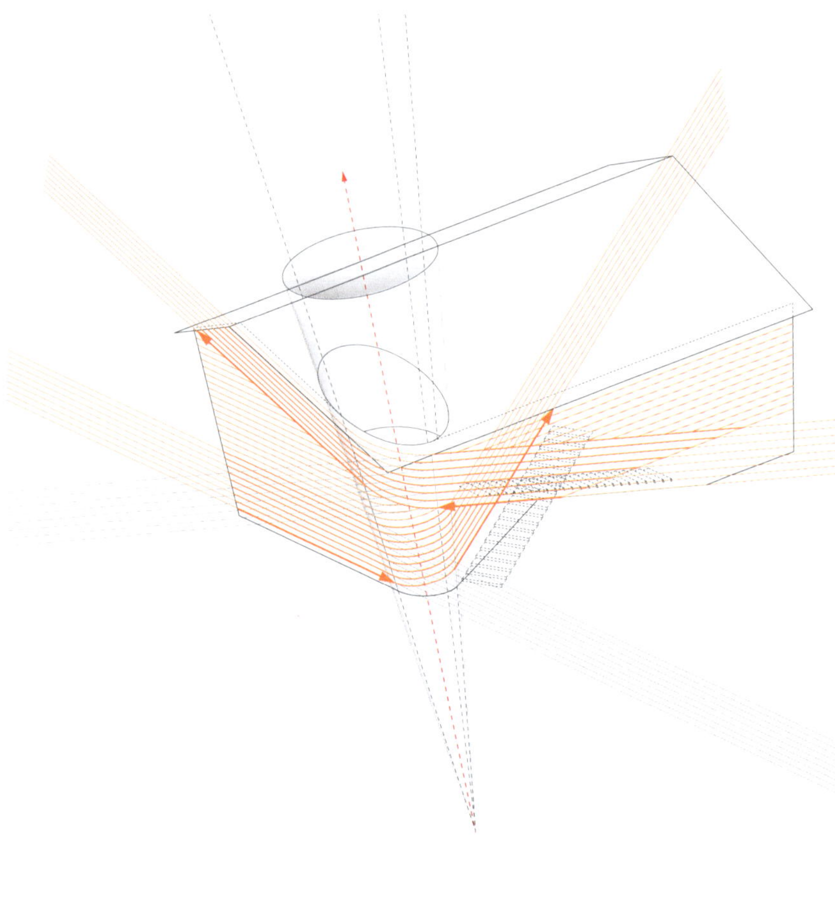

04 Multiple geodesic trajectories traced around the conical corner

05 Exterior view

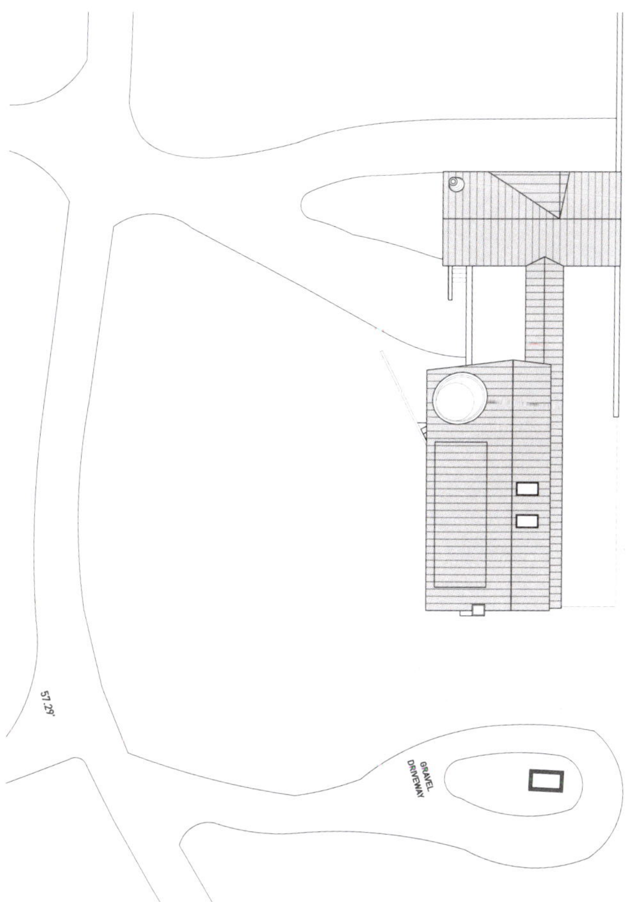

06 Siteplan

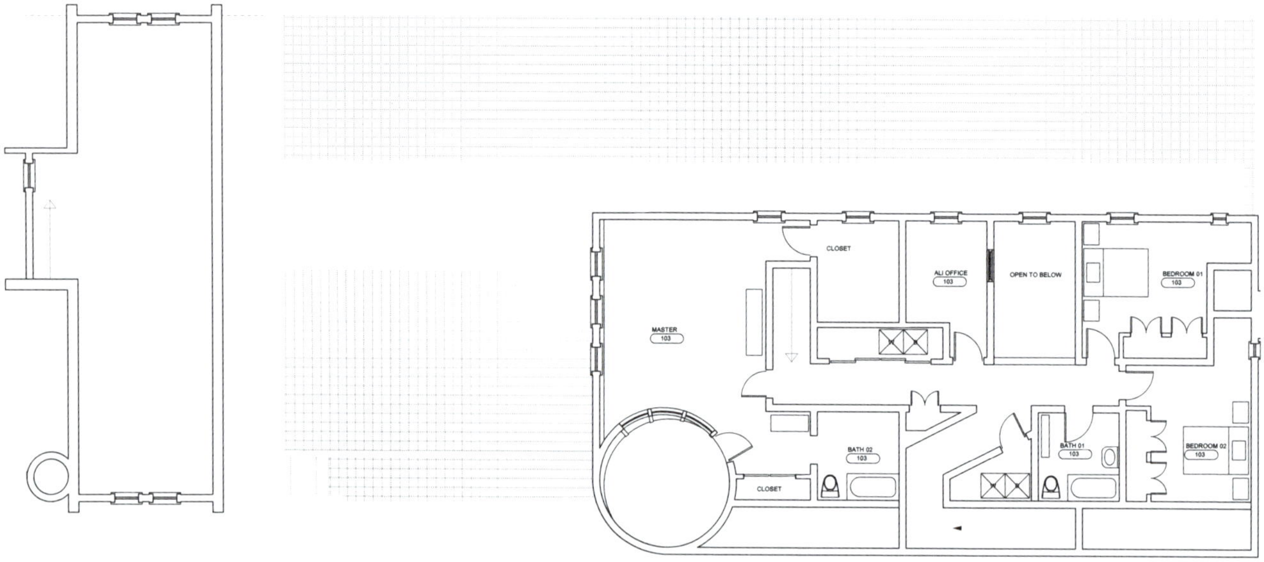

07 Second floor plan

08 View of approach from west

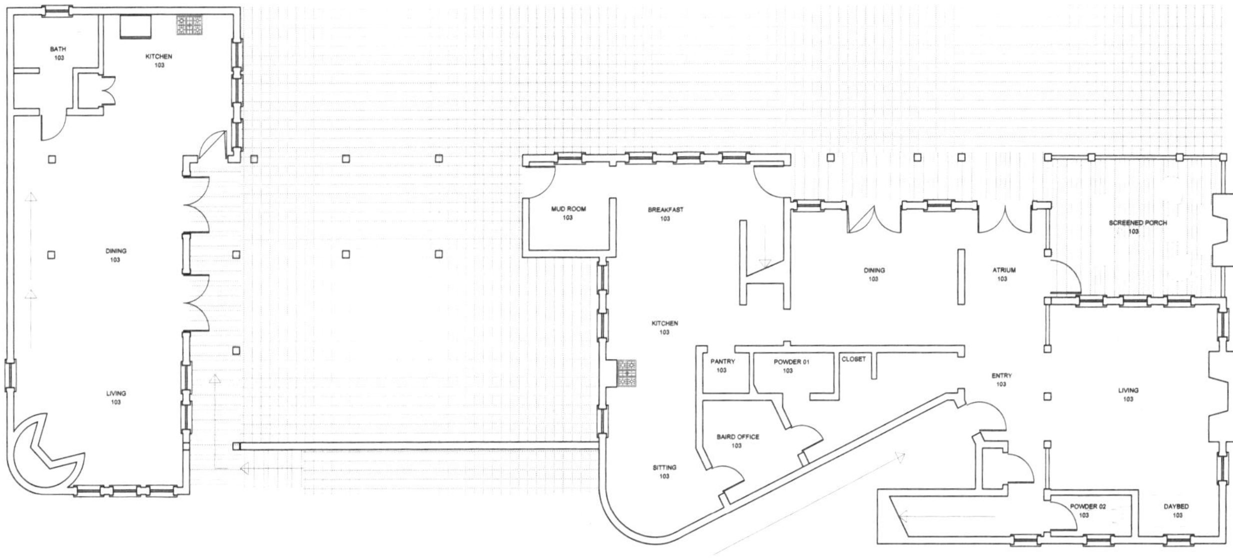

09 First floor plan

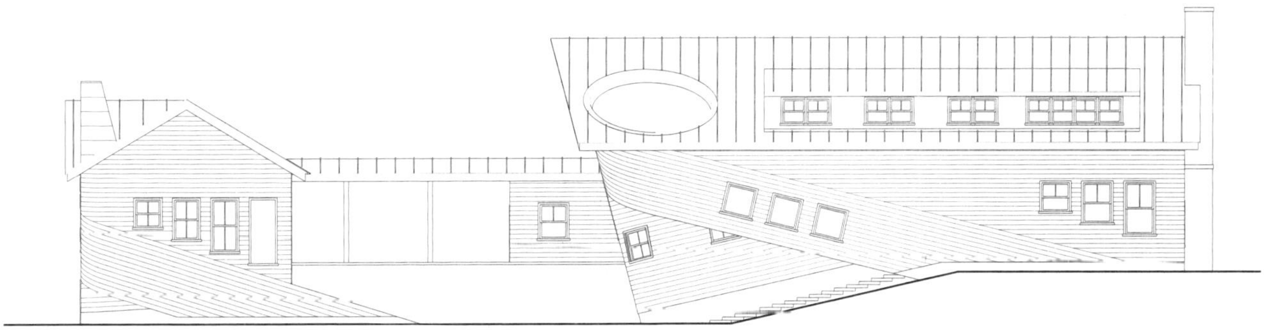

10 West elevation

FAÇADE AND ORGANIZATION

The shallow slope of the geodesic siding parallel to the exterior entry stair pushes the main arrival hall to the south, defining the more formal areas of the house (**09**). The interior stair from the main hall to the upper level is aligned with the front façade, and generally aligns with the opposing slope seen on the main elevation (**10**). The circulatory route from the entry hall to the atrium, along the back porch, mud room, covered connection to the guest house, and the patio stair is conceptually continuous—a looping circuit that keys into the elevational slopes of the geodesic siding.

01 View from atrium floor

Conic Knots

Plasticity Competition
2014

Because they are curved in one axis and straight (or ruled) in the other, cones can operate as the geometric interlocutor between the curvilinear and the planar/orthogonal. Conic Knots deploys two pairs of cones, each tangent to the floor, to produce a rotationally symmetric composition of geodesic planks in an institutional atrium. Composed of discrete geometric parts, the developable ribbon surfaces interlock in space, suggesting a unified surface subject to elastic and topological transformation.

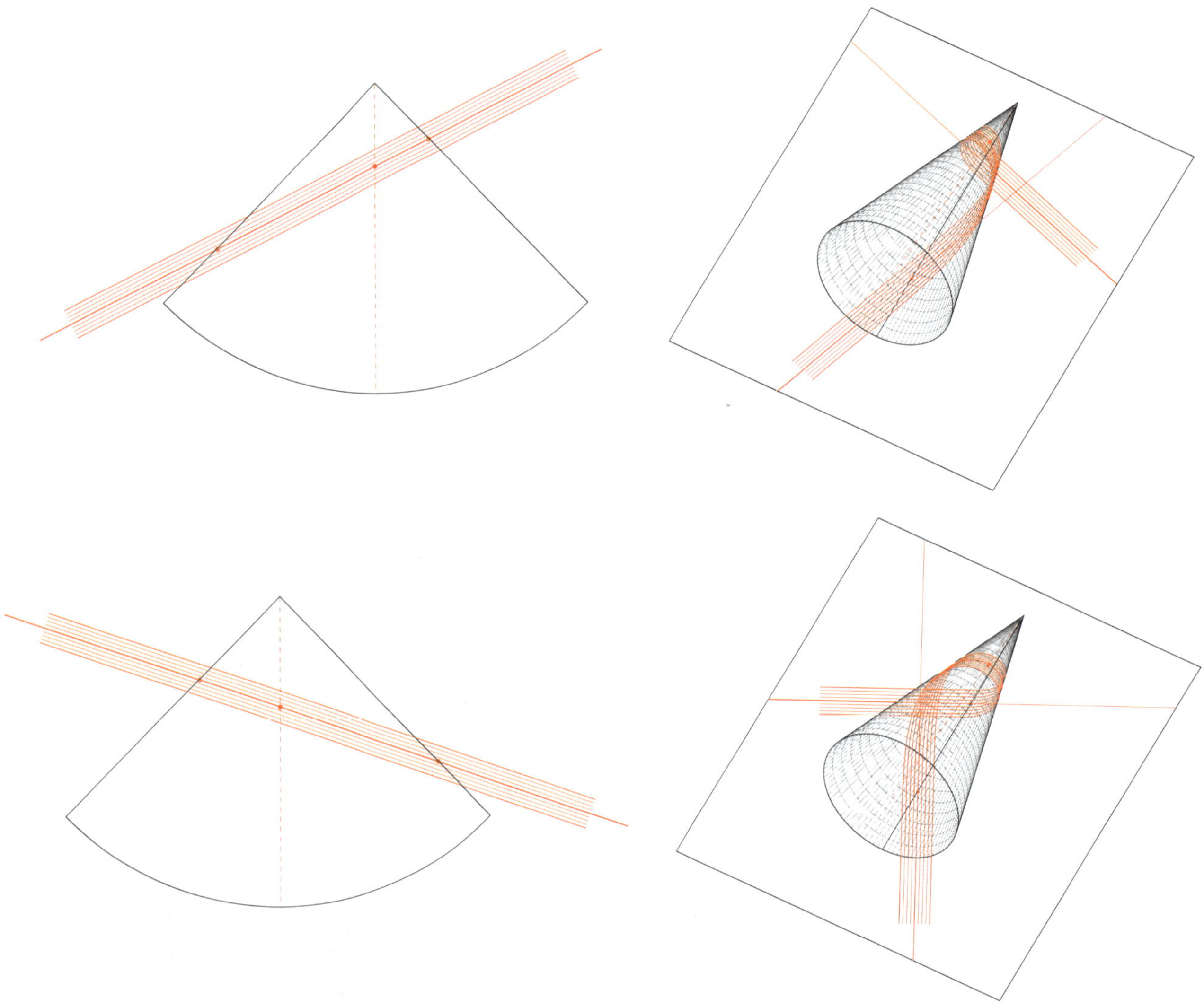

02 Variations of geodesic development

GEODESIC DEVELOPMENT

The shortest distance between any two points on a given surface is known as a geodesic line. Multiple offset geodesic lines may be drawn on a surface to subdivide it into geodesic planks. When developed onto a plane, these geodesic lines (of cones) become straight and parallel, demarcating the boundaries between contiguous planks. The isometric relationship between the two-dimensional developed state and three-dimensional form allows conventional dimensional lumber, plastic, or other flat stock to produce various smooth and piecewise continuous form.

Conic Knots uses two pairs of discrete cones, each tangent to the floor along a horizontal generator, the specific profile angle (~14.48°) of these congruent cones dictates that a full geodesic loop will be tangent to perpendicular lines on the floor (**02**). Each of the cones has been trimmed along specific geodesic lines to produce the resulting sculptural ribbons in a rotationally symmetric organization (**05**).

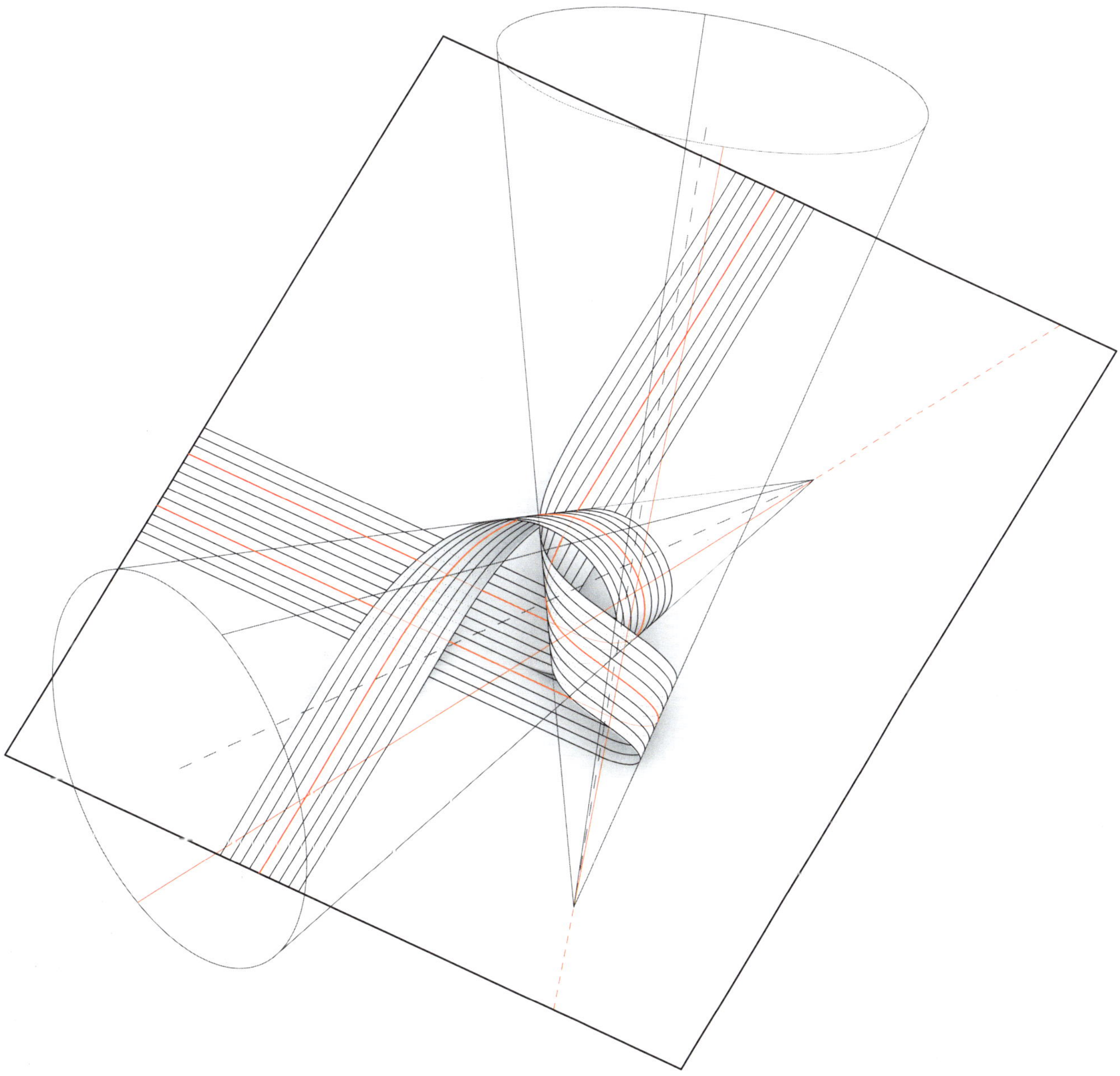

03 Piecewise continuous cones tangent to the floor

04 Aerial view of atrium

SITE SPECIFIC GEOMETRY

The acute profile angle (~14.48°) of the four cones dictate that the tangent extensions of the geodesic lines on floor are perpendicular, allowing the composition to key into the orthogonal grid of the atrium. The developable ribbon surfaces interlock in space, suggesting a topological transformation of a three-dimensional rug. The calibrated composition of several discrete geometric parts produces the formal reading of unified surfaces subjected to plastic deformation.

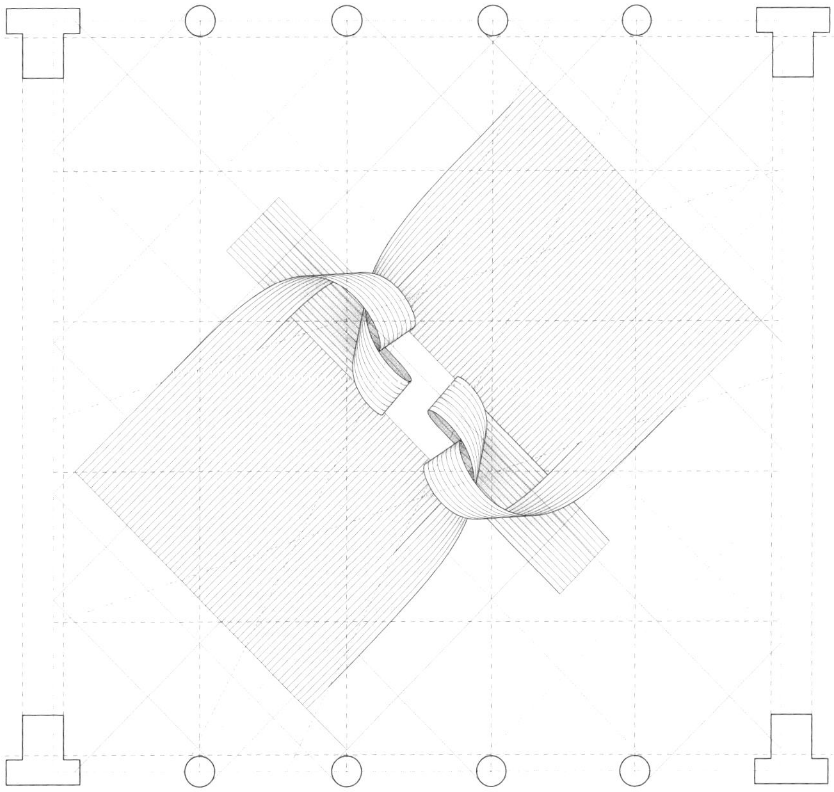

05 Plan

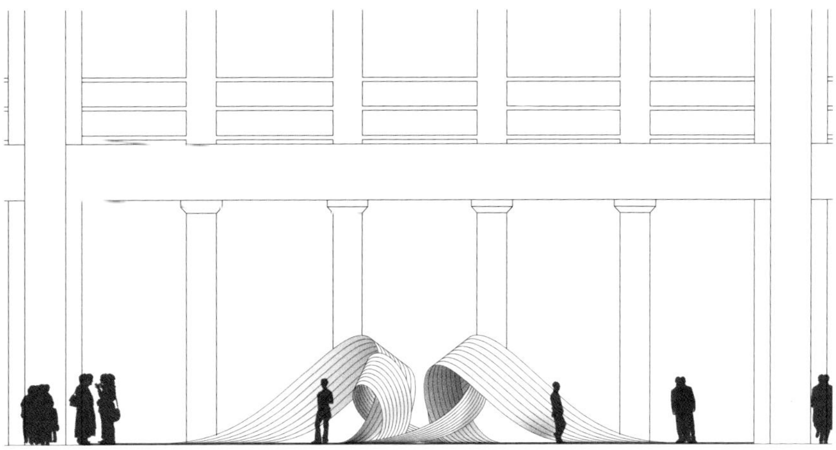

06 Elevation

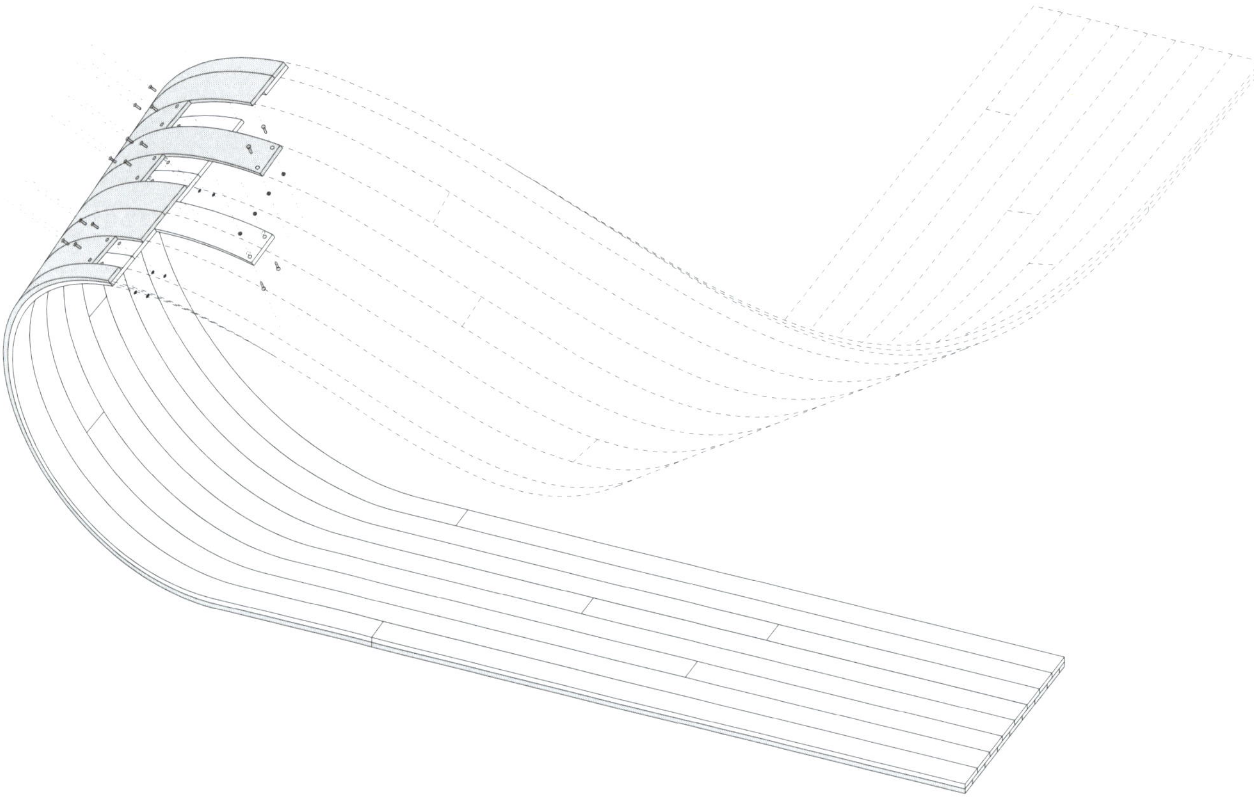

07 3d view showing lap joint detail

08 1:12 model

MATERIALITY AND STRUCTURE

Custom and unique parts are kept to a minimum. Factors influencing material choice and construction sequence relate to minimum bending radii, material k-value, maximum length of available materials, etc. The surfaces of Conic Knots are comprised of two-ply polycarbonate planks bolted together via a longitudinal lap-joint detail (**07**). Precise CNC pre-drilling of counter-sunk bolt holes on the planks facilitate accurate layer assembly. The dimensional difference between the inner and outer radii of curvature provide additional structural stiffness, which is welcome, as developable surfaces concede two-way "shell action" in favor of their geometric and fabrication advantages.

09 1:12 model

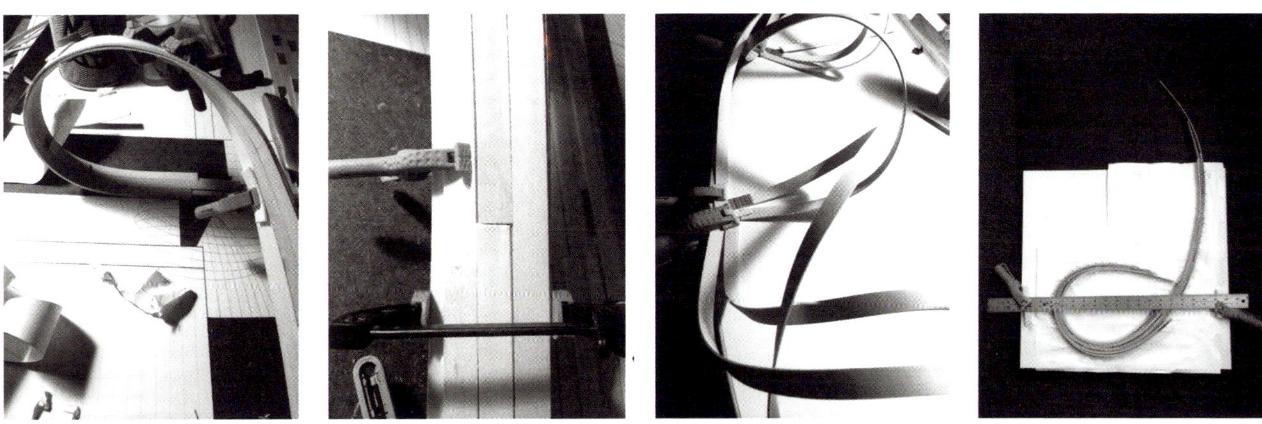

10 1:12 model construction

01 Eduardo Catalano (1917-2010), Catalano House (1954)

Doubly Ruled House

North Haven, Maine
2013

A surface is doubly ruled if it contains straight ruling lines in two directions-i.e. through any given point there are two distinct lines that lie on the surface. There are only three types of these surfaces: the hyperbolic paraboloid (hypar), the hyperboloid of one sheet, and the plane. The Doubly Ruled House deploys all three geometries in the production of a three-dimensional armature for space making.

Though the investigation of these surfaces was mainly the purview of 19th-century differential geometers and mathematicians, doubly ruled surfaces had been in sporadic use in architecture as early as the 17th century[1]. Well-behaved in projection yet complex in three dimensional space, their characteristics proved instrumental in addressing formal and linguistic predicaments of the Baroque period. It was not until the 20th century that these surfaces were deployed as a primary language of architectural and structural expression.

The Eduardo Catalano House (1954) is a distilled example which showcases the geometric properties of the hypar. Elegantly fusing the sculptural horizontality of the exterior with a minimalist orthogonal plan, the house embodies a synthesis of modernist and structuralist agendas.

The Doubly Ruled House exhibits a hybrid of the hypar and hyperboloid. The ruling line subdivisions of its piecewise continuous compound roof/enclosure serve as geometric armature, related to the volumetric and linear extrusions of the interior. By addressing the horizontal and vertical projections as equivalent, it takes the Catalano House to another dimension.

1 Robin Evans, "Comic Lines", The Projective Cast, MIT press (Cambridge 1995), p.305.

02 Exterior view

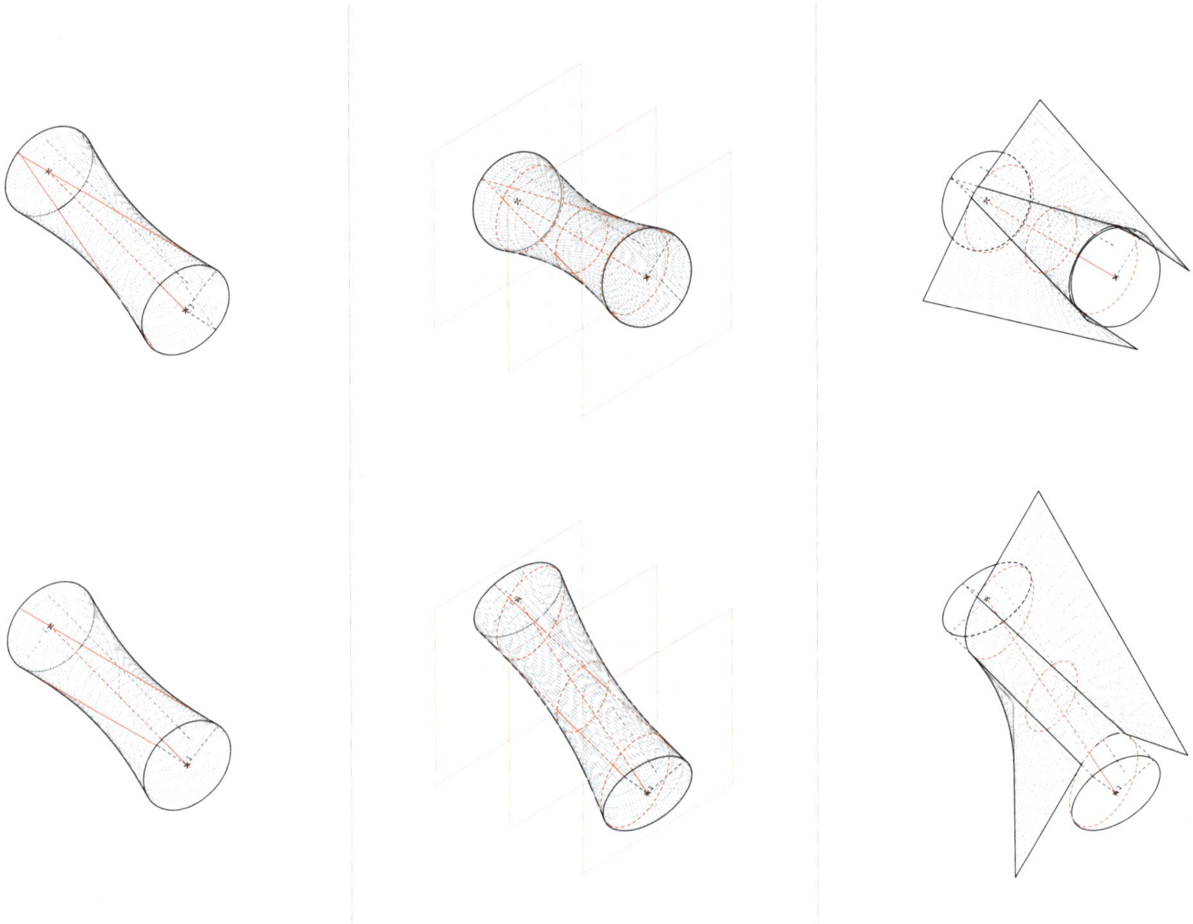

03 Piecewise continuous assemblies of hyperboloids and hypars along parallel and intersecting generators

04 Projective relationships between orthogonal interior elements and doubly ruled compound surface

PROJECTIVE ORTHOGONALITY

For any given hypar surface, there exists an orientation(s) such that both U and V curve fields of ruling lines produce an orthogonal grid in horizontal and vertical projections. For each of these specific orientations, there also exists a unique hyperboloid which can be stitched in a smooth and piecewise continuous manner. The vertical and horizontal projections from this piecewise continuous three-part surface comprise the orthogonal armature of the house (**05**).

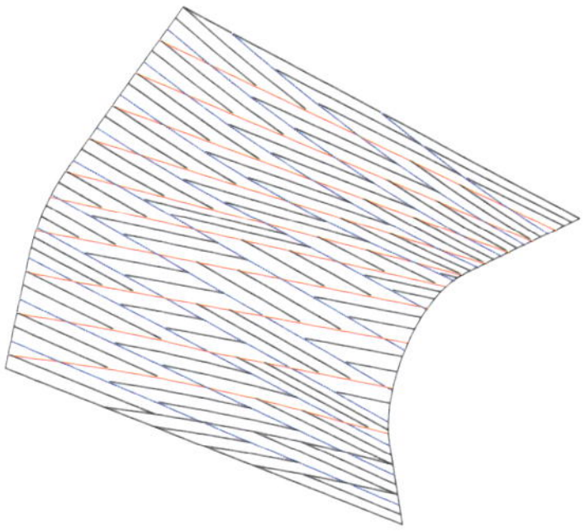

5.1 Parquet style

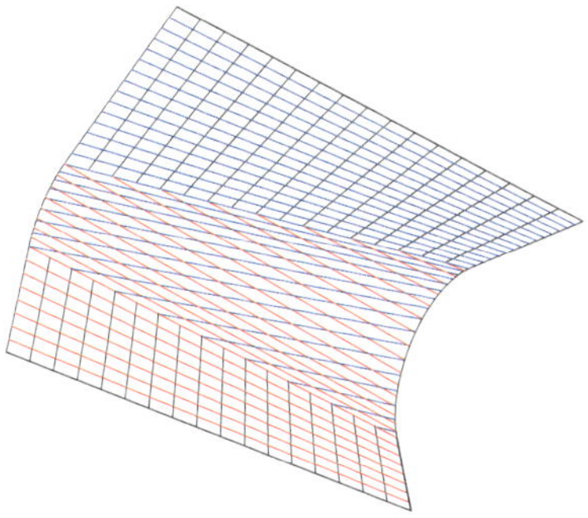

5.2 Native ruling line subdivision

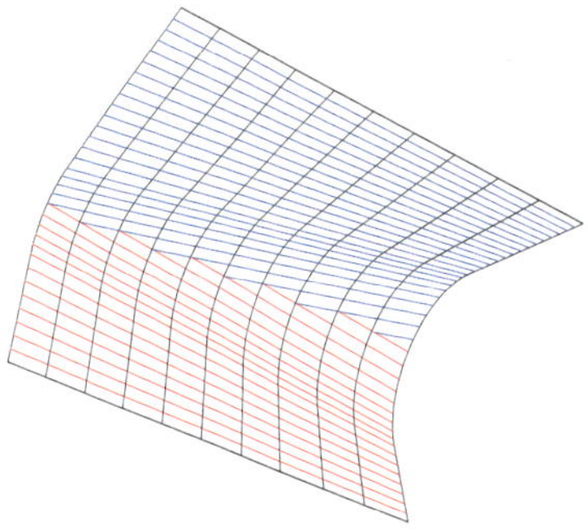

5.3 Chevron joint

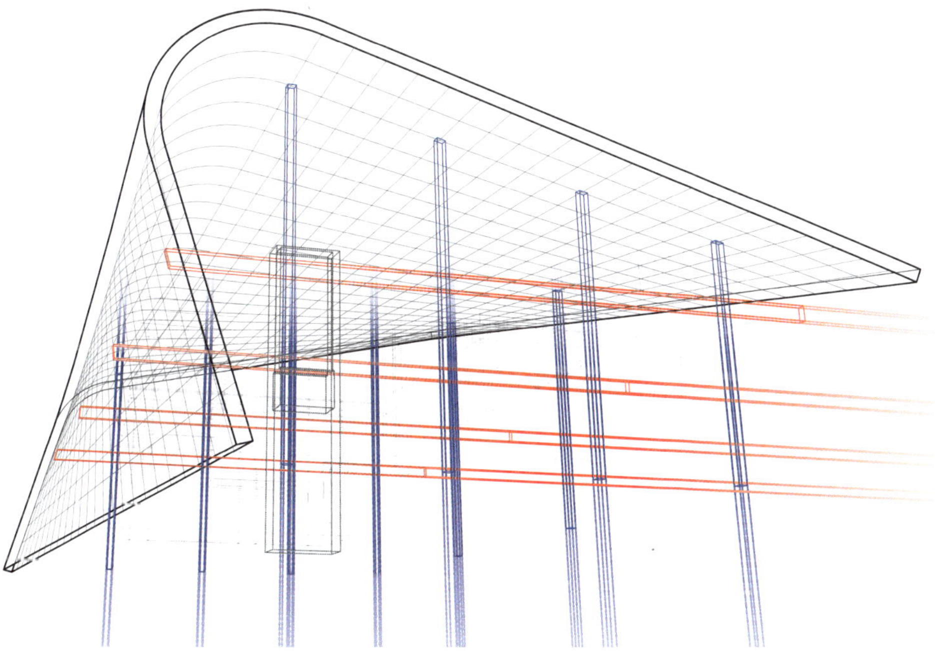

06 The piecewise continuous surface as armature for orthogonal projection

HYPAR/HYPERBOLOID SURFACE SUBDIVISIONS

Varying methods of subdivision exhibit a geometric contradiction of the compound doubly ruled surface. Though the surfaces are smooth and continuous (G1) across their contiguous edges, the native ruling line subdivisions across these edges are discontinuous. Alternative subdivision logics (**05.1-05.3**) may read more continuously, but the curving lines across the surfaces will concede some fabrication advantages.

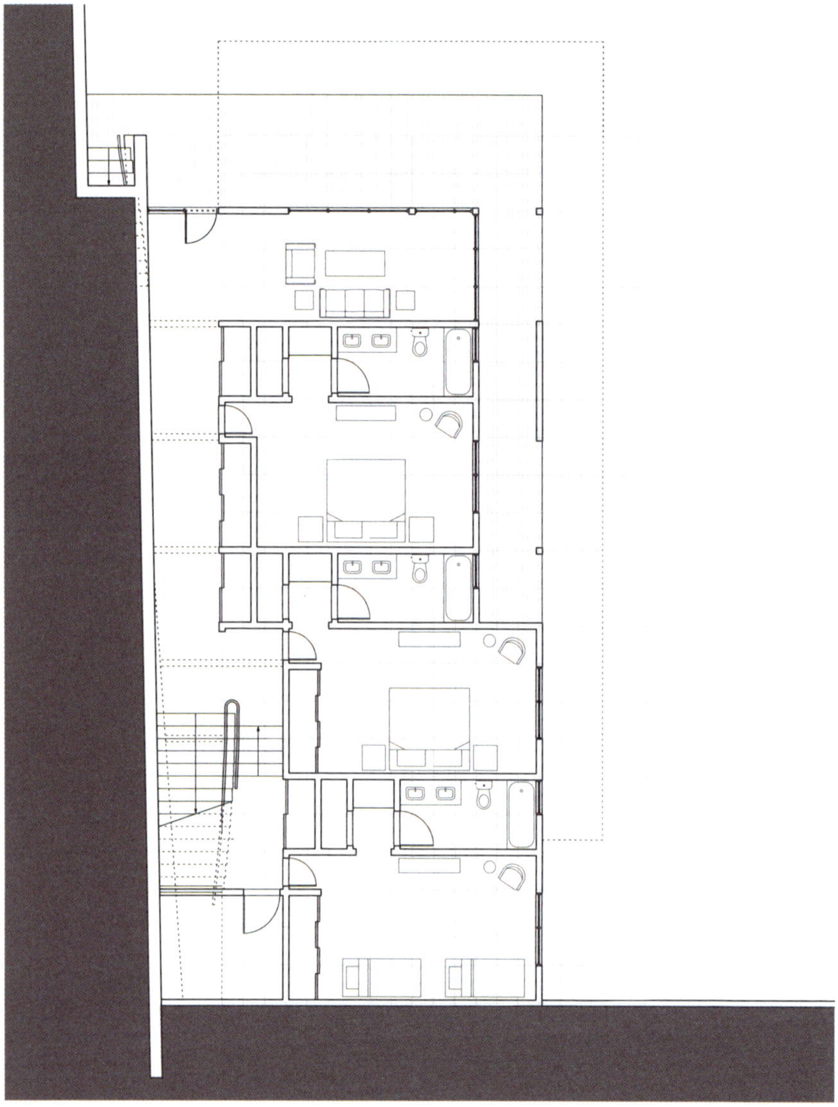

07 Lower level plan

08 Lower level

PROJECTIVE ELEMENTS

The upper level entrance occurs beneath the most acute bend of the continuous roof (**10**). The plan is dense at the entrance with extruded volumes for office and kitchen programs, powder room, and closets. The density dissipates toward the east, allowing more commodious space for living room, dining, and views to the landscape.

Governed by the projective relationships of the doubly ruled hypar surface, the extruded volumes meet the continuous ceiling along straight line edges (**04**). Horizontally extruded elements of the lower level such as beams, floor slab, and treads have a similar relationship with the hypar wall (**08**), thus making these opposing orientations conceptually equivalent (**06**).

The intrusion of the main stair leading to the lower bedroom level shears the blocks of cellular program, creating a slight irregularity of the exterior foot print, which serves to terminate the wrap-around porch at the lower level (**07**).

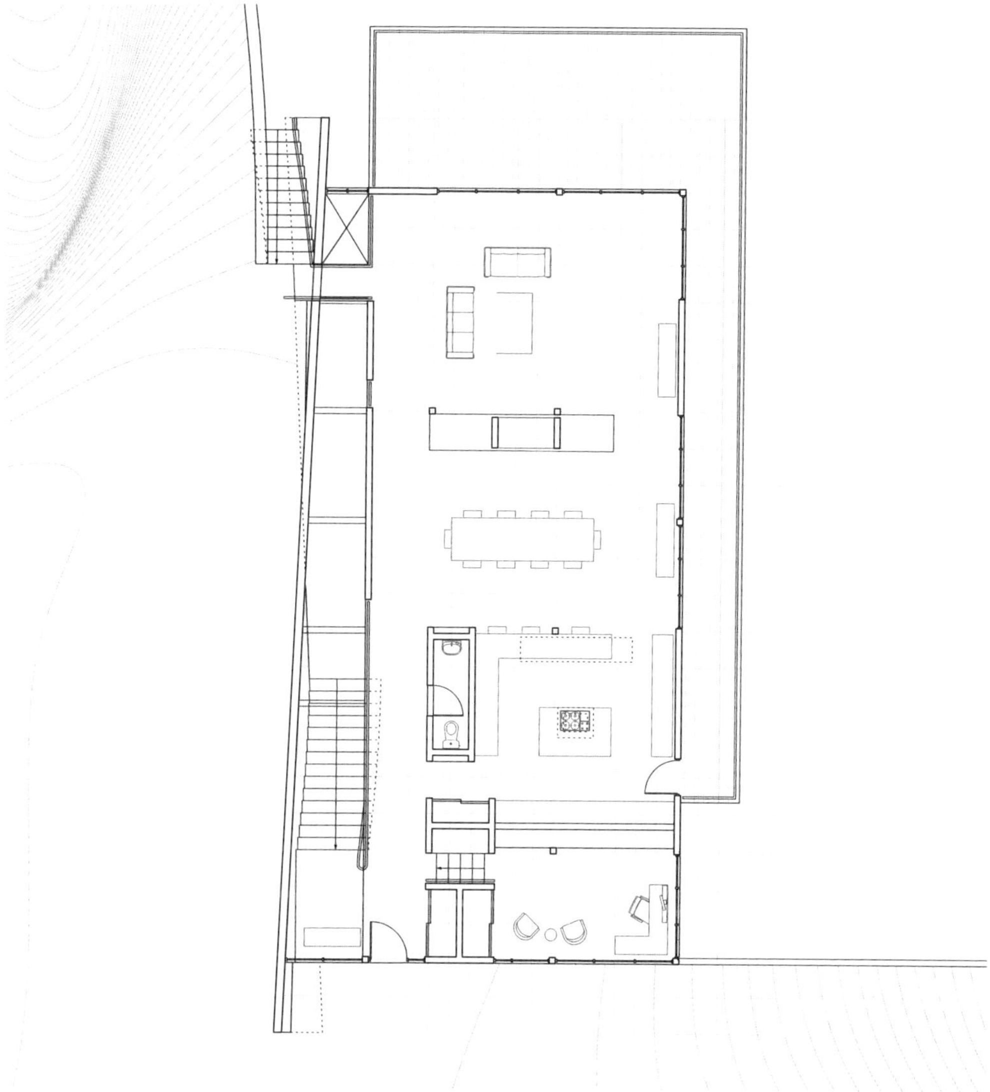

09 Upper level plan

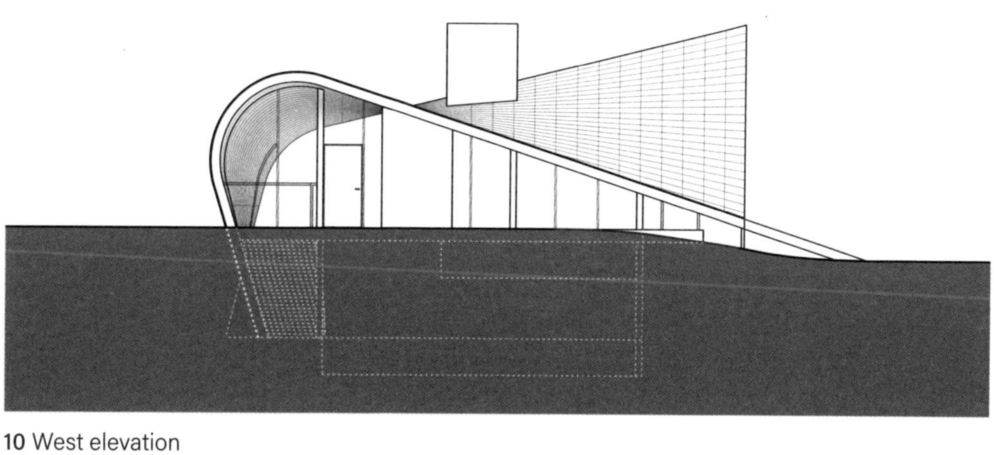

10 West elevation

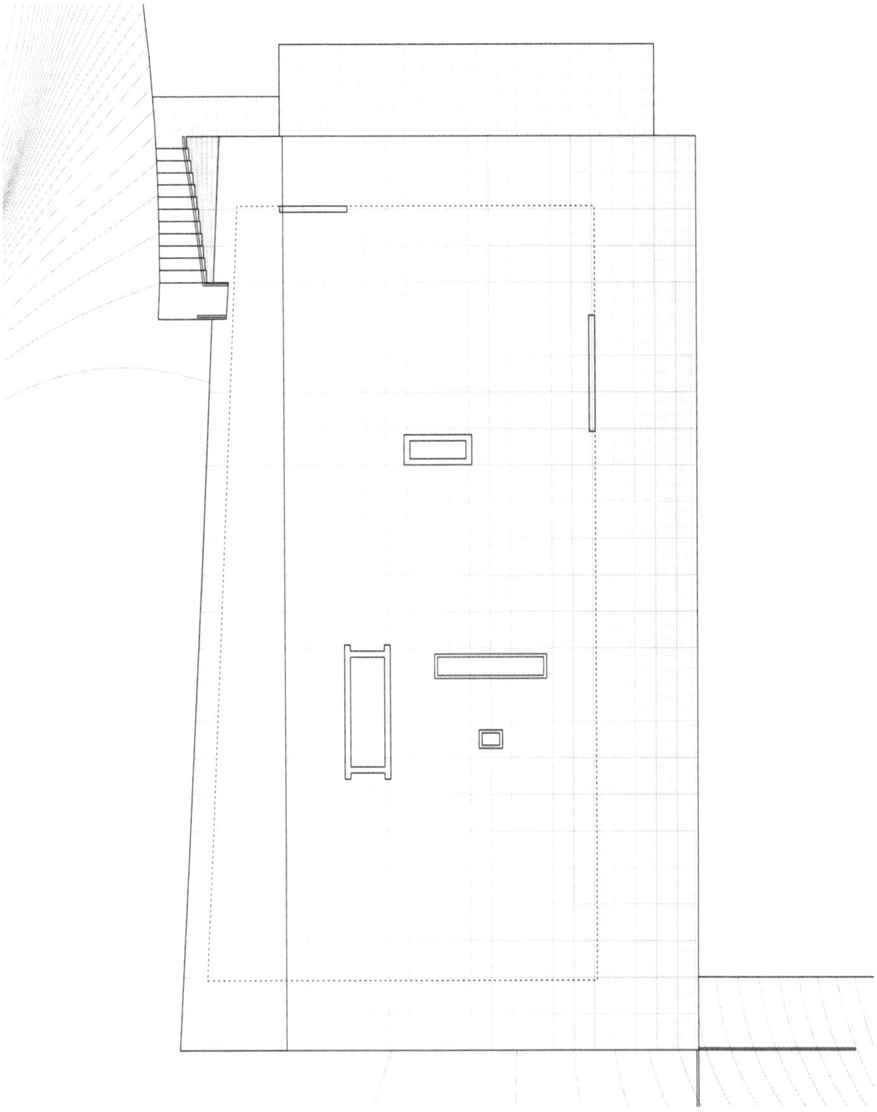

11 Roof plan

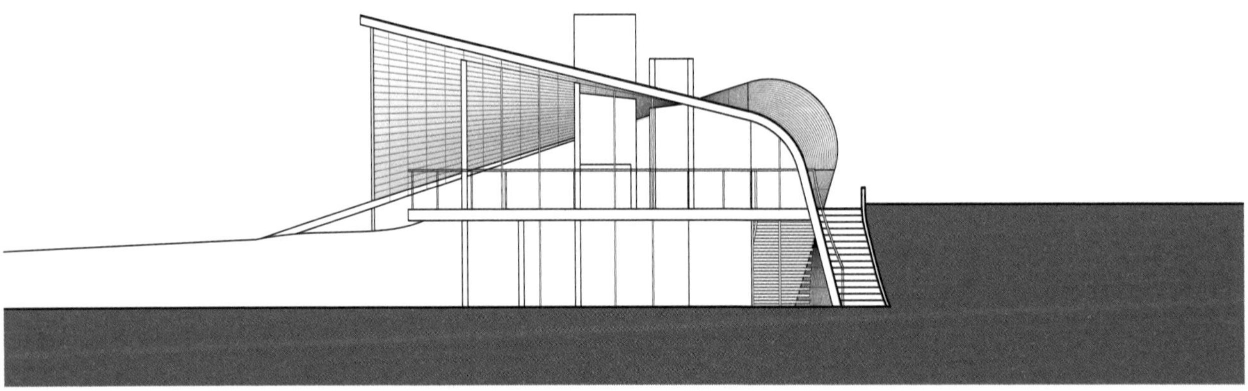

12 East elevation

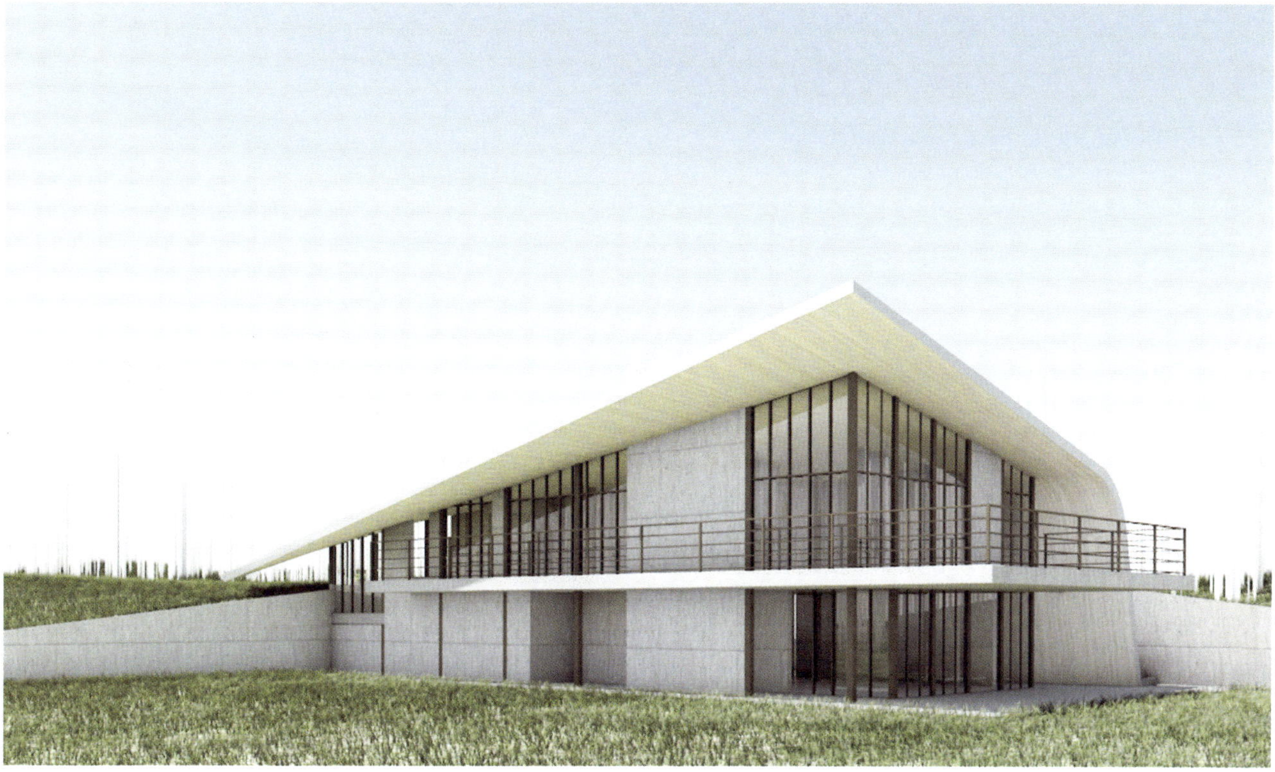

13 Exterior view from northwest

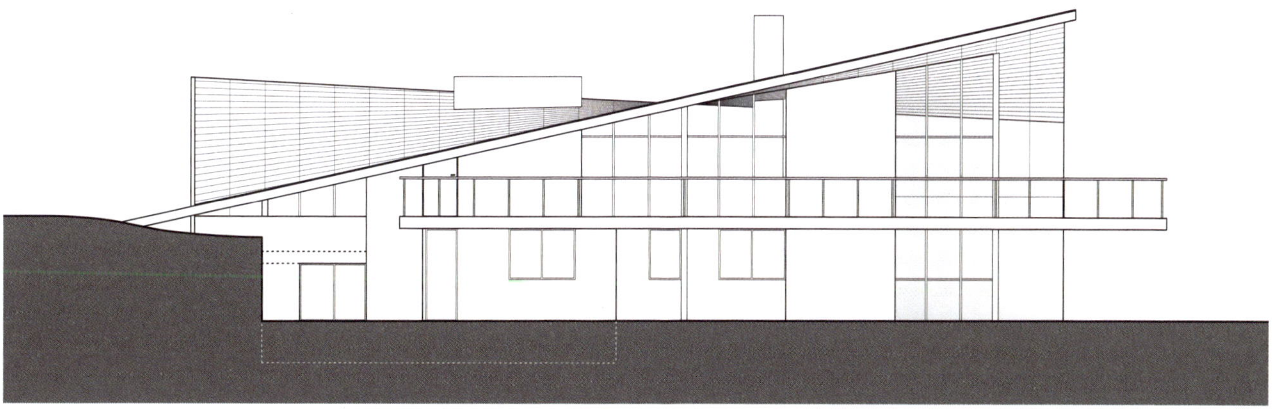

14 North elevation

01 View from the northwest

Wrap Music

Hungarian House of Music Competition
Budapest, Hungary

2014

Seriality, rhythm, texture, and proportion relate to the linguistic and expressionistic characteristics of both music and architecture. These descriptive and metaphorical comparisons are well-worn, yet their applicability endures. Themes of periodicity, repetition, scale, harmonics, global/local conditions, linear and non-linear narratives continue as fruitful topics of investigation for musical and architectural composition alike. In lieu of tonal differentiation, Wrap Music deploys a continuous architectural surface which choreographs a spatial experience as the metaphorical embodiment of the act of musical listening.

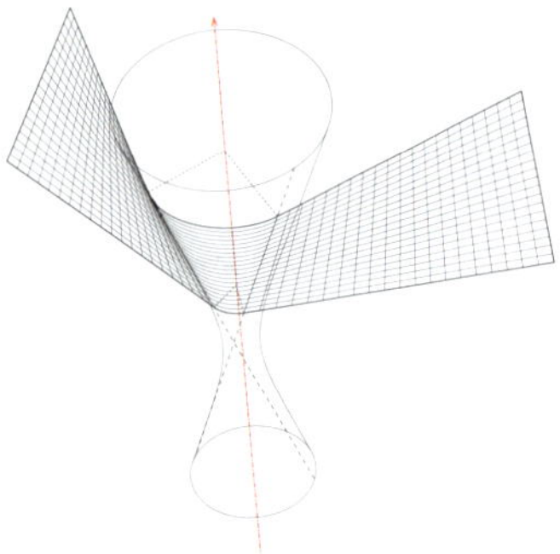

02.1 Projective orthogonal hyperboloid corner: hypars stitched to mirrored generators

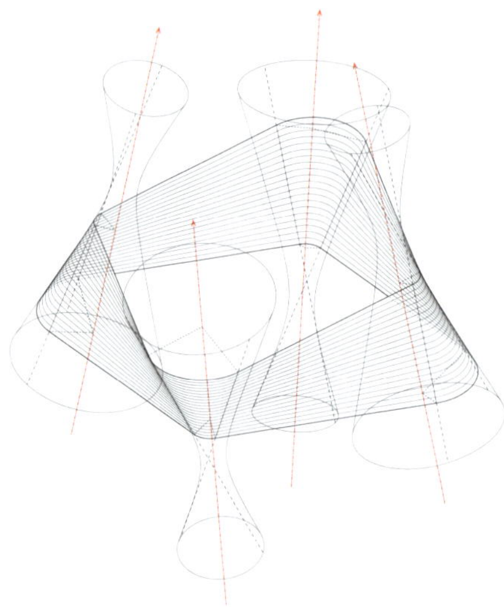

02.2 Full projective orthogonal loop

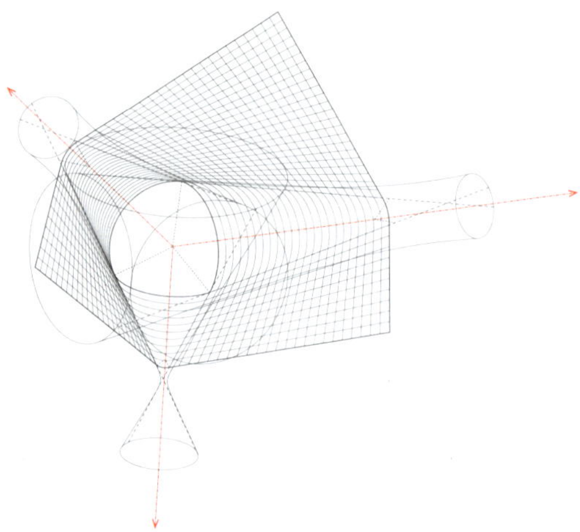

02.3 3-axis projective orthogonal corner (capped with sphere)

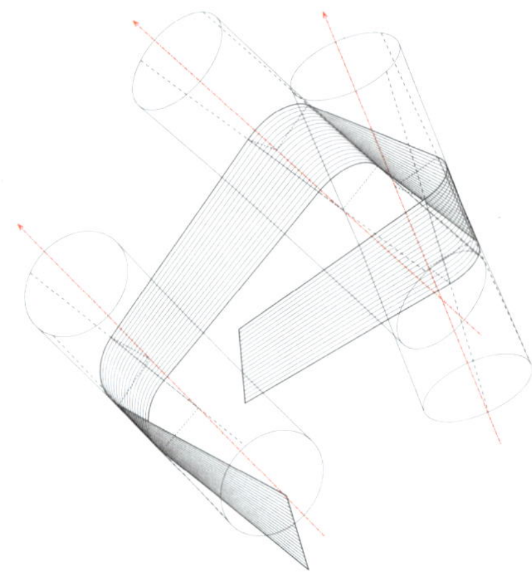

02.4 Non-orthogonal projection (ramping)

03 Musical ribbon

04 Gregorian chant notation

MUSICAL NOTATION

The visual qualities of music in written (indexical) notation resembles a variety of historical analog devices such as music boxes and associated media. Physical artifacts such as punched cylinders and flat coded ribbons embody sequences of discrete data points, allowing calibrated machines to convert these sets of information into melody and song. While sheet music operates as a symbolic representation, the analog music box is the actual artifact whose physical operation determines and produces the specific aural form signified by the visual aesthetic.

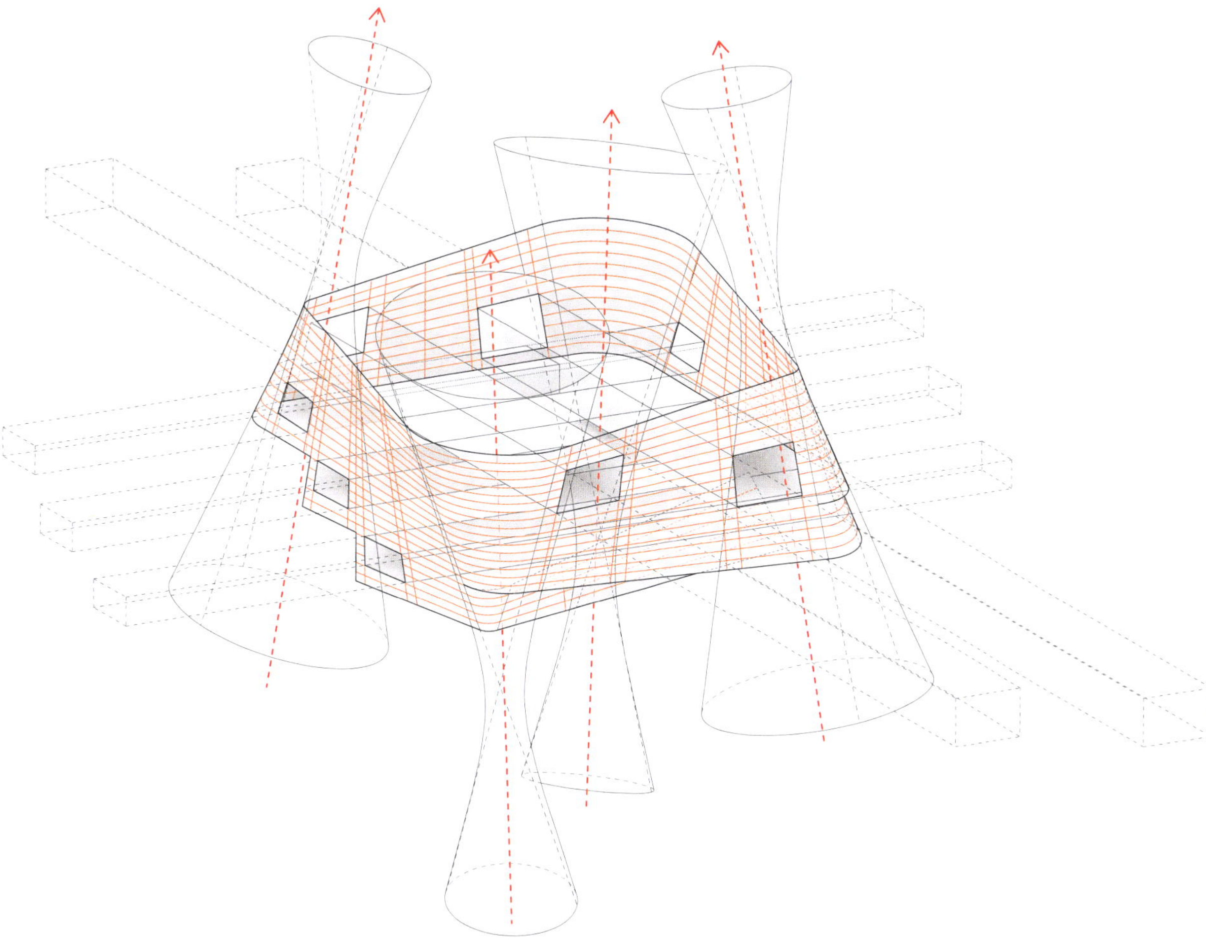

05 Projective relationship of doubly ruled wrapper and interior orthogonal volumes

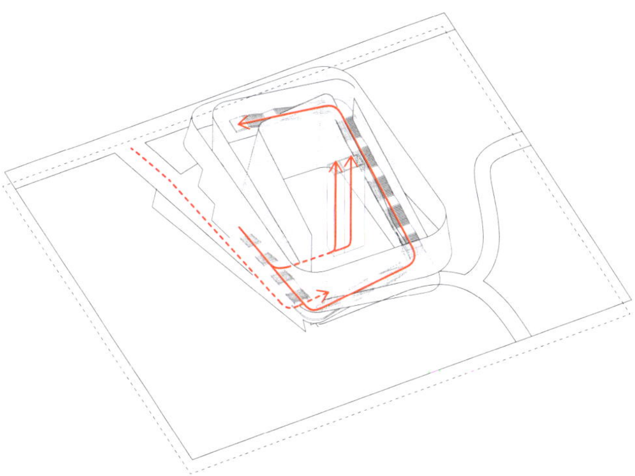

06 Circulation around Grand Promenade and vertical core

INTERIOR ORTHOGONAL ORGANIZATION

For any given hypar surface, there exists a particular projection such that both U and V curve fields of ruling lines produce a two-way grid of parallel lines (This is the view parallel to the surface normal at the hypar saddle). For some hypars, these U and V grid projections are perpendicular, allowing orthogonal planes and volumes to projectively align with the hypar ruling lines. There also exists a unique hyperboloid (of one sheet) which can be stitched in a piece wise continuous manner to any two hypars, enabling the production of a smooth exterior skin composed of many discrete parts. The column grid, vertical walls, and horizontal floors/ceilings which project from the hypar walls comprise the orthogonal armature of Wrap Music's interior spaces.

SITING

From the city, the primary pedestrian approach is from the southeast, with service and loading entrances on the northwest. Due to the compact massing, orientation has little to no effect on solar gain. The small apertures perforating the façade produce a variety of views and lighting conditions at the perimeter. Larger windows exist on the northwest façade to provide views toward the lake.

07 View of main southeast entrance

SPATIAL ORGANIZATION AND CIRCULATION

The interior concept is to provide an extremely rational and dense spatial core inside of which new interactive musical experiences can happen. The inflection and nesting of the hypar-hyperboloid composite surfaces produces a thick zone of sectional continuity and circulation wrapped around the more densely packed core of galleries and museum spaces. This thick and continuous perimeter allows one to partake in dynamic sectional overlooks as it allows patrons to recalibrate their relationship to the exterior.

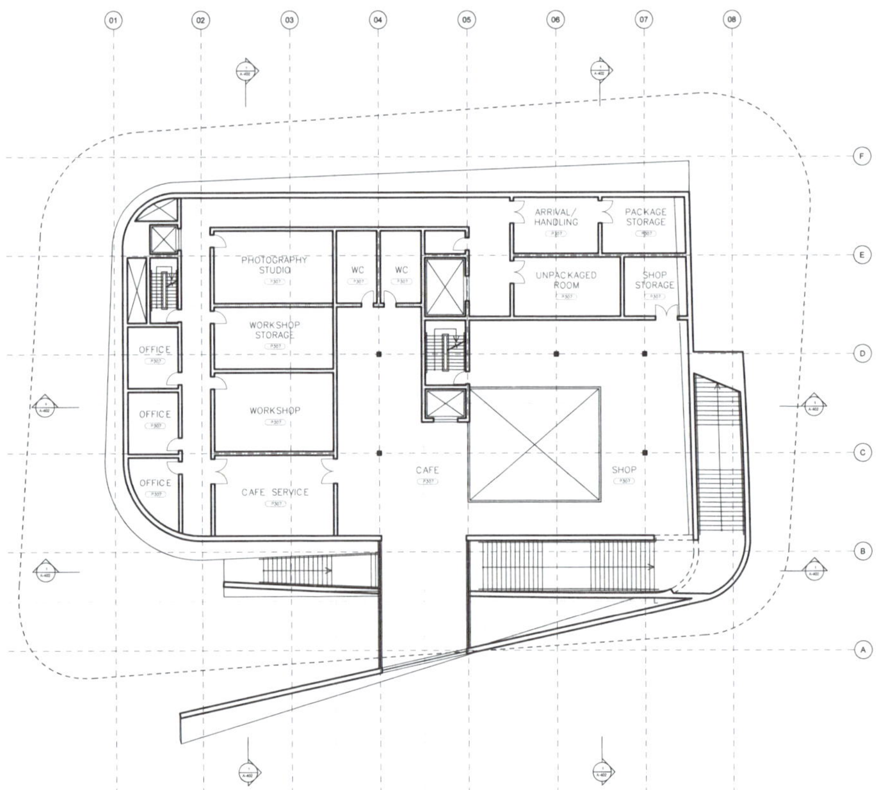

08 Second floor plan (offices, gift shop and café)

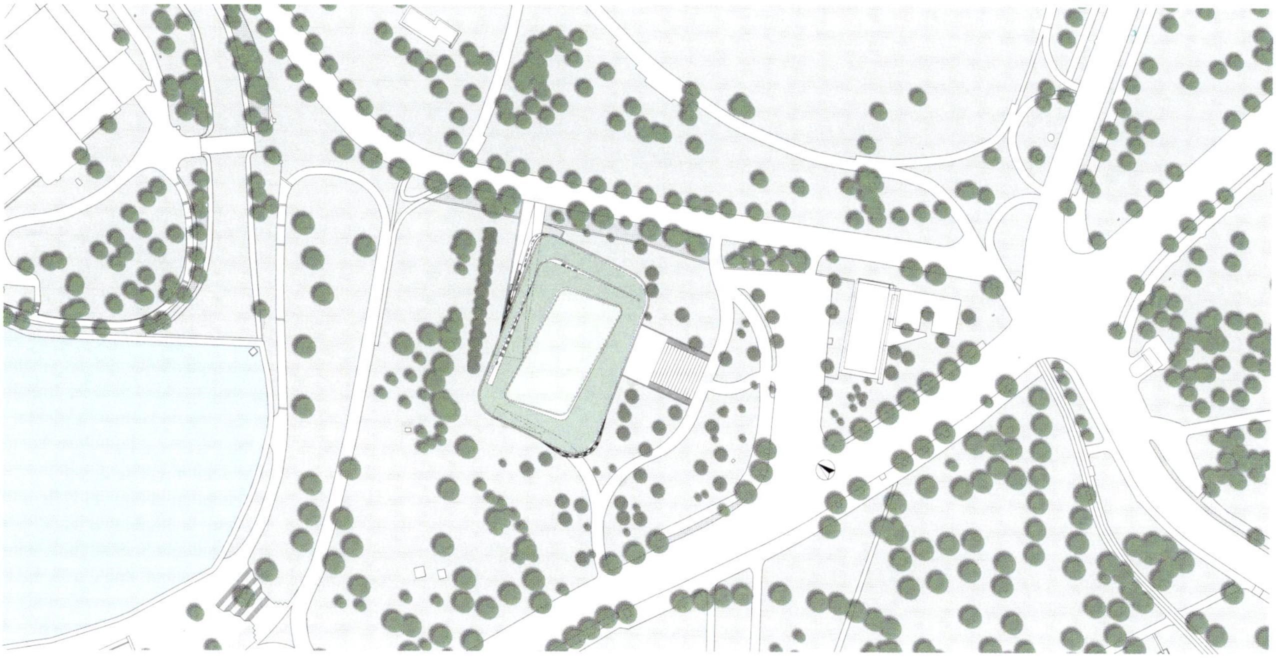

09 Site plan

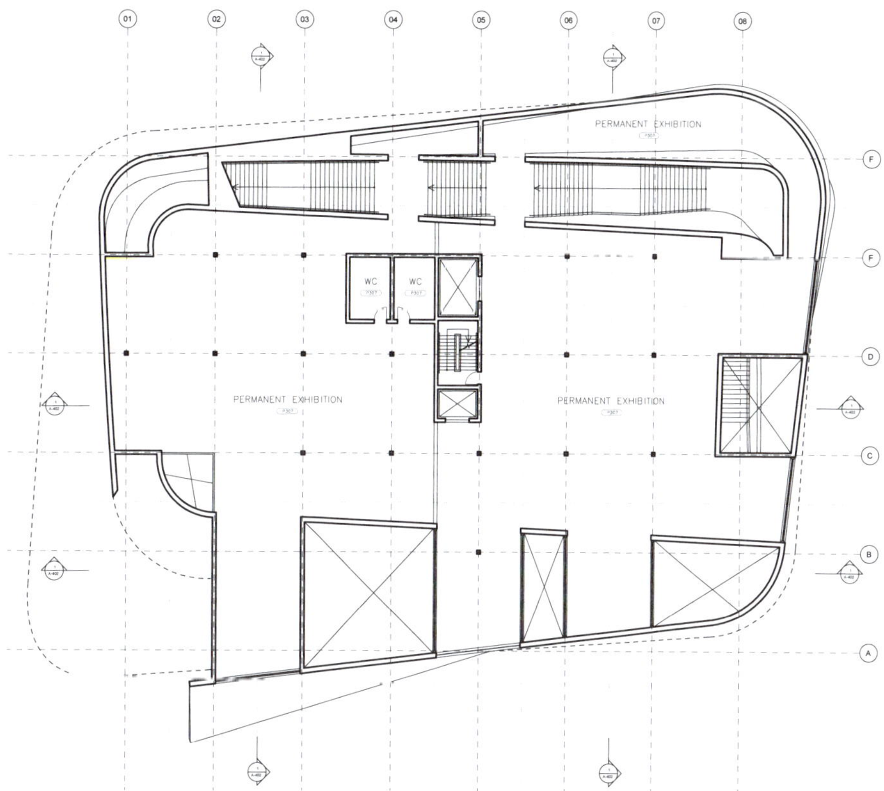

10 Third floor plan (main galleries and programmed bridges)

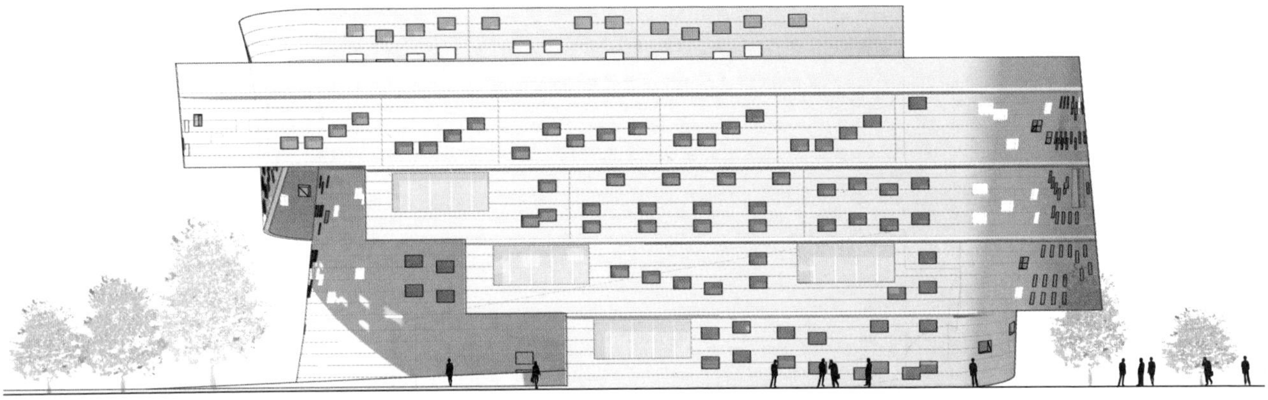

11 West elevation

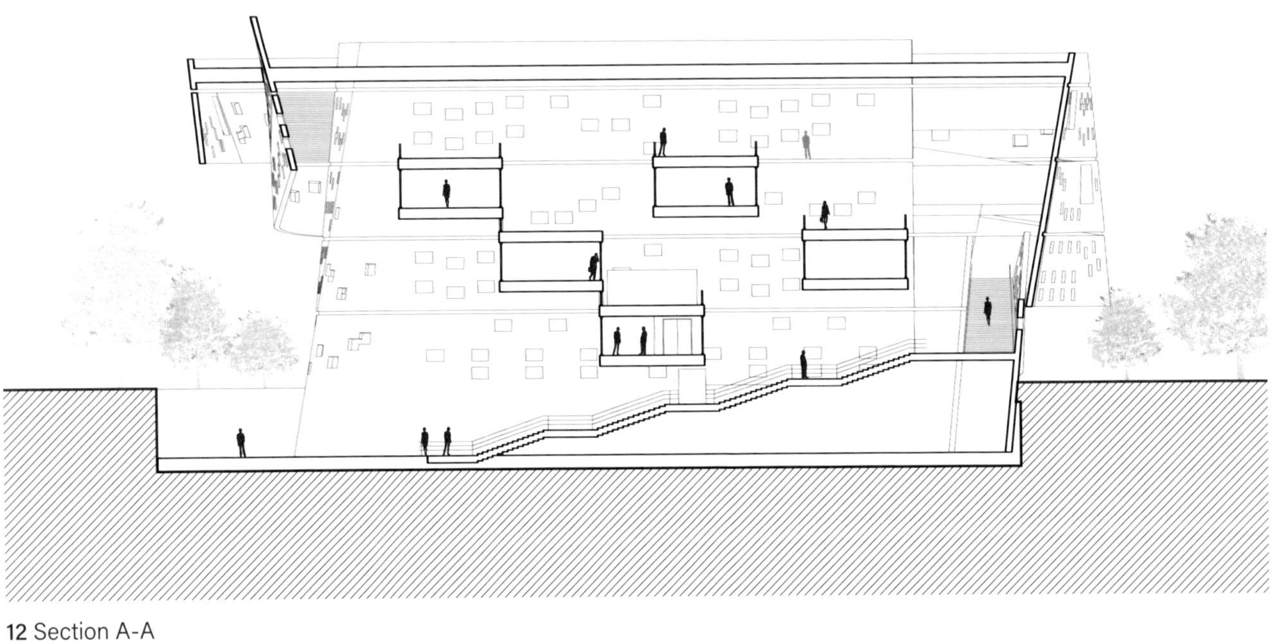

12 Section A-A

OCCUPIABLE POCHÉ

The main promenade exists between the exterior skin and an interior façade wrapped around the galleries. Programmed "bridges" extrude to connect these two surfaces, didactically exhibiting the projective relationship of the orthognal volumes with the hypars. These bridges mark locations within the promenade, providing means of wayfinding while producing sectional overlaps and visual access between various areas of the museum.

13 Museum circulation in thick zone between interior and exterior

14 Overlooking promenade and other programmed bridges

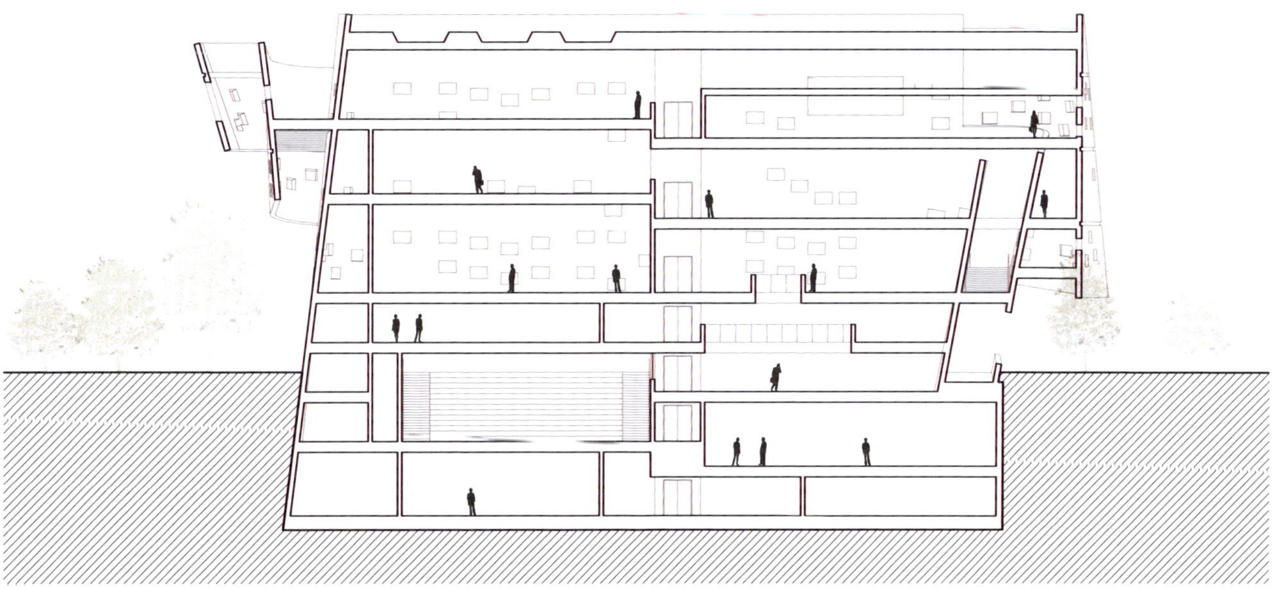

15 Section B-B

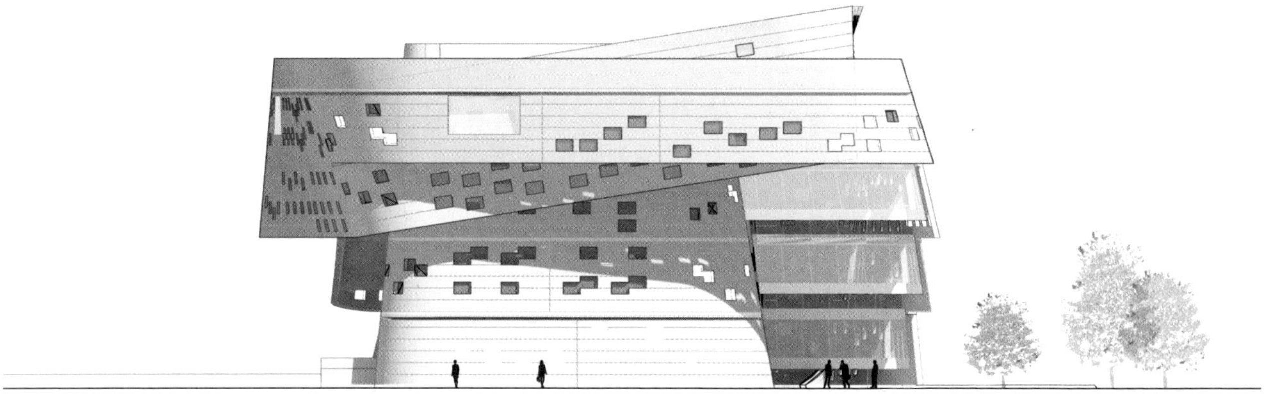

16 North elevation

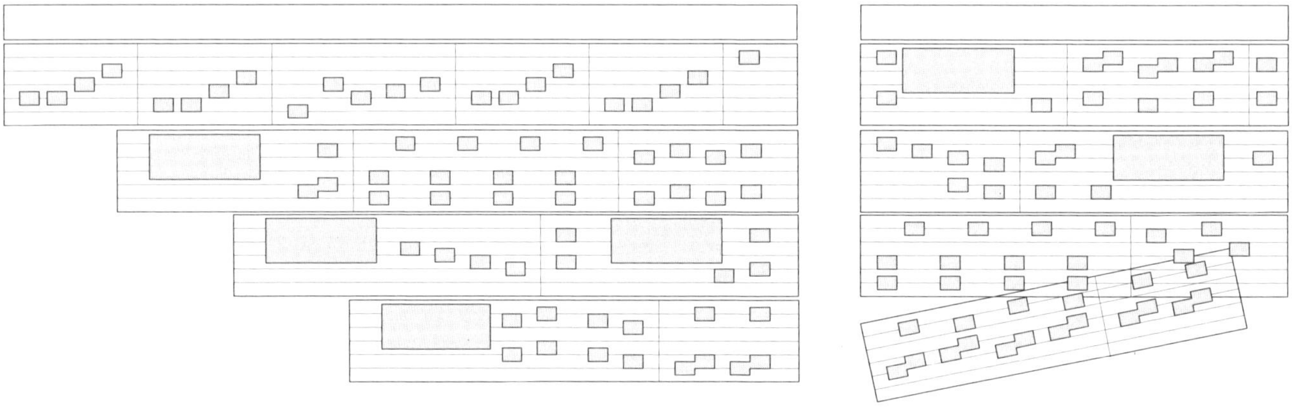

17 Elevations of the discrete hypar surfaces of the exterior wrapper

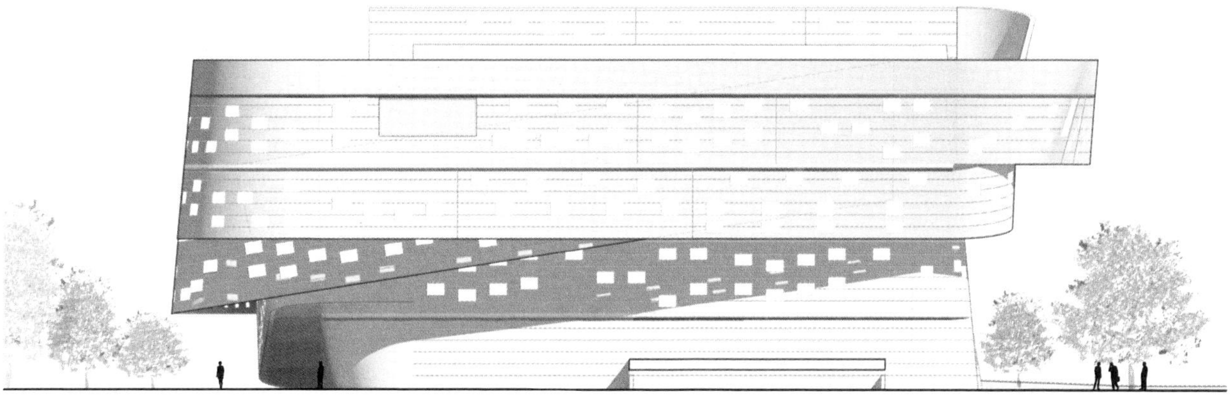

18 East elevation

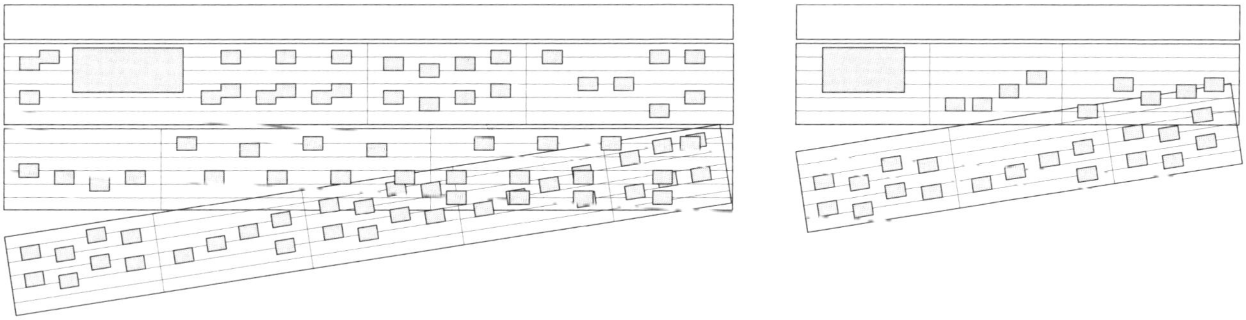

Magnetic Z

ART OMI
Ghent, New York
2020

Magnetic Z is a constructed study and composition of geodesic planking behavior. It is comprised of two primary surfaces which exhibit opposing formal properties—curved vs. planar, high resolution vs. low resolution, continuous vs. discrete. These surfaces bound a figural promenade of ramp and stairs, which acts as a spatial hinge in the landscape, providing new vantages of the visitor's surroundings, a sense of movement and play, and a respite from the elements. The title alludes to the phenomenon of magnetic north, which deviates from true geographic north. In this case, the leaning axes of the outer conical surface and the inner frustum tower deviate from a true vertical orientation, otherwise known as the z-axis.

01

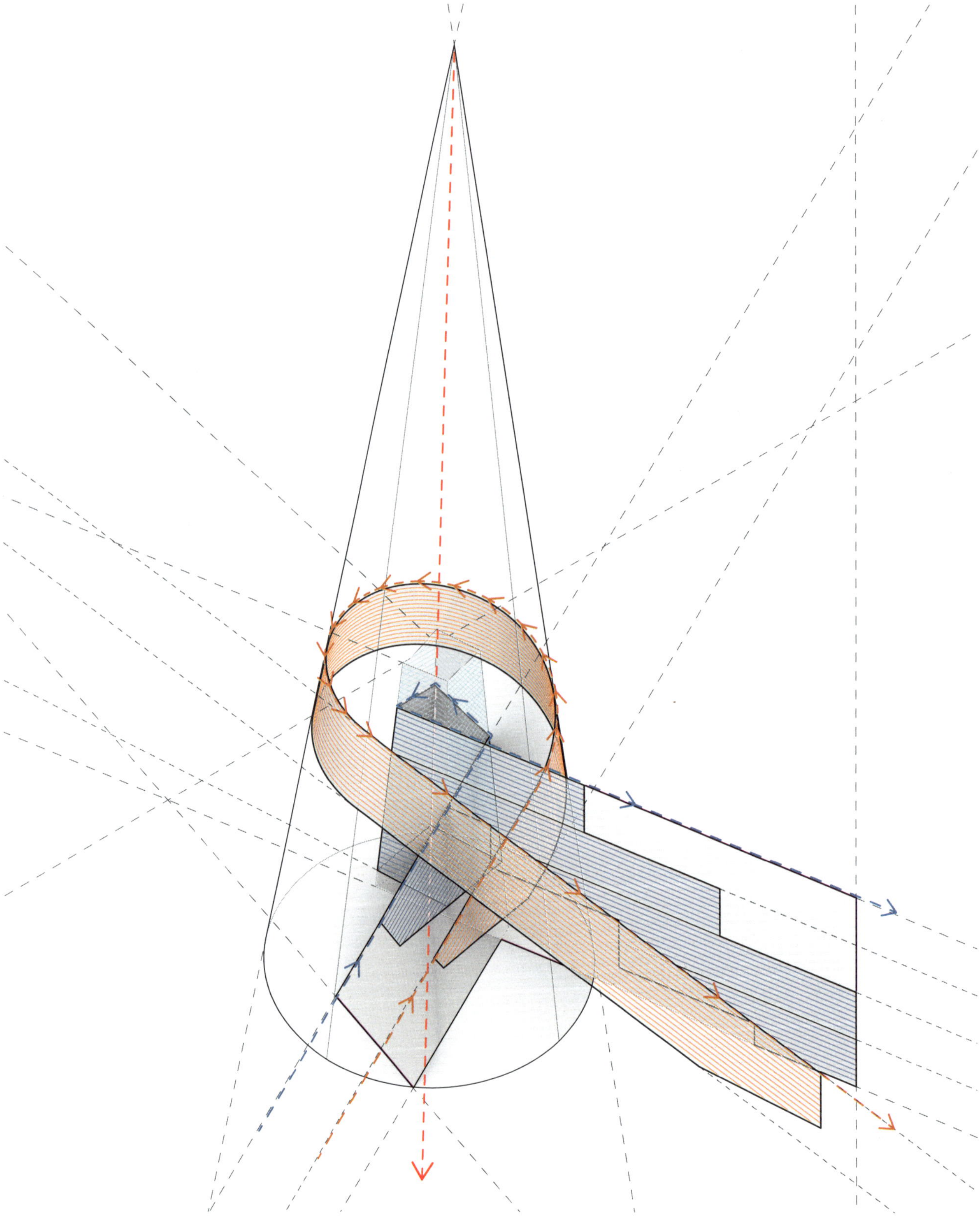

02 Outer and inner geodesic ribbons operate at different resolutions–high and low, respectively

HIGH-RES/LOW-RES

The leaning cone is positioned tangent to both plumb planes of the outer guard walls (orange) of the ramp and stair–i.e. two of the ruling line generators of the cone lie in these planes. The profile angle of the cone is calibrated such that its curving geodesic lines are tangent and continuous with the sloping planks of the ramp wall and the sloping planks of the stair wall.

The plank orientation of the inner (blue) surface is also aligned with the slope of the stair at one end. As the planks wrap around the frustum, the plank lines only change direction at each angular fold, resulting in significantly less re-orientation than the continuously changing conical geodesics. After three discrete folds around the frustum, the geodesic lines of the blue surface are not parallel with the ramp (unlike the cone). They slope up to the right instead of down (**04**). To acknowledge the ramp slope in a different way, the silhouette of the blue wall steps down in a sawtooth manner.

Whereas the geodesic behavior on the cone is continuous and high-resolution, the discrete angular turns of the frustum and the resulting stepped wall profile represent low-resolution manifestations.

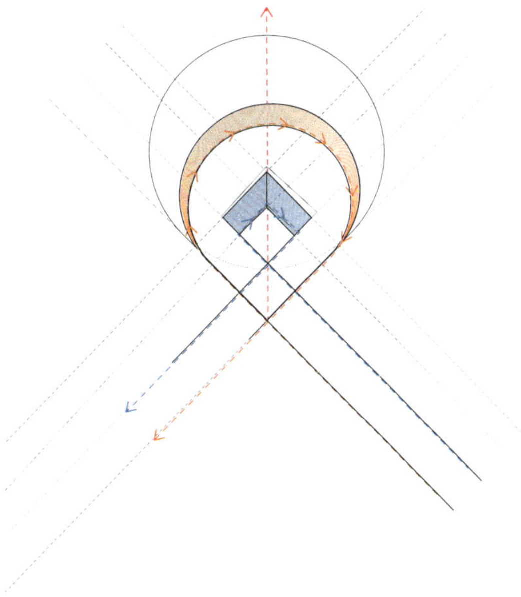

03 Plan diagram

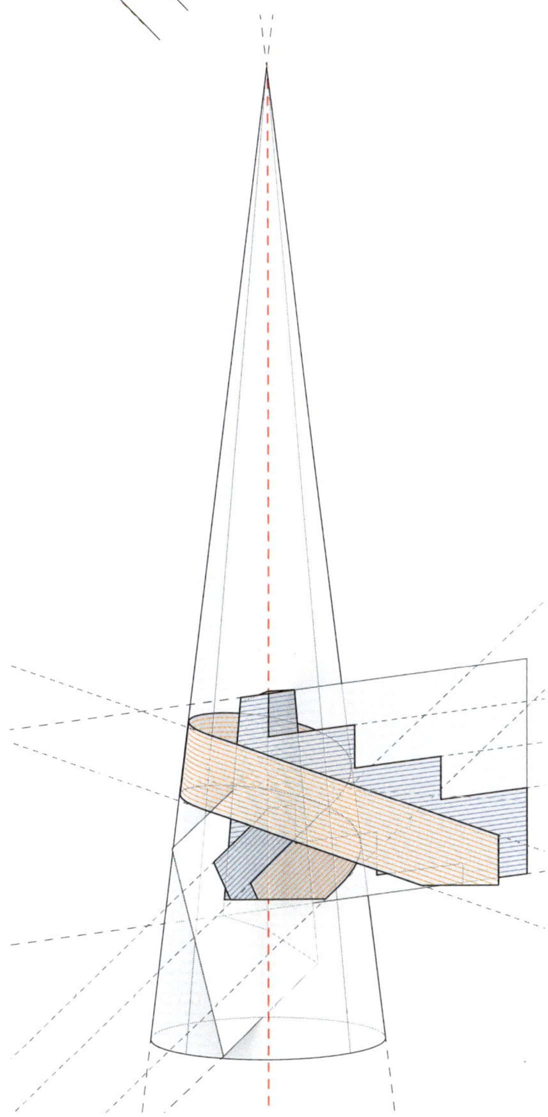

04 Elevation diagram

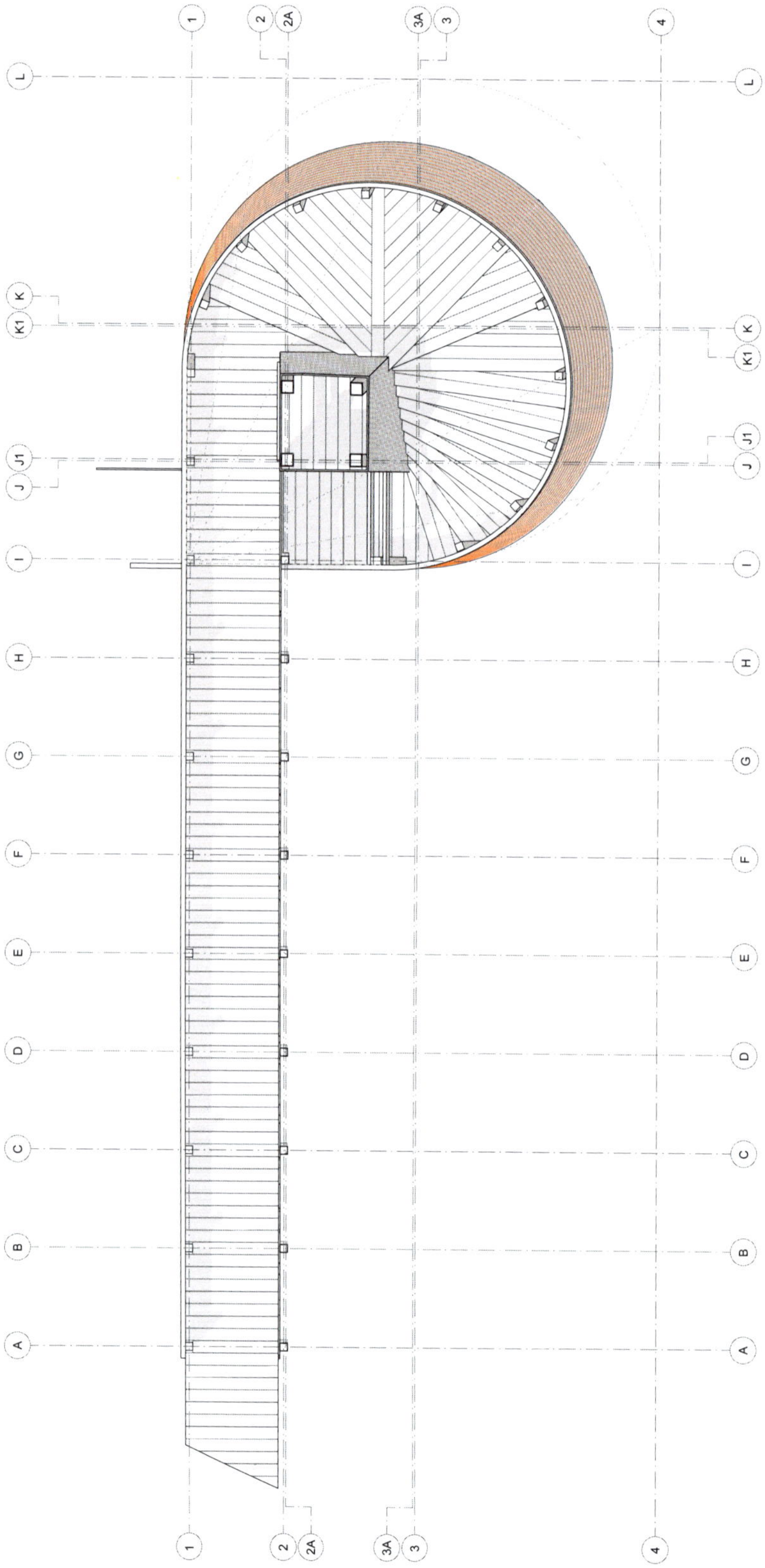

05 Plan

GEOMETRY AND STRUCTURE

The geometries of the planar frustum and the cone are calibrated to facilitate the construction of both. The most oblique 6"x6" corner post of the frustum is the central axis of the leaning cone. This allows the tapered cantilever assemblies to pivot around this axis to support the elevated deck while accurately structuring the cone.

06

RULING LINE NAILERS

The centerline of 4"x4" posts are precisely positioned along the ruling lines of the cone. These posts serve as nailers for the steam bent pine boards which comprise the conical surface.

07

PLANAR TRANSITION

The curving geodesic plank surface of the cone transitions to the plane of the straight stair guard wall. The (taller) 4"x4" post where this tangency occurs marks the last ruling line generator which points to the (unbuilt) apex of the cone high above (**09, 14**). In plan projection, the apex is located at the intersection of the outer edges of the ramp and straight stair (**05**).

08

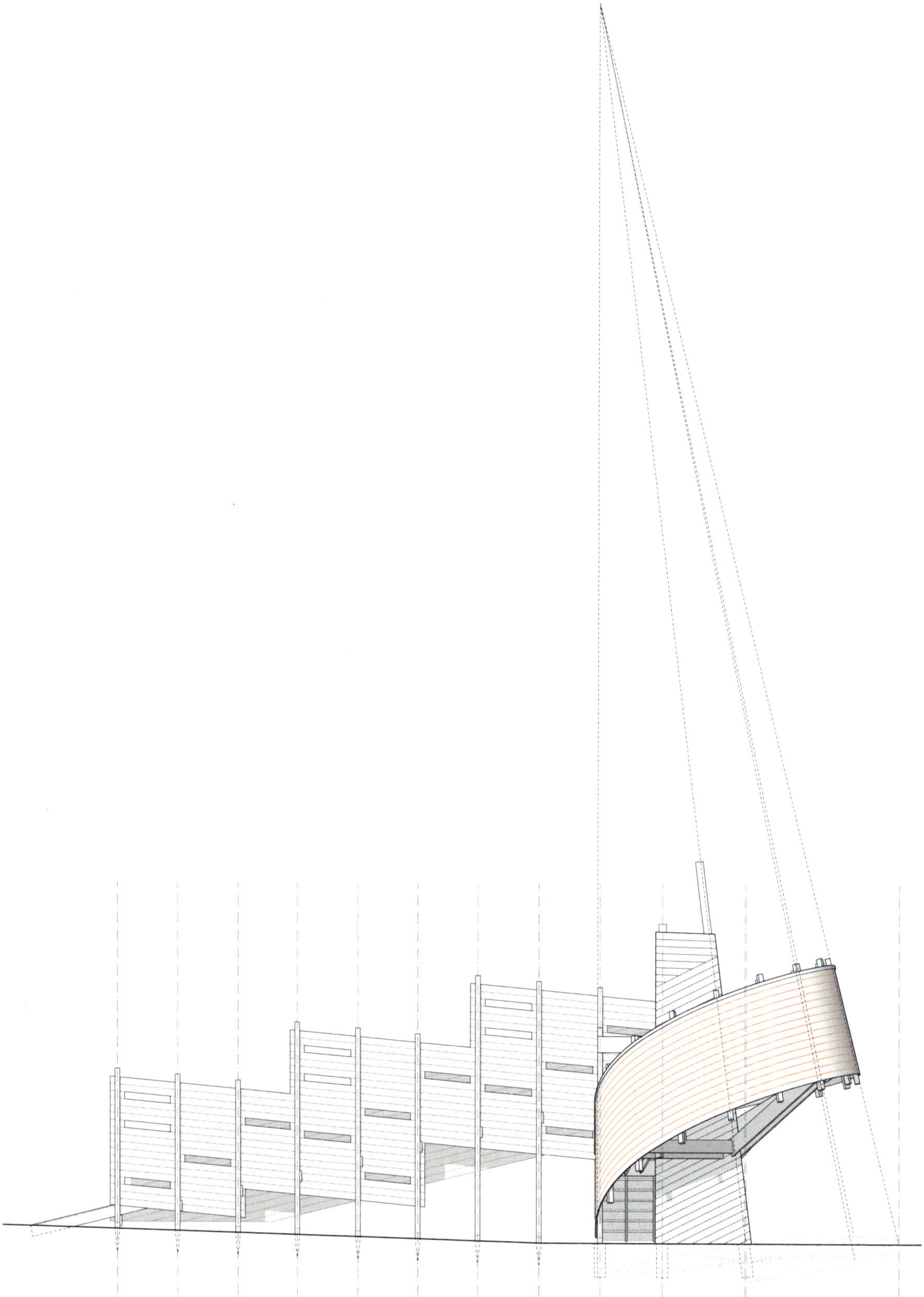

09 Elevation

10

11

PERIPATETIC LOOP

Numerous walking paths lead vistors to various pieces and installations in the Art Omi sculpture and architecture parks. Both ramp and stair of Magnetic Z are aligned deliberately with two paths, making its peripatetic loop of vertical circulation part of the curatorial circuit of the landscape.

12

13 Ramp

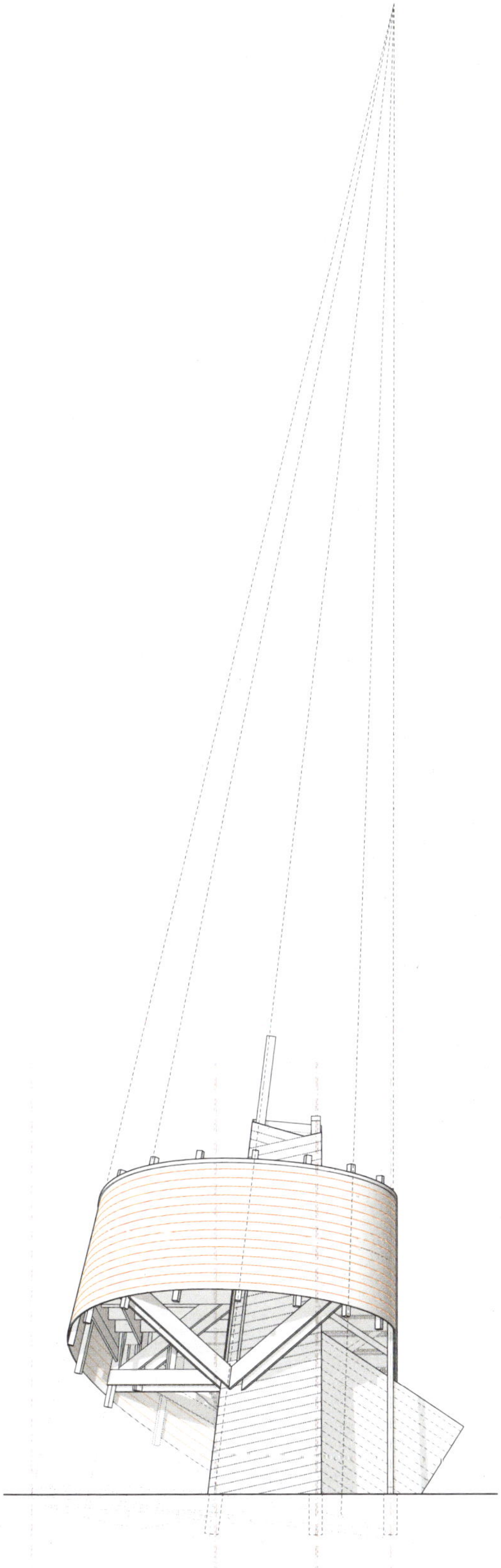

14 Elevation

15 Staircase

Circumvolute_00

2021

Circumvolute_00 deploys methods of geodesic planking to produce a continuous two-sided closed loop ribbon, wrapping around two host volumes–a cylinder and a tetrahedron. The ribbon is partially coincident with each of these volumes before migrating to the other in an endless cycle. It serves as a referent "Urform", a vehicle to explore dialectics that are constantly present in architecture–curvilinear/planar, high-res/low-res, continuous/discrete. The scalability of the form and its technique allow it to serve as a geometric springboard for other architectural explorations, projects, and processes. It models both material and geometric behaviors, each subject to further design differentiation.

01

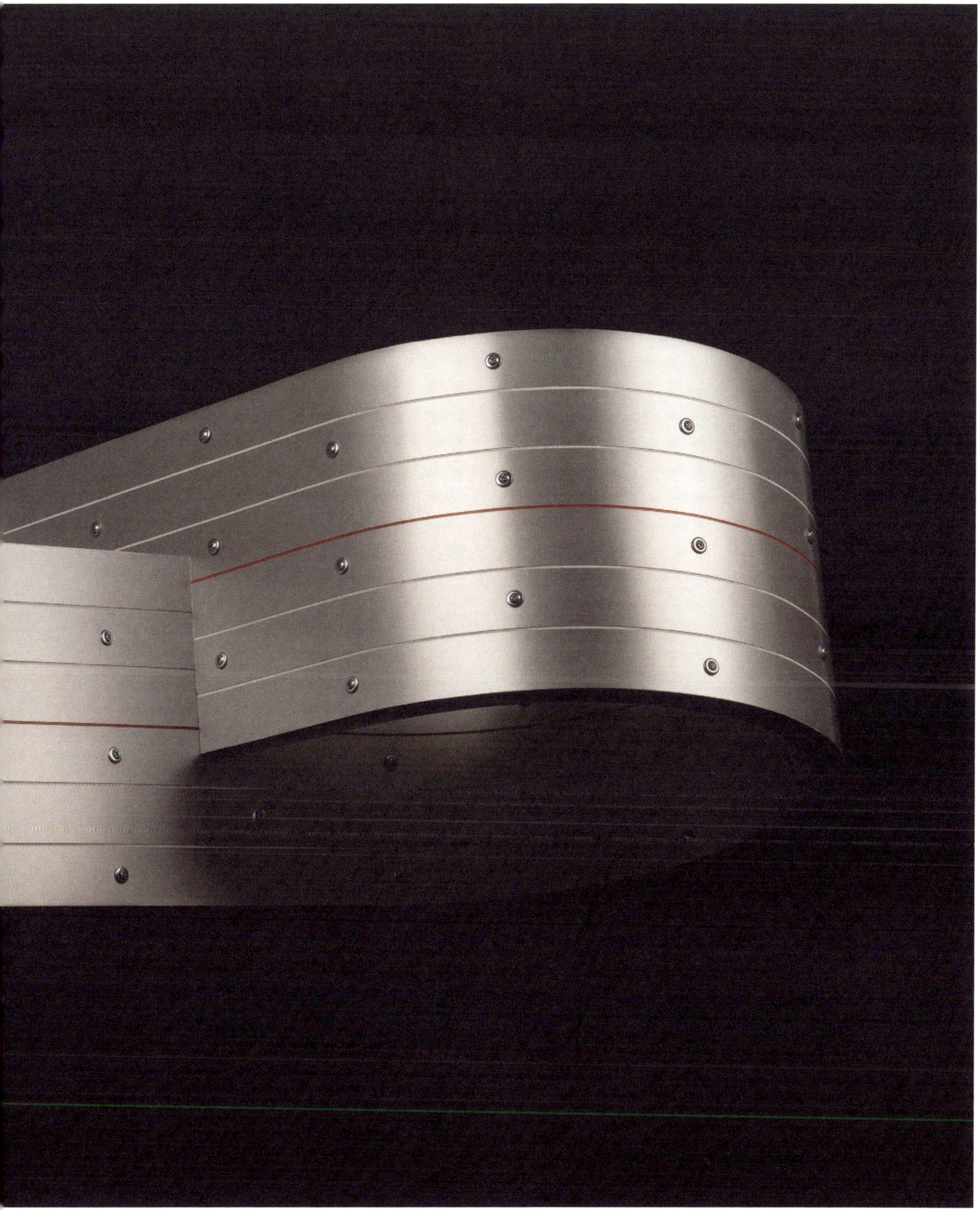

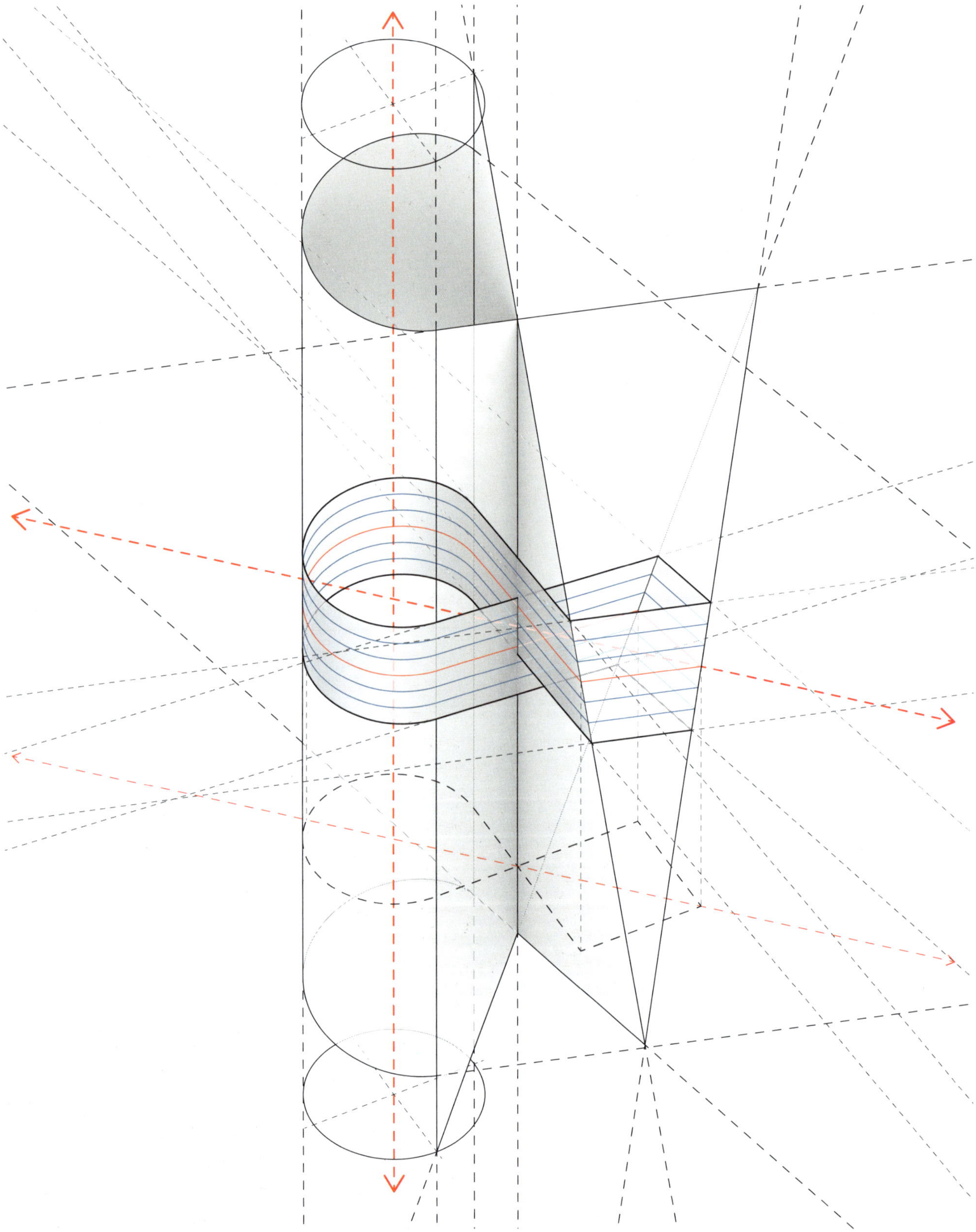

02 Continuous figure eight geodesic ribbon turning around host volumes

EQUAL AND OPPOSITE

The behavior of any geodesic line moving across a surface depends on its initial orientation and the curvature of the surface. The non-zero curvature of the cylinder is constant, causing the geodesic to continuously bend into a helical form. For the tetrahedron, the zero curvature of each plane dictates that the only change in direction of the geodesic occurs at the three discrete dihedral folds. Despite their geometric differences, the cylinder and the tetrahedron are calibrated to "turn" the geodeisc ribbon in space in equal and opposite directions, facilitating the closed loop.

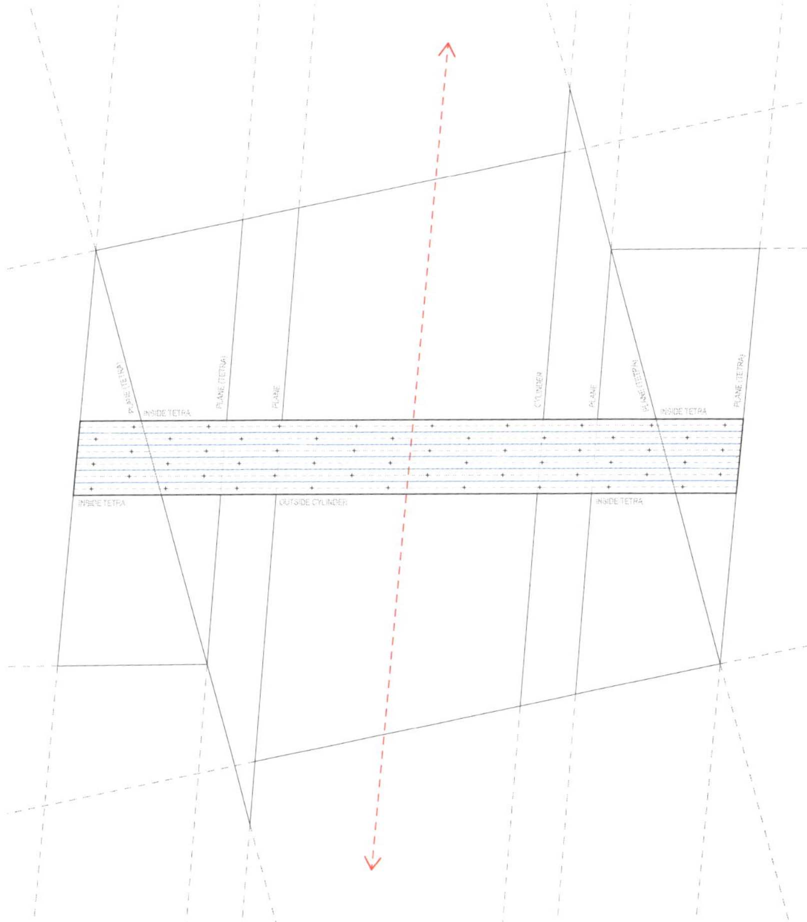

03 Developed elevation and bolt pattern

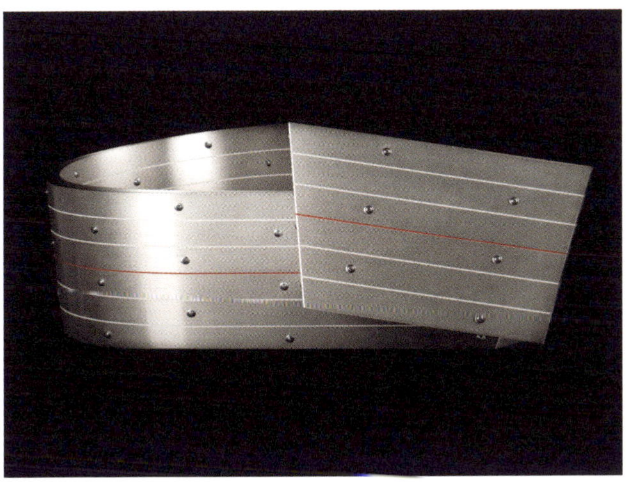

04

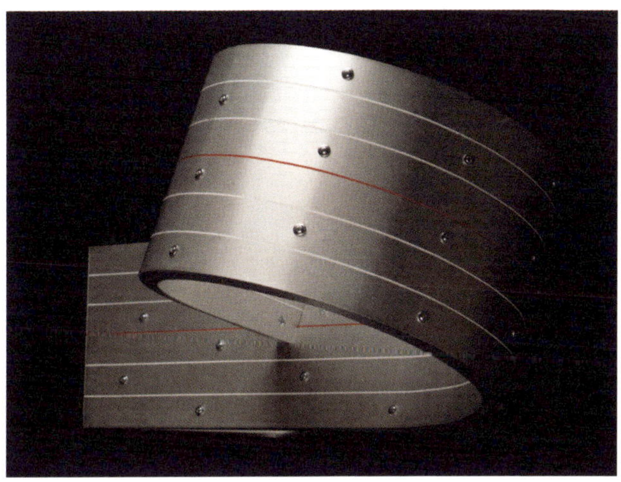

05

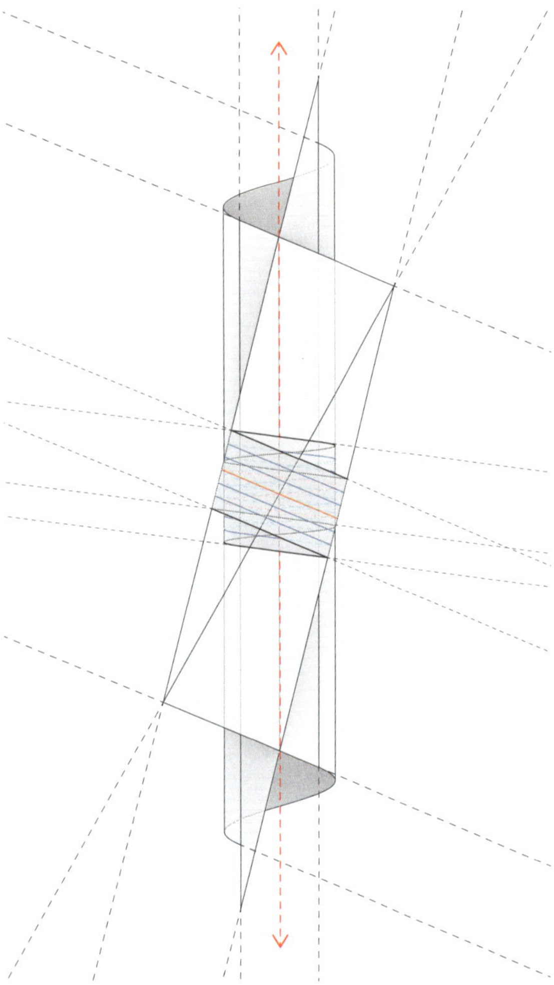

06 Elevation 01

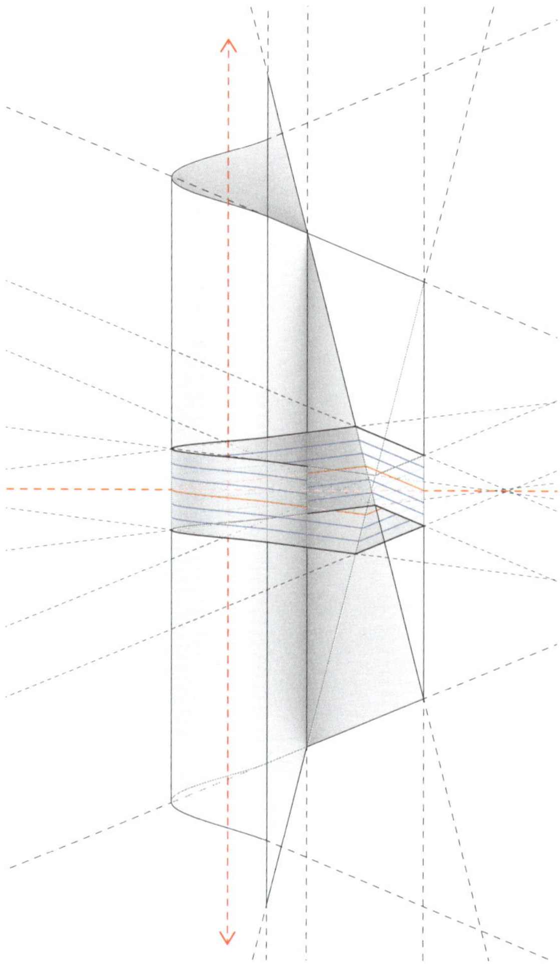

07 Elevation 02

08 Fabrication

CONTINUOUS AND DISCRETE

Because of its constant non-zero curvature, the cylinder turns the geodesic lines continuously into helices. The tetrahedron must taper upward in one (plan) axis and downward in the perpendicular (plan) axis to counteract (in three discrete folds) the spiraling disposition of the cylindrical geodesics.

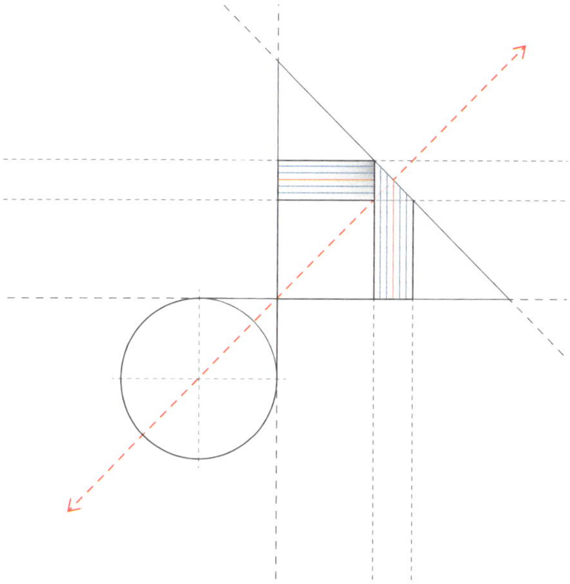

09 Plan

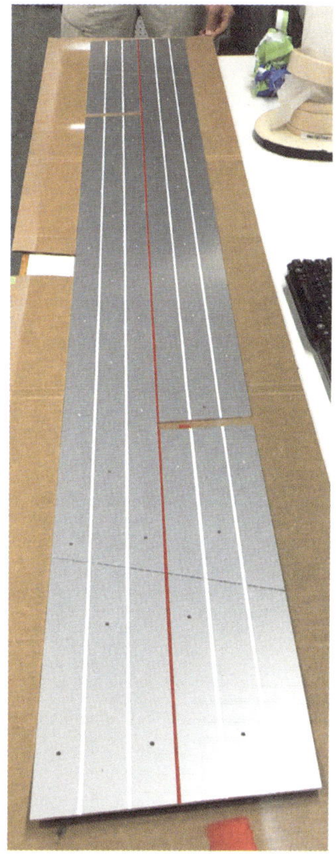

10 Developed sheet

MATERIALITY AND CONSTRUCTION

The double-sided ribbon is made of two 1/16″ aluminum sheets—measuring approximately 10″ x 94″—scored, drilled, and cut on a large-format Zund cutter. Though its plane figures are trapezoidal, the dihedral angle of the 3/4″ plywood substructure is 90°, facilitating fabrication. Using techniques of geodesic planking, the continuous strips are curved, folded, and fastened to the plywood substructure, producing the double-sided closed loop form. The staggered bolt lines call out the ruling lines of the cylinder.

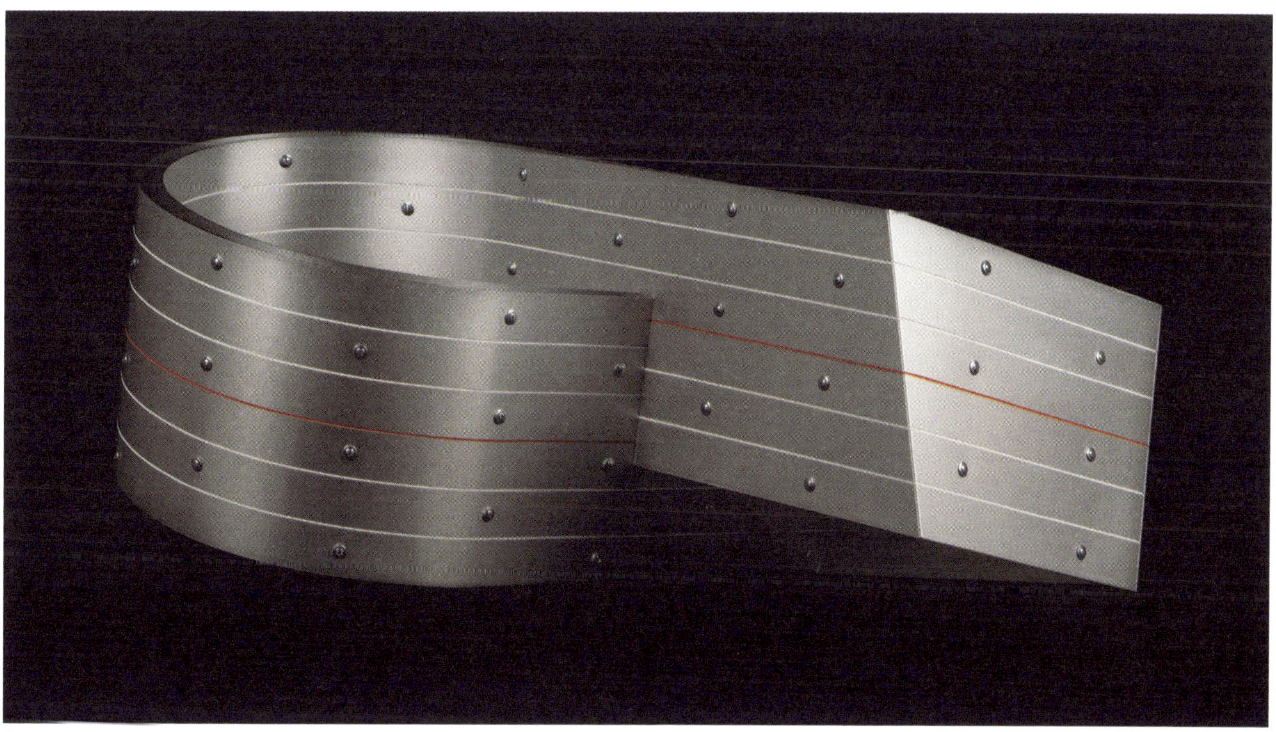

11

01 Street view

Geodesic Garage
2022

Surface and circulatory continuity is arguably more important for parking garages than other architectural types. While helical guard rails are commonly used in the vertical circulation of many parking garages, Geodesic Garage uses the technique of planar geodesic folding to extend this logic to the remaining majority of the building. The geometric behavior of the planar folds requires a typological mutation of typical garage organizations while also producing the serrated aesthetic of its exterior. A typical one-way up, one-way down double helix ramp system unfurls into an oscillating A-B-A–B sequence of layered parking surfaces, whereby each geodesic guardrail inflects to accomodate geometric and programmatic requirements.

PLANAR GEODESICS

Geodesic planking typically refers to how a ribbon behaves across a curved developable surface. Planar ribbons folded across successive oblique lines manifest similar behavior of redirection in three-dimensional space, abeit in a less continuous manner. Exhibiting this low-resolution geodesic behavior, the normal orientation and direction of extrusion predictably changes across each discrete fold. The desired plan angle and elevational slope determine a unique fold line for each turn. Cones revolved at specific locations serve as auxiliary geometries in the construction and determination of the fold lines (**04**).

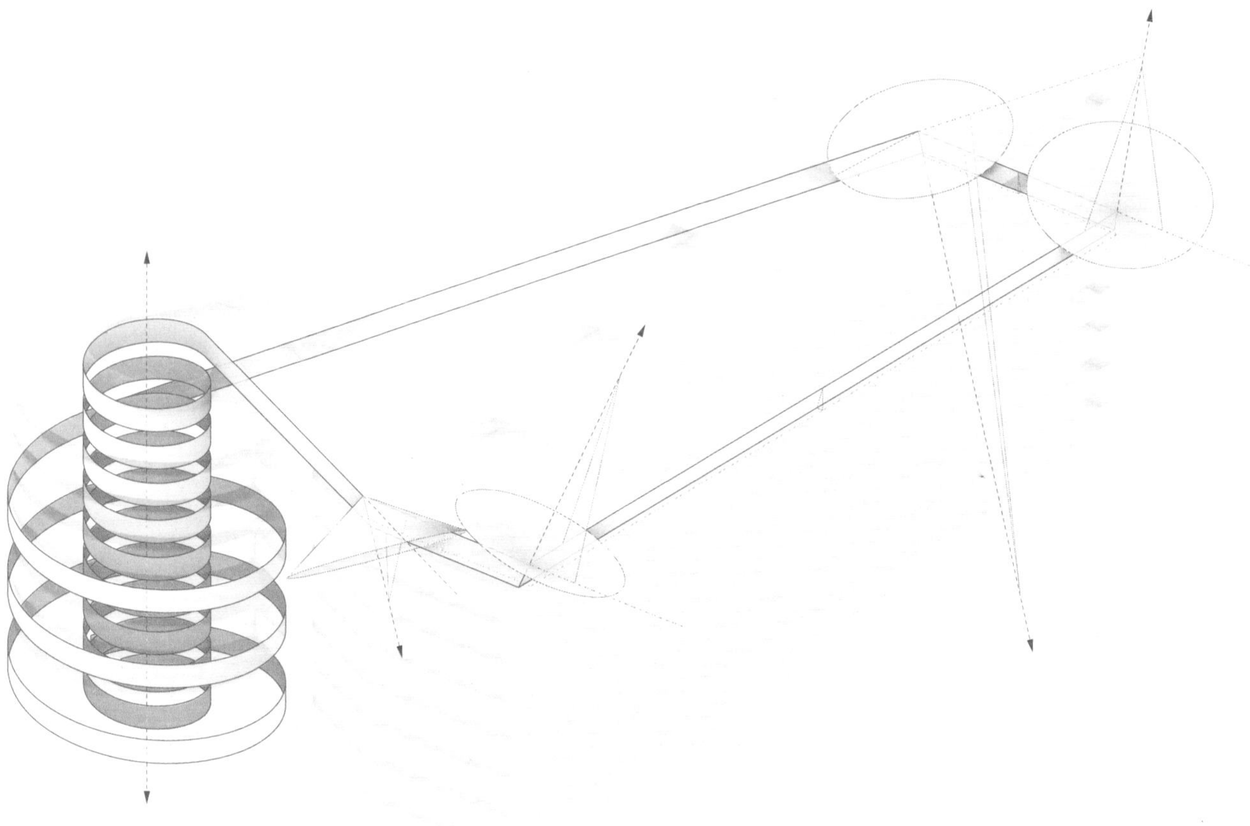

02 Continuous geodesic ribbon, curved and planar

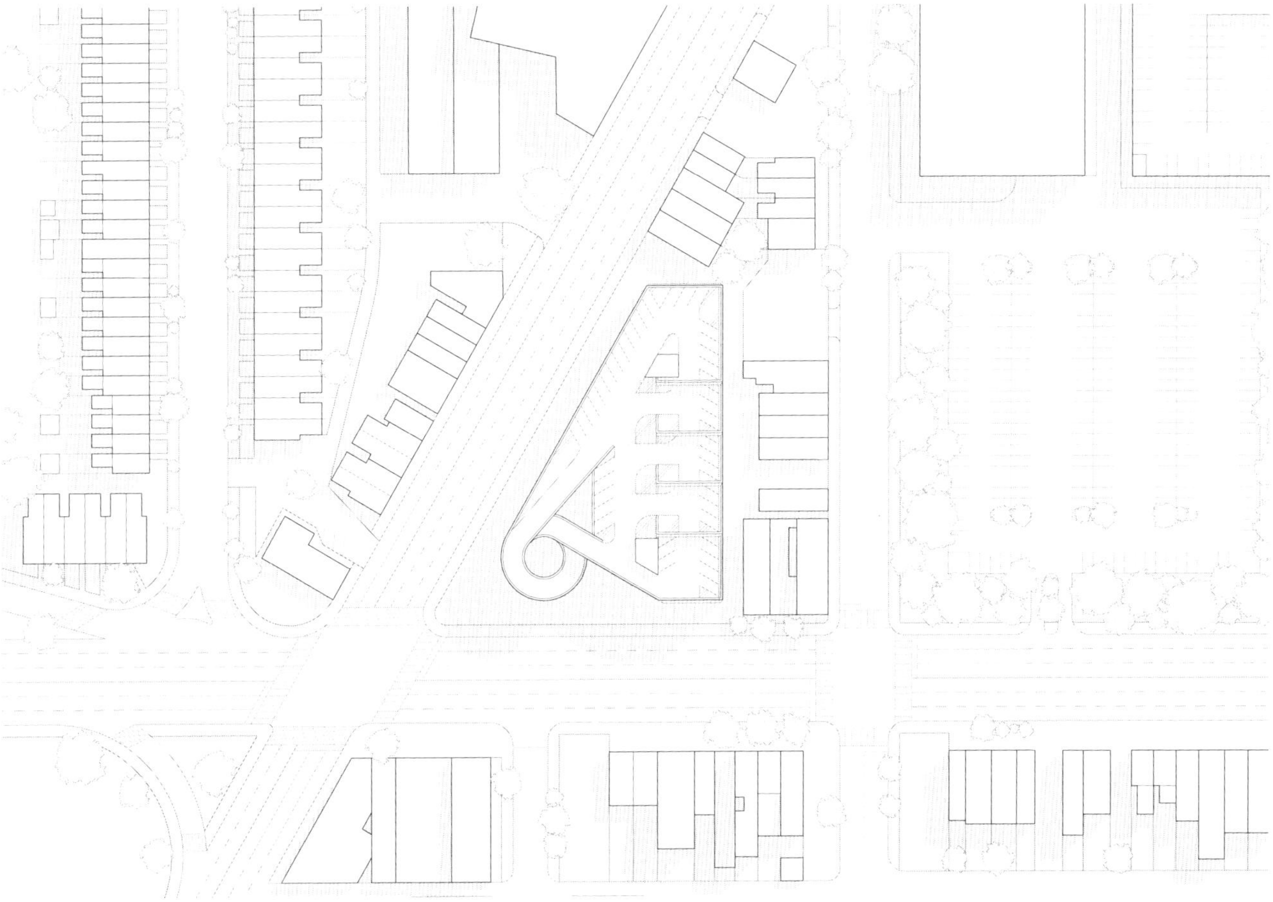

03 Site plan

SITING

The 60° angle of the site is well suited to prominently exhibit the helical ramps at the major street intersection (**01**). Connecting bridges peel away from the ramps and spread into broader parking surfaces which are staggered and layered. The technique of planar geodesics shapes the guard rails and allows the garage to fill the trapezoidal site.

04 Fold line construction

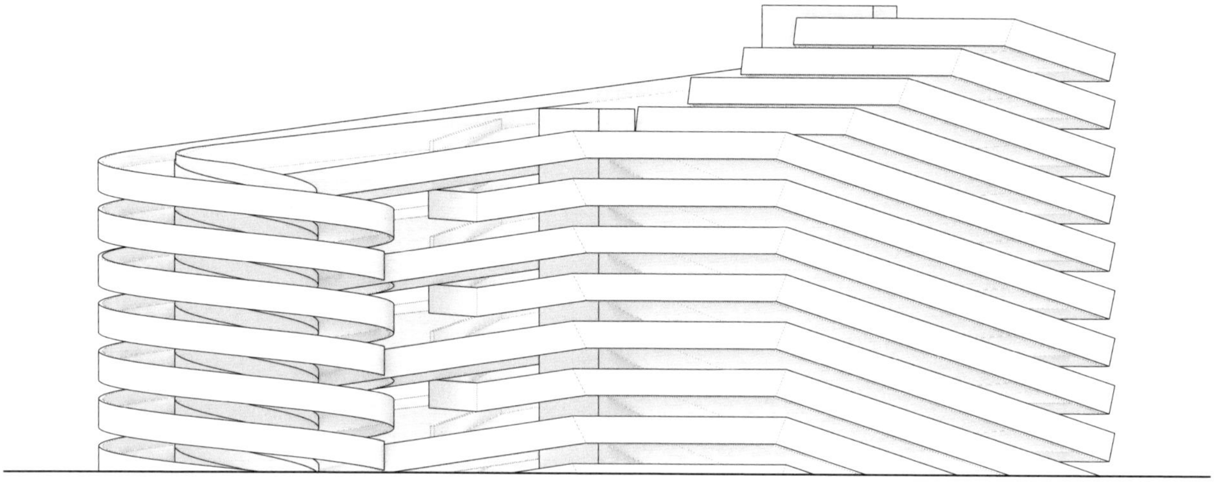

06 Elevation

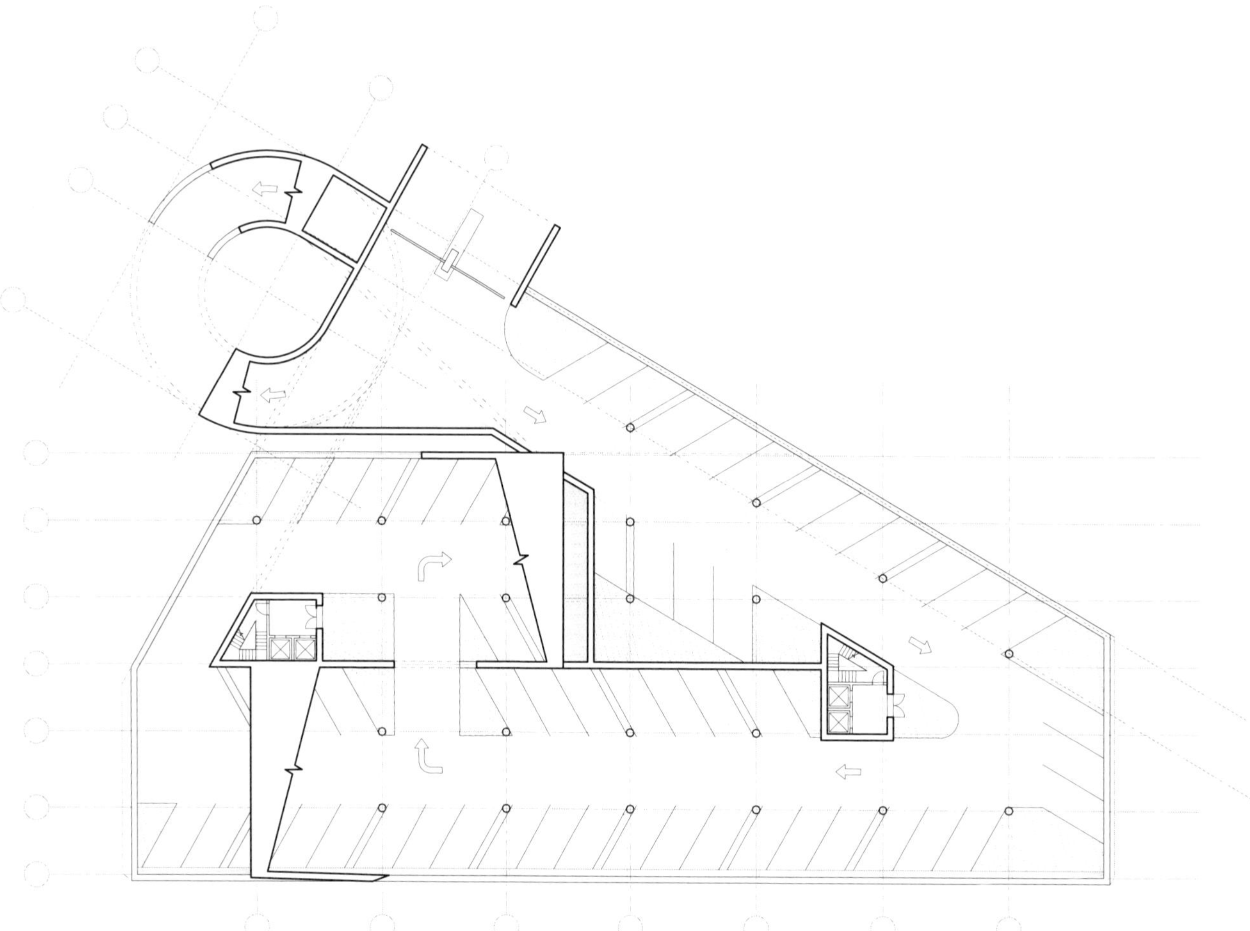

07 Ground level plan

08

CURVED AND STRAIGHT

The formal dialectic between curvilinear and planar is apparent in this architectural example. The sloped parking surfaces and irregular site shape demand that the planar geodesic ribbons (bounding most of the plan area) inflect in section at variable angles. This conveys a more contingent aesthetic, responsive to geometric and programmatic needs.

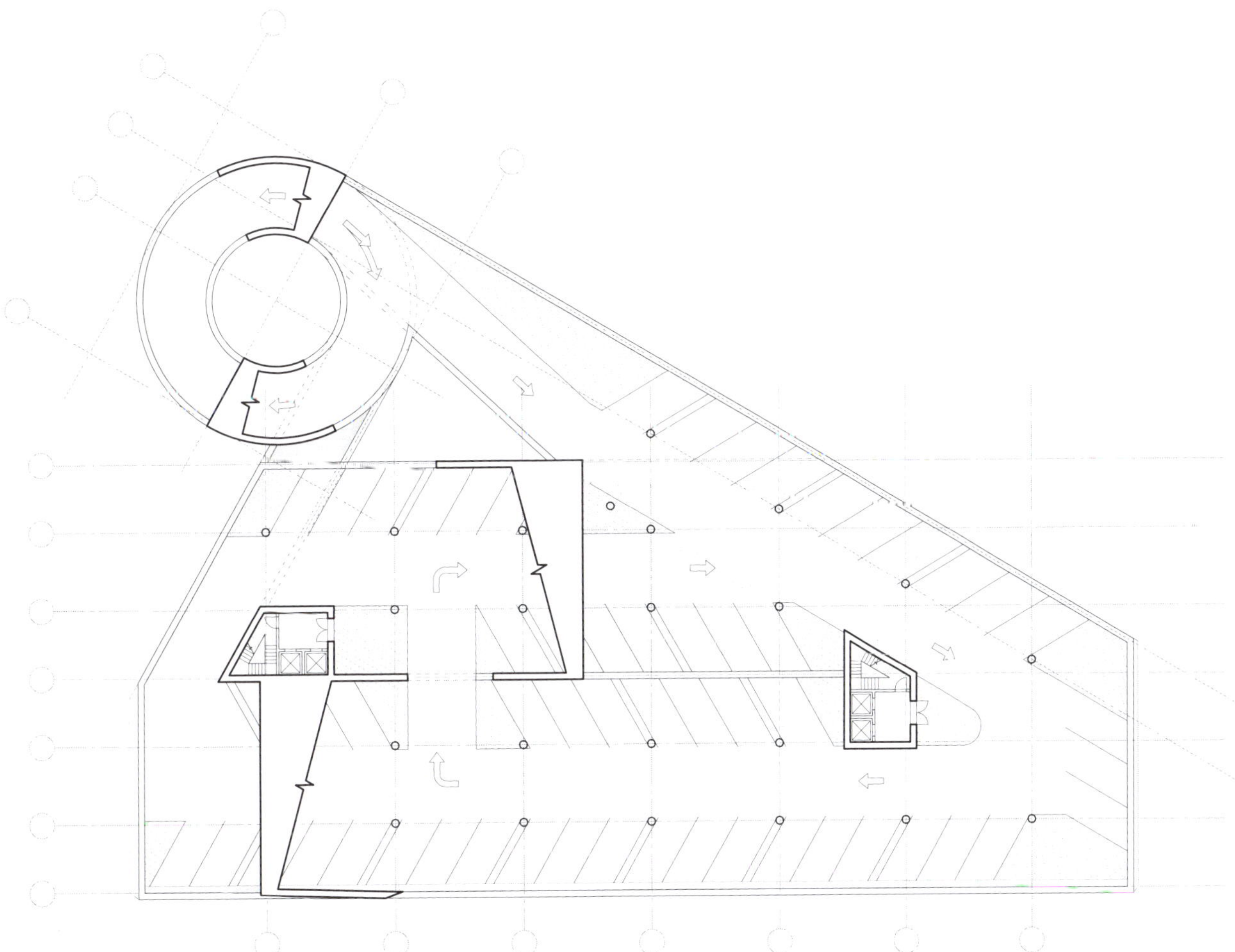

09 Typical plan

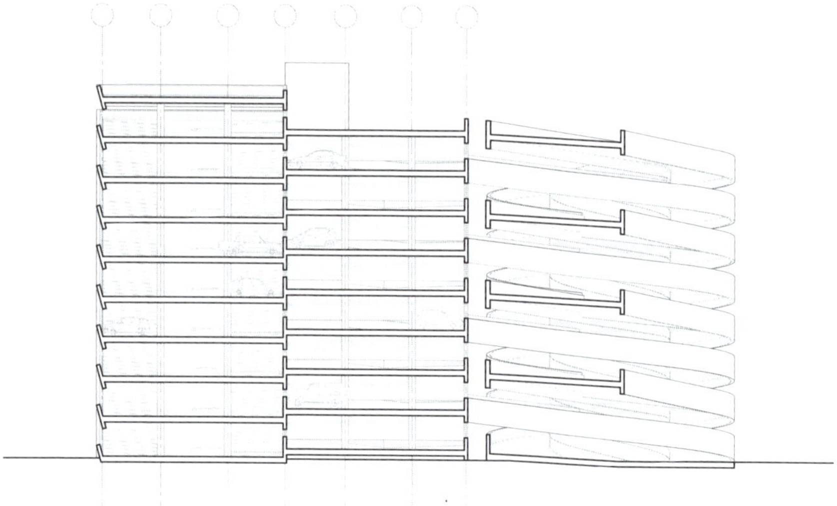

10 Section

11 Helical ramps unfurl into broader layers of parking surfaces

2014

GEODESIC HOUSE 02

PROJECT TEAM:
Cameron Wu
Iman Fayyad
Ashley Takacs

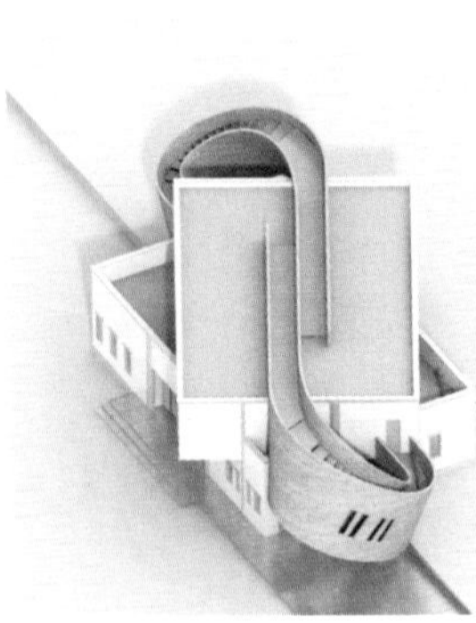

2015

GEODESIC HOUSE 03

PROJECT TEAM:
Cameron Wu
Iman Fayyad
Ashley Takacs

2012

CONEY INLAND

PROJECT TEAM:
Cameron Wu
W. Gavin Robb
Taylor Dover
James Leng
Mark Lewis
Jennifer Ly
Alex Watchman
Max Wong

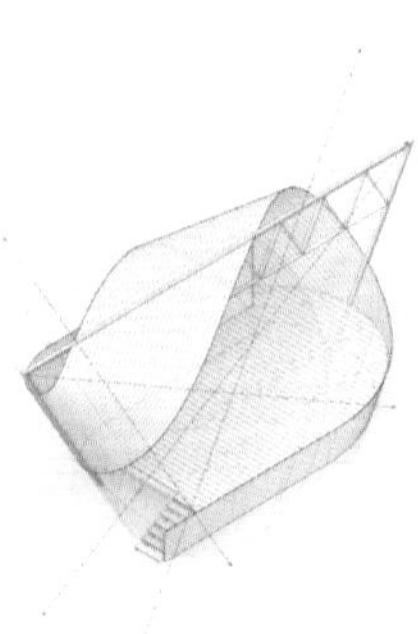

2016

CHRYSALIS

PROJECT TEAM:
Cameron Wu
Iman Fayyad

2011

ATLANTA HISTORY MUSEUM COMPETITION

PROJECT TEAM:
Cameron Wu
Jeffry Burchard (collaborator)
Ted Baab
Marcela Delgado
Mark Lewis
W. Gavin Robb

2012

NOTRE DAME DE L'ASSOMPTION CATHEDRAL COMPETITION

PROJECT TEAM:
Cameron Wu
W. Gavin Robb
Drew Cowdrey
Iman Fayyad

2017

GEODESIC HOUSE 06

PROJECT TEAM:
Cameron Wu
Milos Mladenovic

2017

GEODESIC HOUSE 07

PROJECT TEAM:
Cameron Wu
Milos Mladenovic

2014-15

EPKER HOUSE GEODESIC HOUSE 01

PROJECT TEAM:
Cameron Wu
Iman Fayyad
Max Wong

2014

CONIC KNOTS PLASTICITY COMPETITION

PROJECT TEAM:
Cameron Wu
Iman Fayyad
John Morrison
Max Wong

2014

DOUBLY RULED HOUSE

PROJECT TEAM:
Cameron Wu
Iman Fayyad
Michael Peguero

2014

WRAP MUSIC

PROJECT TEAM:
Cameron Wu
Iman Fayyad
Jonathan Rieke
Niki Murata
Yurina Kodama

2020

MAGNETIC Z

PROJECT TEAM:
Cameron Wu
Anna Kerr
Lisa Ramsburg
Grey Wartinger
Cole Cataneo
Jasen Domanico
Julian Gonzalez

2021

CIRCUMVOLUTE_00

PROJECT TEAM:
Cameron Wu
Jasen Domanico
Julian Gonzalez

2022

GEODESIC GARAGE

PROJECT TEAM:
Cameron Wu
Julian Gonzalez
Jasen Domanico

ACKNOWLEGDMENTS

The forms and ideas in this book have been influenced by numerous friends, colleagues, and students over the course of many years. I first thank my teacher Preston Scott Cohen for introducing me to projective geometry—one of many historical motivators of architectural form. His unyielding curiosity and contagious enthusiasm for architectural thought and pedagogy have significantly altered my own intellectual trajectories. Equally important has been the encouragement and advocacy of Monica Ponce de Leon, who continues to provide an environment conducive to informed architectural experimentation. I am greatly indebted to many other teachers and mentors who have afforded me valuable knowledge and guidance, including Toshiko Mori, George Legendre, Mack Scogin, Merrill Elam, Jamie Carpenter, Robert Levit, Jorge Silvetti, Luis Rojo, K. Michael Hays, Harry Cobb, Wes Jones, Farshid Moussavi, Antoine Picon, Sanford Kwinter, Richard Sommer, Hashim Sarkis, Nader Tehrani, Sarah Whiting, and Mario Gandelsonas. My understanding of architecture continues to transform directly from debate and discussion with fellow teachers in the studio and classroom. These colleagues include, but are not limited to Michael Meredith, Jeffry Burchard, Darell Fields, Andrew Witt, Scott Cohen, Monica Ponce de Leon, Paul Lewis, Grace La, Christine Boyer, Eric Howeler, Florian Idenburg, Forrest Meggers, Stan Allen, Mariana Ibanez, Elisa Silva, Nancy Nichols, Liz Diller, Beth Whittaker, Marshall Brown, Iman Fayyad, Megan Panzano, Sylvia Lavin, Sean Canty, Carl D'Apolito-Dworkin, Erin Besler, Ingeborg Rocker, S. E. Eisterer, J Jih, V. Mitch McEwen, Jesse Reiser, Dan Sherer, Chris Hoxie, Jenny French, Anda French, Jay Cephas, John May, Guy Nordenson, Kiel Moe, Spyros Papapetros, Jon Lott, Beatriz Colomina, Andrew Holder, and Katy Barkan. Gratitude is especially due to those who collaborated to produce the projects, including W. Gavin Robb, Alex Watchman, Max Wong, Ashley Takacs, Taylor Dover, Mike Burton, James Leng, Mark Lewis, Ted Baab, Hyojin Kwon, Milos Mladenovic, Cole Cataneo, Grey Wartinger, Michelle Deng, Anna Kerr, Lisa Ramsburg, Julian Gonzalez, Jasen Domanico, and Lee Onbargi. I owe a profound debt to Iman Fayyad whose curiosity, critical eye, and skillfulness collaboratively developed most of the geometric techniques and projects in this book. Her love of geometry and contributions to the work presented here are immeasurable. Thanks to the publishers and editors of the journals in which some projects in this book have previously appeared. In particular, I would like to thank Cynthia Davidson for her support and advocacy. She has not only provided generous publishing opportunities, but has worked tirelessly to provide keen editorial feedback ensuring the writing conveys difficult concepts lucidly. For the publication of this book, I owe many thanks to Olga Pipnik and Ricardo Devesa at Actar Publishers for their careful editing, graphic design, and seemingly inexhaustible patience. I would like to thank my parents, Dr. Yenching and Geraldine Wu for many years of support, opportunities, and encouragement, along with my brothers Mark Wu, Christopher Wu, and Jonathan Wu, and their families. Love and thanks to Imogen and Lucy. Finally, to my wife Carroll, I offer profound gratitude and deepest apologies for having pushed your love, understanding, and patience beyond endurance.

IMAGE CREDITS

All images © Cameron Wu courtesy the author except:

CASE STUDIES

Sickergill Bridge

01 Unknown photographer. "Sickergill Skew Bridge". Source: *A Practical Treatise on Segmental and Elliptical Oblique or Skew Arches* by George Joseph Bell. 1896.
06 Unknown photographer. "Sickergill Skew Bridge over the River Raven at Renwick, near Penright, under construction, showing the helicoidal coursing of the stones". Source: *A Practical Treatise on Segmental and Elliptical Oblique or Skew Arches* by George Joseph. 1896.

Trompe At Abbaye Toussaint d'Angers

01 Coyau. "Trompe de l'abbaye Toussaint d'Angers". Photograph. Source: *Wikimedia Commons*. October 4, 2008. (Free to use under creative commons license BY-SA 3.0)
03 Hôtel d'Angoulême Lamoignon, Baptiste Androuet du Cerceau Paris France. 1589. Source: Photo courtesy the author.
04 Hôtel de Bullioud. Philibert de l'Orme. Lyons France. 1536. Source: Photo courtesy the author.

Église Saint-Pierre

01 Weil, Richard. "Eglise Saint-Pierre, Le Corbusier, Firminy". Photograph. Source: *Flickr*. October 12, 2008. (Free to use under creative license CC BY-SA 2.0)
04 Weil, Richard. "Eglise Saint-Pierre, Le Corbusier, Firminy". Photograph. Source: *Flickr*. October 12, 2008. (Free to use under creative license CC BY-SA 2.0)

IKMZ Brandenburg University of Technology

01 Huthmacher, Werner. "IKMZ BTU Information, Communications and Media Centre, Cottbus, Germany." Photograph. Source: *Detail Magazine, no 6*, 2005. © Werner Hutmacher
05 Huthmacher, Werner. "IKMZ BTU Information, Communications and Media Centre, Cottbus, Germany." Photograph. Source: *Detail Magazine, no 6*, 2005. © Werner Hutmacher

Aula Medica

01 Aula Medica. Solna, Sweden. View from southwest. Photo ©Patrik Lindell
05 Aula Medica. Solna, Sweden. View from east. Source: Photo courtesy the author.

Saint-Andrew the Apostle Parish Church
01 Kawasumi, Akio. "Saint-Andrew The Apostle Parish Church, Makati 1967". Photograph. Source: Jean-Claude Girard. *Leandro Valencia Locsin: Filipino Architect*. Birkhäuser, 2021. ©Akio Kawasumi
02 Saint-Andrew The Apostle Parish Church, 1967. Interior. Source: Photo courtesy the author.
04 Saint-Andrew The Apostle Parish Church, 1967. Entry detail. Source: Photo courtesy the author.

Springtecture B
01 Kitajima, Toshiharu. "Springtecture B, View of the west front". 2002. Photograph. © Shuhei Endo Architect Institute.
07 Kitajima, Toshiharu. "Springtecture B, Detail of the south front". 2002. Photograph. © Shuhei Endo Architect Institute.

520 West 28th Street
01 "Untitled". Photograph. © Hufton + Crow.
07 520 West 28th Street. Façade detail. Photograph. Source: Photo Courtesy the author.

Precious Blood Parish Church
01 Kalen, Henry. "Exterior of Eglise du Precieux-Sang". August 22, 1968. Photograph. Source: University of Manitoba Archives & Special Collections.
06 Kalen, Henry. "Eglise du Precieux-Sang". August 22, 1968. Photograph. Source: University of Manitoba Archives & Special Collections.

Catalano House (44-45)
01 Stoller, Ezra. "Catalano House". Exterior. Photograph. January 1, 1955. Source: Esto Ezra Stoller Archive (file 49Q.004.jpg) ©Ezra Stoller/Esto.
03 Stoller, Ezra. "Catalano House". Interior. Photograph. January 1, 1955. Source: Esto Ezra Stoller Archive (file 49Q.014.jpg) ©Ezra Stoller/Esto.

Luce Memorial Chapel
01 Pei Cobb Freed & Partners. "Luce Memorial Chapel, Campus of Tunghai University in Taichung, Taiwan". 1963. Exterior. Photograph. © Pei Cobb Freed & Partners.
05 Pei Cobb Freed & Partners. "Luce Memorial Chapel, Campus of Tunghai University in Taichung, Taiwan". 1963. Interior. Photograph. © Pei Cobb Freed & Partners.

Via 57 West
01 Via 57 WEST. Bjarke Ingels Group. 2020. View from southwest. Photograph © Nic Lehoux
05 Via 57 WEST. Bjarke Ingels Group. 2020. Aerial view. Photograph © Iwan Baan

PROJECTS
Geodesic House 03
01 Andrea Palladio. Villa Gazzotti. Bertesina, Italy. 1542. Plan. Source: Scamozzi, 1778.

Epker House (Geodesic House 01)
01 H. H. Richardson. The Stoughton House. Cambridge, MA. 1880. Source: Photo courtesy the author.

Magnetic Z (Art Omi)
01 Cameron Wu. Magnetic Z. Art Omi. Ghent NY. 2020. View from northeast. Photo © Bryan Zimmerman
10 Cameron Wu. Magnetic Z. Art Omi. Ghent NY. 2020. View from southwest. Photo © Bryan Zimmerman
11 Cameron Wu. Magnetic Z. Art Omi. Ghent NY. 2020. View from north. Photo © Bryan Zimmerman.
12 Cameron Wu. Magnetic Z. Art Omi. Ghent NY. 2020. Ramp view. Photo © Bryan Zimmerman.
13 Cameron Wu. Magnetic Z. Art Omi. Ghent NY. 2020. Ramp detail. Photo © Bryan Zimmerman.
15 Cameron Wu. Magnetic Z. Art Omi. Ghent NY. 2020. Stair detail. Photo © Bryan Zimmerman.